WATCH-DOGS: THEIR TRAINING AND MANAGEMENT

LIEUT.-COLONEL RICHARDSON.

LIEUT.-COLONEL RICHARDSON.

[*Frontispiece.*

WATCH-DOGS:

THEIR TRAINING and MANAGEMENT

By Lieut.-Col. E. H. RICHARDSON

(Late Commandant of the British War Dog School in the Great War) :: :: :: Author of "War, Police and Watch-dogs," and "British War Dogs"

WITH SEVENTEEN ILLUSTRATIONS

SECOND EDITION

LONDON: HUTCHINSON & CO.

PATERNOSTER ROW

1924

CONTENTS

CHAPTER		PAGE
I.	THE STORY OF THE WATCH-DOG	9
II.	THE NECESSITY FOR A WATCH-DOG	27
III.	THE USES OF A WATCH-DOG	32
IV.	THE CHOICE OF A WATCH-DOG	49
V.	HOW TO PURCHASE A DOG	56
VI.	TRAINING DOGS	66
VII.	HOW TO FEED YOUR DOG	97
VIII.	EXERCISE AND GROOMING	105
IX.	A DOG ON ITS TRAVELS	112
X.	BREEDING DOGS AND REARING PUPS	122
XI.	THE DOG'S HEALTH	132
XII.	KENNELLING	155
XIII.	MAN-TRACKING AS A PROTECTION	159
XIV.	DOGS IN THE GREAT WAR	180
XV.	DOGS FOR THE POLICE	260
XVI.	BRITISH V. GERMAN POLICE DOGS	266
	CONCLUSION	276

LIST OF ILLUSTRATIONS

Lieut.-Colonel Richardson - - - *Frontispiece*

FACING PAGE

"Halt! Who Goes There?" - - - 32

Training Dog to Gunfire - - - 32

Training the Dog to Pursue in Face of Revolver Fire - 50

Training an Airedale to Save Life - - 52

Training in Obedience - - - - 52

Mr. Lloyd George's Guardian for Stormy Times - 98

Royal Interest. Queen Alexandra and the Empress of Russia Inspecting Lieut.-Col. Richardson's Military Airedales - - - - - 130

The Duke of Connaught Asks Questions. Military Dogs at Naval and Military Exhibition - - 150

Man-tracking Bloodhounds at Aldershot - - 160

In the Trenches, Morocco. Riff War, 1911 - 182

School of Instruction. Training Military Dogs - 182

Messenger Dog. Message Being Inserted in Collar for Return to Headquarters - - - 200

Message Received. A Distance of Three Miles has been Covered by these Dogs - - - 200

Typical Group of Messenger Dogs - - 210

One of Lieut.-Col. Richardson's Airedales Trained to Lay Signal Wire on a Supposedly Dangerous Zone and thus to Save Human Life and Time - - 210

Group of Army Guard Dogs - - - 234

Watch-dogs: Their Training and Management

CHAPTER I

The Story of the Watch-dog

"The Almighty, who gave the dog to be the companion of our pleasures and of our toils, hath invested him with a nature noble and incapable of deceit. He forgets neither friend nor foe; remembers, and with accuracy, both benefit and injury. He hath a share of man's intelligence, but no share of man's falsehood. You may bribe an assassin to slay a man, or a witness to take his life by false accusation, but you cannot make a dog tear his benefactor. He is the friend of man save when man justly incurs his enmity."—Sir Walter Scott.

Is there anything new under the sun? Over and over again, in these latter days, one has seen old habits and customs refurbished and set forth as new experiences, until investigations prove they are as old as the hills.

There is a wave of unrest and turmoil sweeping over the world—a clashing of arms, an upheaval of evil will-power. The "Have-nots" threaten the "Haves," and honest toil is nowadays called labour. *To have*, without effort on the part of the individual, is the dominant idea of a section of the community. The old predatory instinct has revived with astonishing vigour since the war. Man preys on man, and relentless individuals pursue the honourable citizen with cruel and often ferocious intention. It is a fact nowadays that many a man leaves his home in fear and trembling, when he bids farewell to his wife and little ones, and goes out to his daily work. What may happen during his absence? What is there to protect them in the event of attack?

And so he seeks a solution for his difficulty, and all unknowingly goes back to the same idea as held by his brother the cave-man, on the subject thousands of years ago! He gets himself a good watch-dog, and puts it in charge of his womankind. Ages ago the night wind howled round the mountainside, and lifted the hanging leaves over the cave's mouth, giving a watcher without a glimpse of the drowsy woman and children within by the glowing logs, where they lie awaiting their lord's return from the chase. The semi-wild dogs are with him, assisting in the pursuit of the quarry, and ever becoming more useful and adaptable to their master, and one day the woman, with terrified gestures and primitive mouthings, pours forth a tale of fear: an enemy's stealthy tread . . . a moment of terrible danger . . . a terror of the lonely cave.

The inborn instinct to defend his woman and his young surges with furious determination within the cave-man, as he grasps his weapons with intent there and then to dash forth to slay his enemy. But the woman's loneliness comes to him again; what can he do? How can he leave her unprotected while he goes forth to fight or to the chase? His roving eye falls on the dog skulking at the mouth of the cave. He takes him in, and lets him lie beside the logs. He feeds him, and exults as he sees the response to his attentions. He sees the animal's pricked ears, rising fur, and snarling teeth at the strange footfall without, and also notes the loving response to the fondling offered to this new denizen of the cave by the children.

In time this first watch-dog, and others with him, are installed as recognised guardians of the cave family, and so began the long line of home canine guardians, through times of swamp, and times of sand, of wattle and reed, and later of castle and camp and fort and temple. Man found that he could not work all day and watch at night as well, and the dog readily and effectively co-operated with his master in the protection of his household at night, so that man could rest.

There are representations of the guard dog on many of the monuments which have been excavated in Egypt at various times. Many of these date from extremely ancient periods, and it is well known that the Egyptians held dogs in high estimation on account of their utility for guardian purposes, and there is much evidence to show how greatly their fidelity and courage was appreciated. We hear of them guarding the entrances to the cities, temples and palaces, or as sentries for the flocks and herds from marauding tribes, and also from wolves and other wild animals.

We find that Sirius was called the Dog star, on account of the regularity of its appearance. Gazing up into the glittering heavens, the farmer observed a glorious star, whose appearance always coincided with the rising of the Nile, which would bring him all he desired for his land. His simple mind was impressed with the fidelity of the star, and casting about for the most faithful thing he could think of to compare it with, he remembered his dog, and so we get this far-distant thought echoing down the ages, and finding a response in the hearts of all who know and understand dog nature.

From earliest times he has ever been the sharer of man's dangers, joys and labours, and if one thinks over the animal creation carefully, one can easily see that, while there are other animals who enter into one or two of these categories, the dog is the only one who, with an unqualified and ardent *desire*, of his own accord enters into all three of them.

In this connection I may mention a legend, which has always appeared to me exactly to express the difference in the attitude of dog towards man, as compared to any of the other animals. It is said that, soon after the Creation, a great chasm opened up, and man found himself on one side, and all the animals on the other. All the animals remained indifferent and acquiesced in the situation, with the exception of the dog. He commenced to whimper uneasily, and with imploring eyes essayed to attract the man's attention across the widening chasm. The man turned and saw the dog's despairing eyes. "Come to me!" he said. The dog jumped, and just reached the opposite side with his front paws. "You shall be my friend and comrade," said the man, and leaned over and drew the dog up to safety beside him.

This story typifies the wonderful co-operation between

man and dog, and it cannot be applied quite in the same way to any other animal.

Blaze, a writer on the dog in 1843, says: "The dog being a symbol of vigilance, it was thus intended to warn princes of their constant duty to watch over the welfare of their people. The dog was worshipped principally at Hermopolis the Great, and ultimately in all towns in Egypt."

The city of Cynopolis was built in honour of the dog, and priests celebrated solemn festivals in its honour.

The famous watch-dog Kitmer is interestingly alluded to in an article by Colonel Hamilton Smith in 1861, who says: "Even the Mohammedans, while they shrink from his touch as defilement, are compelled to recognise the courage and fidelity of the dog. He, moreover, is lifted into the region of the supernatural by no less an authority than the Koran. Three animals, and only three, are permitted to share the joys and repose of Mohammed's paradise. The camel, on which the prophet rode during his famous flight from Mecca, the ass of Balaam, and Kitmer, the dog of the seven sleepers, who, with his master, entered the cave in which, year after year, they lay wrapped in mysterious slumber, who fell asleep with them, and who, with them, was at last raised to receive the reward of his care and fidelity. The Mohammedan legend asserts that, as the seven youths were on their way to the cavern, in which they intended to take refuge from their heathen persecutor (the Emperor Decius), they passed Kitmer and attempted to drive him away, upon which God caused him to speak, and he said: 'I love those who are dear unto God; go to sleep, therefore, and I will guard you.' So Kitmer 'stretched forth his legs in the mouth of the cave,' and during his sleep of three hundred years turned himself from side to side like his masters."

There are, however, dogs of other breeds depicted on the ancient temples of Assyria, and which have been brought to light during excavations. Some of these show a large-headed dog somewhat like a St. Bernard. A collar of leaves, or of leather, or of metal wrought in design, is round the neck. The name of the dog is also frequently given, and generally indicates some form of prowess.

A very wonderful picture on part of the furniture of Tutankhamen's tomb shows the King engaged in the chase. Close to his chariot are two large dogs of mastiff appearance. They are provided with heavy collars of armour type—3,000 years ago.

For many centuries the shepherd tribes used dogs for guarding their flocks, and the "sheep-dogs" of the period had very serious duties to perform, apart from keeping the flocks and herds together. It must be remembered that they were really of vital necessity for war-like purposes in their daily work. Owing to the savage and war-like state of the tribes of the world for many centuries, the possessor of flocks and herds, or valuable property of any description, was never safe from massed attacks from envious neighbours, and had to be perpetually on his guard.

After all, war, as we now understand it, is only a more organised form of this same spirit, and it is difficult to distinguish in any way between the dogs deputed to guard the mountain passes leading to the pastures of their masters, or of those posted on the battlements of the castle, and the modern sentry dog, standing alert with pricked ears, listening for the stealthy tread of the Boche across No-Man's-Land, or of the guardian of the magazine or canteen. In fact, these sheep-dogs of olden times are almost entirely spoken of in the light of guardians, and it is not until considerably later in history that there is any mention of them taking part in driving the sheep, or aiding in any way after that peaceful manner. But it is interesting to note how very ancient, nevertheless, is the association of the sheep-dog with sheep, and it is therefore not to be wondered at that the modern animal takes so instinctively to the idea of this useful method of turning its capabilities to account.

Not only were there human marauders to be feared, during these early times of which we are speaking, but the persons of both the keepers and their flocks were in constant danger from attack by bands of ferocious wolves. These guardian dogs, watchful and alert through the dark hours, must have been supremely valuable, and terrific and desperate must the conflicts have been at times, when the prowling hordes attempted to break through the guarding cordon.

Evliya Effendi, the Turkish traveller of the seventeenth century, when commenting on many things, mentions dogs. He says : " They are the size of asses, and fierce as lions from Africa, in double or triple chains, covered with rich cloth, and wearing silver collars and neck rings. They perform everything they are told to perform, and if bid to do so, will bring down a fellow from horseback, however stout a fellow may be. The shepherds look on these as their companions and brethren, and do not object to eat out of the dish with them."

It is curious to study the differing attitudes of the various early races of the world towards the canine race. The Egyptians loved and venerated it, and no doubt this very fact greatly contributed to the dislike and contempt felt for it by the Jews. To them the dog was an outcast and a pariah, a frequenter of middens and an alien from man, who should have been his friend. In the chapter on training I shall have more to say on the psychology of the dog, and will only point out the fact here that, according to the attitude adopted by man to the animal creation as a whole, and to the dog in particular, in an equal degree for better for worse does the response return to him.

The Jews found them useful as scavengers, and they also used them with their flocks. We find in Job xxx. 1 : " Whose fathers I would have disdained to have set with the dogs of my flocks."

But they never recognised the wonderful mental qualities of their dogs, which only required cultivating. Other races of the world at the same period did so, however.

Thus we find the Aryans were great dog lovers, and associated the dog with some of the most solemn moments in the human life. We find there was a belief that a dog accompanied the departing soul on its journey to heavenly places, as companion and guardian, and it was the custom, very often, to introduce a dog into the death-chamber, so that the dying person should be comforted by the sight of the creature of whose race a member would keep him from loneliness on his journey.

Nevertheless, in spite of the attitude on the part of the Jews, it would appear that at one time they must have had a high understanding of the dog, as we find that Caleb, the faithful and discerning spy of Israel, seems to have had the sense of faithfulness attached to him, and that his name means " dog of God."

Renan, writing on this in his " History of the People of Israel," says: " Often with names of this kind, 'El' " (which means God) " was omitted, Irham being used instead of Irhamel, Caleb instead of Calbel. This last name, irregular as it is, need not create any surprise, for Dog of El was an energetic way of expressing the faithful attachment of a tribe to the God to which it had devoted itself."

It will be remembered that when Moses sent a representative of each of the tribes to spy out the land " flowing with milk and honey," Caleb was the only one of them who showed fidelity to the Lord's command, and recommended that the children of Israel should go forward and possess it, and also the courage to believe it could be done, whereas the other spies allowed their fear of the fierce and gigantic people of the land completely to obscure the remembrance of the solemn trust and injunction placed on them as a people. On account of this fidelity of attitude on the part of Caleb we find the following promise given to him:

" But my servant Caleb, because he had another spirit with him, and hath followed me fully, him will I bring unto the land whereinto he went and his seed shall possess it."

The fulfilment of this promise is later on spoken of: "And Joshua blessed him, and gave unto Caleb the son of Jephunneh the Kenezite, Hebron for an inheritance . . . because he wholly followed the Lord God of Israel."

The object of quoting this at length is to accentuate the fact that the fidelity of this Jewish hero is inevitably associated with the dog, as it was the custom of this race to bestow names on individuals according to certain mental characteristics manifested by the person. Companionship from the dog is, however, hardly ever mentioned in Jewish writings, one exception being the dog in Tobit (Apocrypha) which is spoken of on two separate occasions as accompanying the young man Tobias on his journeys: " And the young man's dog went with them."

One can well imagine how useful the watching and attacking qualities of the dog would be to the early war-like and turbulent inhabitants of the world, especially when it is remembered that before the invention of gunpowder there would be no method of disposing of the enemy, except at close quarters where the dog would be a very useful auxiliary.

The Romans and Greeks were quick to appreciate this fact, and we find the deeds of their fighting and guarding dogs extolled in song and story. Homer writes:

> " Nor last forget thy faithful dogs, but feed
> With fattening whey the mastiff's generous breed
> And Spartan race, who for the fold's relief,
> Will prosecute with cries the nightly thief:
> Repulse the prowling wolf, and hold at bay
> The mountain robbers rushing to their prey."

Herodotus, speaking of the veneration of the Egyptians for many of their animals, states that when the household dog died the family used to shave themselves—a sign of mourning; and he adds that this was a custom obtaining in his own time.

Pythagorus taught a quaint idea, that at the death of a person the soul entered into an animal, and whenever one of his favourite disciples died, he had a dog held up to the mouth of the dying man, asserting that it was the animal most worthy to receive the departing spirit, and to perpetuate the human virtues.

Cicero extols the use of guard dogs, going so far as to give some rather minute directions as to their proper management. Thus among other things, he very sensibly points out that, in order to utilise the guarding propensities of the dogs at their highest degree at night-time, the animals should be allowed to rest in the day-time, so that they should be more alert at night.

Plutarch and Pliny both mention war dogs in their writings. The dogs were employed as a means of defence against enemy attack, and also as actual weapons of attack. They were used thus at the siege of Mantenea, and King Cambyses also employed large numbers in his campaign in Egypt.

There is a story related that when the King of the Spartans was besieging Mantenea, he discovered treachery among some of his own forces, and that provisions were being carried into the town by night. He stopped this by surrounding the town with a cordon of dogs, which no one was able to penetrate owing to the vigilance of the animals.

When Philip of Macedon made war against the Thracians, the latter took to the forests, and the only satisfactory means he had of tracing them was by using dogs.

It is related that the garrison at Corinth were asleep after a lengthy carouse, and were only saved from a surprise attack from the enemy by the faithful watch-dogs on duty on the ramparts, who neither slumbered nor slept, but remained, unlike the men, faithful to their trust. They were ever afterwards held in the greatest reverence by the garrison.

In their accounts of their incursions all over the world, we find a constant repetition of the statement that the Romans took dogs with them, and, in fact, that they recognised in the latter a necessary and reliable auxiliary in warfare; thus we find them in constant use as guards and sentries for their camps, and for the ramparts of their towns. They were taken in large groups when the Roman legions penetrated into the Sahara against the Samarantes.

Marius, a Roman consul, gives an interesting account of how, at the Battle of Versella, 101 B.C., against the Teutons, the Romans, having overcome the defending forces, found they then had to take into account very seriously the hordes of dogs which were organised and furiously urged against them by the "blonde-haired women of Wagenburg."

The particular species of mastiff which inhabited Britain was much prized by the warriors of middle Europe, and in their incursions into these islands large quantities were annexed. The finest specimens were considered fit gifts for kings, and were placed as guardians to palace, temple and fort.

Another breed of the same vehement nature was the Molossian of Epirus. These were used in war, and were immensely loved by their owners, because, besides displaying a very brave and courageous spirit, they also became intensely devoted to their masters. Allian relates that one of them so greatly distinguished himself with his master in the battle of Marathon, that his effigy was placed on the same tablet as his master. It is, as a matter of fact, extremely probable that they were buried in the same tomb.

It is also interesting to observe that, on the column of Marcus Aurelius in Rome, dogs are represented fighting beside the men, clad in mail, and with spiked collars.

Vegetious, the Roman historian, alludes to the dogs used by the Teutonic tribes against the Roman legions. Large and powerful dogs were at all times greatly prized. Sometimes they were supplied with complete suits of armour, consisting of a body-covering and a headpiece. In Madrid Museum there is an interesting specimen of this accoutrement mounted on a stuffed dog.

Certain of these are described by a writer—Camerarius—in his book, "Living Librarie or Historical Meditations," printed in 1625. He says: "The dogs of Albania bring under all other beasts, throttle bulls, kill lions, stay all that is thrown against them; and therefore are very famous in histories. We read that Alexander, going to the Indies, received two of them, which the King of Albania presented him with. These dogs grow very high, and bark with a stronger voice than the roaring of lions."

Perhaps the dog of Andronicus, the King of Constantinople, was of this race. "This Prince was much hated because of his villainies and mischiefs, and made himself be guarded, not only with companies of strange soldiers, but also with a very great dogge, who made no bones to fight with lions, and could turn a man all armed off his horse. The guard kept watch in the night a prettie way from his chamber, and at his chamber door this dog was tied, who at the least noise that was, made a terrible barking."

Andronicus seems to have trusted dog more than man.

Camerarius also narrates a curious instance of guard dogs distinguishing between Christians and Turks. This, however, is quite to be understood by all who have studied the question of scenting powers in dogs. They learn to distinguish the scents of different races very readily, and also between communities of people. It will be observed that differing modes of living and also of food produce varying scents in people, and communities living together have each their distinctive scent. This also applies even to the men of different regiments, and I have found that dogs can quite easily detect a man of a regiment belonging to another than their own.

"The Rhodians held very strong and well-fortified citie, called the Castle of S. Peter, in a place of the firme land, over against the Isle Coos, being the only retrait for the Christians of Asia, that saved themselves from being slaves to the Turkes. The enemy was master of all without and about this place, in so much as the citisens could not safely fetch wood or other fuel for their use. Some bodie had told the Venetians strange things of the sence and service of the dogs that were within the Citie, to the number of fiftie, all of which the Inhabitants put forth every night (as it were) for Sentinels. If during the night, these watchers met with any Christian, they would receive him, and with fawning and joy conduct him into the Citie: contrariwise, if they discovered a Turke, they would first keepe a great barking, and then falling upon him, pull him down and then teare him in pieces. These are the words of Sabellicus.

"At Renes in Brittaine, at Saint Malo, and at Saint Michaels, they keepe a great many dogs, that watch and ward both night and day, as I have heard reported by many. Plutarch showeth that it is an ancient custome; for he saith, That the enterprise of Aratus, which he undertooke for the freeing of his countrey, had like to have bin mar'd, by the watchfulness of a dog. By this it appeareth, what moved Socrates to sweare commonly by the dog, as Plato noteth; who thereby would point out an unmatchable faithfulnesse, such as is seene in those creatures."

Camerarius also quotes another writer, Pierius, who shows forth the faithful and discerning qualities of guard dogs by stating that ancient authors had written that:

"Near to Mount Gibell, in Cicilia, there was a temple builded to Vulcan, the groave whereof was guarded by dogs (as M. Marlianus also reporteth, that in old Rome, before Vulcan's chappell, in the Flaminian Cirque, were certain dogs that would never barke but against church-robbers), which would run with great fawning to meet the good and devout Pilgrims; but if any that were villainous and dishonest came thither, they were miserably torne in pieces by those dogs."

Ulysses Androrandus wrote, in 1607, a work on natural history, and in this he describes certain dogs of middle Europe as " terrible and frightful to behold, and more fierce and fell than any Arcadian curre. . . . In build he resembles the hound. He ought to be gentle to his own household, savage to those outside it, and not to be taken in by caresses. He should be robust, with a muscular body, and noisy in his deep bark, so that, by his bold baying, he may threaten on all sides, and frighten away prowlers. He should have a fierce light in his eyes, portending the lightning attack on the rash enemy. He should be black in his coat, in order to appear more fearful to the thieves in the daylight, and being of the same shade as night itself, to be able to make his way quite unseen by enemies and thieves."

Camerarius also refers to two other writers, Coelius Rhodiginus and Alexander of Alexandria, who write as follows :

" The faithfulnesse of a dog hath been the cause that many have chosen to trust their lives with that beast, and to commit themselves to the good of him rather than of reasonable men. As we read of King Massinissa, who by the barking of dogs freed himself many times from the ambuscadoes that were laid for him, discovered afar off the coming of his enemies, stood upon his guard and, by the helpe, of dogs, sometimes carryed away the victorie. Plinie reporteth to this purpose, that the Colophonians tooke great care to traine their dogs and make them fit for warre, insomuch as they made squadrons of them, which fought in the first rankes with a wonderful boldnesse, and would never give back : above all, they did good service in the night. We read also that the King of the Garamantes, driven by sedition out of his realme, was reestablisht againe by the helpe of two hundred hunting dogs.

" It may bee that Henry VIII., King of England (according to the purport of a letter which his Ambassadour sent from Spire to the King of Polonia, An. 1544, by the report of Olaus Magnus) had an eye to this prompt fidelitie of dogs, when in the armie which he sent to the Emperour

Charles the Fifth against the French King, there were foure hundred souldiers that had charge of the like number of dogs, all of them garnished with good yron collers after the fashion of that countrey: no man being able to say, whether they were appointed to be sentinels in the night, or to serve for some stratagem for obtaining the victorie.

"Strabo saith, that the like was practised in old time, and that the English dogs went to warre with the Gaules: and there is mention of a Procurator or Commissarie that had charge of the dogs of Britanie, in the Emperour's behalfe. And at this day there be some of them found, which Camden calleth Agase-hounds, and named Agasæi by Oppian. Andrew Thenet, speaking of the King of Cephala, writeth, That when he will give battell to his enemies, he commonly mingleth many troupes of dogs among the squadrons of his souldiers. We will hereafter make mention of a dog so couragious in the warre, that the Indians were more afraid of his teeth, than of any other Spanish weapons, and that the owner received extraordinary pay every moneth for the services that were done by that dog."

We get a vivid and also a quaint description of the period in the book on dogs written by Dr. Caius, of Cambridge University, in the year 1576. Comparing his own times with the good old days of King Alfredus, he says: "If a man travelling by the high way of the country under his dominion, chanced to lose a budget of gold, or his cap case farsed with things of great value, late in the evening, he should find it where he had lost it, safe, sound, and untouched the next morning, yea (which is a wonder), at any time for a whole months space, if he sort for it." He continues: "But in this our unhappy age, in these (I say) our devilish days, nothing can escape the clawes of the spoiler, though it be kept never so sure within the house, albeit the doors be lockt, and bolted round about."

In order to cope with this unsatisfactory state of things, he proceeds to describe certain dogs, which were useful in keeping the "theefes" at bay, which people "roge up and down every corner, no place is free from them, no not ye King's palace, not the countryman's cottage." The dog, he says, is called "in the Latin *Canis Culloo*, in English the Dogge Keeper, for he doth not only keepe farmers houses, but also merchants maisons, wherein great wealth, rich substance, and costly stuff is reposed." These dogs seem to have been large sized animals, more or less of the mastiff type, and they possessed apparently many excellent qualifications, as amongst others he mentions that " at his master's voice and commandment, he carrieth letters from place to place, wrapped up cunningly in his leather collar. . . . who lest he should be hindered in his passage useth these helps very skilfully, namely resistance in fighting if he be not over matched, or else swiftness and readiness in running away if he be unable to buckle with the dog that would fain have a snatch at his skin."

Another name for the same animal was *Canis Lunaris*, or Mooner, "because he doth nothing else but watch and ward at an ynche, wasting the wearisome night season without slombering or sleeping, bawing and wawing at the moone,—a qualitiee in mine opinion strange to consider.

"This kind of dogge is also called *Canis Aquarius*, in English Water Drawer.

" And these be of the greater and weightier sort, drawing water out of wells and deep pits by a wheele which they turn round by the moving of their burdensome bodies."

They also seemed to have been used as draft dogs, "because, with marvellous patience they bear big budgettes fraught with Tinkers tools and metal neete to mend kettles, porridge pottes, skellets and chafers, and other trumpery requisite for their occupation and loytering trade, easing him of a great burden which otherwise he himself should carry on his shoulders.

" Besides the qualities which we have already recounted, this kind of dogges hath this principal propertie engrafted in them, that they love their masters liberally, and hate strangers despightfully, where upon it followeth that they are to their masters in travelling a singular safeguard, defending them forcibly from the invasion of villons and theefes, preserving their livffes from losee, and their health from hasard, their flesh from hacking and hewing, and such like desperate dangers for which consideration they are meritoriously termed in Latin *Canis Defensores* or defending dogges."

It may be of interest to remark on the extreme antiquity of this disposition in the dog to guard territory or property. It would appear that this quality of mind is possessed even by carnivorous animals in their wild state. Professor Romanes states :

" Most carnivorous animals in their wild state have an idea of property, and the manner in which certain predaceous carnivora take possession of more or less definite areas, as their hunting grounds, implies an incipient notion of the same thing. From this germ, thus supplied by nature, the art of man has operated in the case of the dog, till now, the idea of defending his master's property has become in this animal truly instinctive."

Mr. Romanes gives an amusing instance of this instinctive habit of guarding in the case of a young puppy which he reared :

" Because I was perfectly certain that, in this case, the idea of protecting property was innate or instinctive. I have seen this dog escort a donkey, which had baskets on its back filled with apples. Although the dog did not know he was being observed, he accompanied the donkey all the way up the long hill, for the express purpose of guarding the apples. For every time the donkey turned his head to take an apple out of the baskets, the terrier sprang up and snapped at his nose ; and such was the vigilance of the dog, that although his companion was keenly desirous of tasting the fruit, he never allowed him to get a single apple during the half-hour they were together."

The desire for speech in the dogs—that is as an audible mode of self-expression—is an instinct on which we depend largely in connection with our watch-dogs. It has been observed that the faculty of expression itself through sound is regulated largely by the environment in which the dog finds itself. Thus Mr. Romanes says : " Ulloa noticed that in Juan Fernandez the dogs did not attempt to bark till taught to do so by the importation of some dogs from Europe, their first attempts being strange and unnatural." Hancock says that " European dogs, when conveyed to Guinea, in three or four generations ceased to bark, and only howled like the dogs, native of that coast. Lastly, it is now well known that the dogs of Labrador are silent as to barking. So that the habit of barking, which is so general among domestic dogs, as to be of the nature of an instinct, is nevertheless seen to vary with geographical position."

During all the ages, dogs have been doing their part co-operating with man in the guardianship of the world, and aiding him in his work and business.

It was after the commencement of the Great War that it was recognised how extremely valuable they could be for various purposes in connection with our soldiers. As despatch-carriers and as sentries they did unrivalled service, and it is impossible actually to estimate the amount of life and property which was saved and preserved through their agency.

Since the Armistice the same co-operation is being carried out, and the dangerous times we have passed through have been greatly mitigated by the protection our watch-dogs have accorded castle, farm, villa and cottage.

In the chapter on Training I have recorded my observations with regard to the influence exercised on the dog by the attitude of mind possessed by its master, and also by that of the majority of minds in its particular environment; therefore for the same reason would facility of expression forsake a dog if it were removed to any land where the inhabitants were less fluent of speech and of ideas. This would, of course, happen in connection with semi-civilised bodies of people. Naturally, their intellects are circumscribed, and as naturally, therefore, their speech is in a much narrower groove. Their dogs will at once reflect this lack, and while their sense of ownership will in nowise deteriorate, they will find other means of communicating their impressions rather than by barking, which is the form of speech of the civilised dog

As a dog becomes very closely in touch with its owner—that is to say, when a dog is fortunate enough to come into the possession of an owner who, while regarding it as a dog, also realises in it the presence of qualities such as reason, honesty, wit, affection, pluck—in fact, the like qualities of the human mind—the desire to exhibit these manifestations of intelligence becomes very strong in the animal. It seeks for every means in its power to reach out to the invitation offered to express these different characteristics, and develops the power of speech to an increasing degree. The bark is made use of in varying tones to express contrasting emotions. There is the short, playful bark, when it is inducing one to accompany it for a walk. This is accompanied by broad smiles and ingratiating little whines; and, finally, the episode is closed with a loud, triumphant bark when the object has been attained, and the expedition has commenced.

There is the bark of welcome, noisy and boisterous, accompanied by much facial expression and bodily gesture. In both these modes of self-expression the clarion note of warning, which is so noticeable in the watch-dog's bark, is absent, and how telling it is in contrast! There is no mistaking it, to one who knows his dog's mind. A dog, thoroughly and suddenly aroused to sudden danger, at once conceives the necessity for warning his master, and the force of his feeling is manifested in a supremely concentrated effort.

With some dogs I have had, I have been able to judge exactly the degree of danger, and what is to be expected, by the quality of the warning bark. I have noticed that when the dog judges that what it sees or hears is of a peculiarly alarming nature, the bark very often is combined with a prolonged howl, and I have often wondered whether some remembrance does not return of the time when the canine ancestors guarded the camps of old on the lonely plains, infested by ravening animals, and the howl was then the only means of expressing the note of warning.

A curious instance of a dog divining danger through sound came under my notice. It was at the time of the terrific explosion of the munition works at Silvertown, Poplar. The sound of the explosion was heard at my house outside London, and in the room in which I was sitting with the dog. The windows also shook, but the impression I received was as of a shot-gun, fired fairly close to the house —a sound which the dog had frequently heard, and which he always resented and barked at in an ordinary way. At the time of the explosion, however, he threw up his head and let forth his most concentrated form of watch-dog bark, in which there was a large proportion of howl, and continued this for some time after the sound, which was practically instantaneous, had ceased. I then knew that something had happened beyond what I myself had grasped.

This habit of barking to let its master know of approaching danger is also due to the fact that the guard dog has been usually placed in such a position outside the camp or house so that it has to exert its vocal power to the fullest extent in order to reach the ears of the owner. For the inverse reason, dogs that are trained for sentry work become more and more silent, as they become interested in their work and accustomed to the conditions. They are always in close contact with the sentry, and feel more in touch with him, so that there is no necessity to bark loudly, but they give him warning by other means, such as low growling, and a very alert attitude. Picket the same dog a couple of hundred yards outside the lines by itself, and it will let the guard know by barking of enemy approach, because it will know that this is the only way it can communicate satisfactorily.

One could write lengthily on speech in dogs. It is a subject which has not been much studied or experimented with, but which opens up immensely interesting possibilities. The most intelligent dogs exhibit the most comical and fascinating ways of communicating their fancies, desires, and mandates. They smile like human beings, they talk —expressing pleasure and annoyance—they scold, they grumble, and are, in fact, never at a loss to clearly express themselves. In fact, the family dog, as everyone knows who is fortunate enough to be in possession of the right sort, rules with a rod of iron, has a very high standard as to punctuality, and other modes of behaviour for the members of the family, and leaves no stone unturned to keep them up to the mark.

CHAPTER II

The Necessity for a Watch-dog.

"There watched before the miser's gate,
A very cur, whom all men seemed to hate,
Quaint, savage, shaggy, with an eye that shone
Like a live coal, and he possessed but one,

. . . . .

His master prized him much. His name was Fang."
—CRABBE.

THE reasons for the acquisition of a watch-dog are fairly obvious. Since the war an immense floating population unattached to any home, to any form of labour, to any uplifting ideals, is unfortunately in our midst. The country at the present time, and until society becomes better organised along the old lines of legitimate supply and demand, cannot support its population. A very large section of unfortunate people are, through various causes, without adequate means of supply, and that the majority remain honest and reputable in spite of all is, indeed, a matter for congratulation. Unfortunately there are others who, to ease the burden for themselves, prey on their fellow-citizens. Never has petty theft been so common as at the present time.

Besides this there are worse evils—clever brains are taking to crime as a means of livelihood. The old Bill Sykes type of ruffian does still exist, but he has also a modern prototype who makes use of much more subtle methods. The modern cracksman's bag of tools contains instruments which our old friend Bill would have considered works of art! I suppose that among the modern fraternity there are those who ply their nefarious "profession" along the more scientific lines, and who disdain, under any circumstances, to attack unarmed men defending their possessions, or defenceless women. One hopes, as long as there are men who refuse to labour honestly with their brains, and prefer to live on the results of the toil of others, that there are among them men of the Raffles type.

Unfortunately, it is apparent that there are many men to whom the value of life has little or no meaning when barring the way to their own desires. They are the pariahs of human society, and there is little doubt that the strain and tension of war, and lack of discipline in the common life, has left us with individuals who, though they do not come under the apparent necessity of restraint, are, as a matter of fact, not absolutely sane, nor capable of real self-control. How many of such people there are among us now it is impossible to say. The sad fact of their presence is often only revealed after some horrible and brutal crime, which displays the cunning and the savagery of a nature whose mental balance is certainly not normal.

The remedy for this condition of society must be left to the community as a whole—to the churches, and to the doctors. That a gradual fundamental remedy will be found there is no doubt, but in the meantime, to face facts, we have to admit that with this class of person we have to take immediate and effectual measures in our own defence.

Now whereas the wit and subtlety of the burglar and the quality of his tools has immensely developed since the Bill Sykes days, the defences of our houses have not altered one whit. It may be said that anyone of ordinary intelligence can enter nearly any house, especially those situated in the country, if he wanted to do so, in spite of bars and bolts, etc. Given a few tools, and the necessary concentration, there is really nothing very serious to stop him.

I recently was asked to supply guarding Airedales for the business premises of an automatic burglar alarm company!

The only thing that would prevent a burglar gaining entrance would be the possibility of danger to himself. This is, and will always be, the trump card of the householder. It used to be said that a light left burning downstairs, a little dog to bark, and the poker, were sufficient to deter the burglar of pre-war days. Well, everything which comes under the heading of a hindrance may be counted to the good, but unfortunately, as I have already stated, we have a different class of intruder to deal with now. He is well versed in the use of fire-arms, and has little scruple in using them. The small dog is certainly a decided nuisance from his point of view, and it is not easy to circumvent its sharp hearing and piercing bark. If the dog is known to have a master who keeps his revolver handy, and has no intention of letting his possessions depart without protest, the combination is one which will certainly give the intending burglar considerable anxiety, and unless the prize is very desirable, he would be well to transfer his attentions elsewhere.

But even the above mentioned difficulties are not always sufficient to stop him, and what of the homes where there are only defenceless women, or are without a male inhabitant of such determination as I have suggested? It is to be feared that it is not sufficient to have only warning given in these cases, but actual co-operation in defence from the dog itself is necessary as well. In the case of houses inhabited by women only, this is certainly the case. There is not the slightest doubt that the gravest risk attends the establishment inhabited by women alone. They are quite without protection, and are at the mercy of any ruffians who may become aware of that fact. A good dog, which will give warning, and is capable of assisting in repelling an attack, and is capable of holding a man up, is one of the best antidotes to this dangerous situation.

Another class of persons which needs special consideration is the gamekeeper, and all those whose occupation takes them to lonely parts at night; also night-watchmen, or workers whose homeward beat takes them across lonely commons or lanes. A dog to patrol beside them is of immense use, and it is unlikely that people thus guarded will be molested.

Ladies who are out walking in country districts by night or day should most emphatically be protected by a good dog, who can come to their assistance in the event of interference. It may be emphatically asserted that it is absolutely unsafe for women to walk out on lonely roads by themselves at the present time.

I have shown in a previous chapter how the possession of dogs was a vital necessity in the daily life of the early races of the world, and it would seem in the present crowded and congested state of society that many of the same difficulties which confronted our early ancestors are with us to-day, and we are beginning to discover, as they did, that a dog is one of the best assistants in the solution of the problem.

For many years I have realised this, and have devoted much time to studying the question of the safeguarding of person and property. My conclusions are set forth after years of experiments with every sort of breed, and under every condition.

To the country and suburban policeman, a good dog is an inestimable boon, as a protection to himself and also to assist him in actually doing his work better, by utilising the quick scenting and hearing powers of the dog.

Owing to the increasing value of dogs since the war, when thousands of valuable animals were destroyed owing to lack of food, it is becoming increasingly difficult to supply dogs for the police, at a price economically practicable, either for the individual policeman to purchase himself, or for their supply from county funds.

During the war I was put in charge, by the War Office, of the dogs trained for the army as messengers and guards, and the whole movement was done on a comprehensive system, whereby the dogs were served out from the War Dog School to the units in the battlefields. In this case, though, animals were presented free to the army for training by private owners all over the country, who were only too thankful to send their canine followers to a place where they would be well fed and cared for during the food shortage, and where their intelligence would be of service to the country. At the time of the Armistice, I represented that the continuation of this War Dog School might be of great advantage to the country, for the purpose of serving out to the police regular supplies of sentry patrol dogs, and incidentally such sentry and messenger dogs as might be required from time to time with the army. It was not considered feasible, however, to continue the school in peace time, and it was therefore closed down. This was a great pity, as soon afterwards the trouble in Ireland began, and a great demand arose for patrol dogs for our troops. None, however, could be supplied, as the large numbers of trained animals which were at the school had been dispersed.

Since then, several occasions have arisen in our national affairs in connection with the army, when a certain number of trained sentry and messenger dogs would have been of immense value, and as regards the police, there is no doubt that nightly, all over the country, trained patrol dogs would be of the greatest protection to the constables themselves, and also to the general public.

CHAPTER III

The Uses of a Watch-dog

"The faithful dog, the natural friend of man,

. . . . .

Watched round his bed at sleep's unguarded hour.

. . . . .

In deeds of death and danger led the way,
And bled unconquered in the doubtful fray.

. . . . .

With nice discriminating nose, inhales
The passing odours in the tainted gales;
And clamorous barks and points his listening ears,
Bristles his wavy back, and fierce defiance growls."

—KNIGHT.

IN the foregoing chapter I have run over the various breeds of dogs, and their qualifications, for the very important office of guardian, and I will now explain the best manner in which to utilise the dog when on duty.

I will first of all discuss the class of dog the necessity for which is perhaps the most in evidence nowadays. It is that one for

THE PROTECTION OF THE TOWN OR SUBURBAN HOUSE

As regards the smaller terriers, I may say at once that many of them are excellent *as additions* to the canine establishment, and their sharp warning bark will always be of service in the house, but as a means of real protection from a serious assault on the premises they are insufficient in these days. Therefore, while not in any way deprecating the assistance these little fellows are able to give, it is better to keep in view the fact that the most effective type of watch-dog for the above is of a medium size, but of sufficient weight in itself to resist and repel an attack from without.

"HALT! WHO GOES THERE?"

TRAINING DOG TO GUNFIRE.

p. 32.

I advocate the Airedale more especially, but whatever breed is decided upon the following directions for management will apply.

In a house of this description it is not to be supposed that a dog is to be on duty outside the house, but that its services are required indoors, certainly at night, and sometimes in the day-time. When off duty the dog can play about the house or garden, but on no account must he be turned out on to the street to roam at will. The best dog will deteriorate if this is done, as he gets into slack habits, and loses his discrimination and acumen in guarding. He may also develop straying propensities and will sometimes remain from home for hours. Futhermore, he runs the risk of being stolen, and it must be remembered that dogs are very valuable indeed in these days, so that expert dog-thieves are always on the look-out.

When our watch-dog is allowed off the premises, therefore, it must be under supervision, and he must remain at home until it is convenient for his mistress or the children to take him with them for a walk. A walk he must have, and while this may sometimes seem to be a trouble, it must be remembered that Jack deserves this consideration in return for the safe guarding of the family. After his return from the walk, it may not be always convenient to let him come indoors. He should then be put into a kennel with a run, or temporarily chained to a kennel. If a dog is given sufficient exercise and liberty it does it no harm whatever to have it under some sort of restraint at certain times during the day, either indoors or outside. In fact the management of the young adult dog is very much on the same lines as that of our children, and it is recognised that youngsters should not be allowed to romp all day, but have to learn self-control and discipline.

It is better for this class of residence that Jack should be indoors when his guarding powers are required. In the day-time he can be allowed the run of the house, but when his really serious work begins at night he should be chained up inside the premises, where he will be in the best position for hearing all over the house, and also nearest the most vulnerable point.

It is generally found that the foot of the staircase in

the hall is the best point for him to lie at night, and he must here be given a comfortable bed, which must be so arranged that it protects him from draughts. Halls are, unfortunately, unless heated, apt to be rather chilly in winter time, and neither man nor beast will thrive if asked to sleep in too low a temperature. Some sort of shelter can usually be devised, however, which need not interfere with audibility.

A great many burglaries take place when the family is at late dinner, and the maids are occupied downstairs. It is a good plan to place the watch-dog in position, therefore, about this time, and leave the bedroom doors open upstairs, so that he can hear any sounds from above. In any case he must go on duty when the family retires to bed, and it is then extremely important that the doors of the lower rooms should all be left open, so that he can hear all over the lower floor, and quickly detect any attempt on the doors or windows from without. Many people give their dog the run of the house at night, but this is a mistake, and there is a psychological reason for chaining the watch-dog to a given point. A dog on the chain is always much more on guard than when loose, and therefore his powers in this direction are accentuated.

Furthermore, he is apt to make for the most comfortable place to suit himself—say the paterfamilias' armchair, which may not necessarily be the best point for hearing.

By the way, I may parenthetically remark, that the surest way to discover which is the most comfortable armchair in a house, is to observe the one selected by the family dog, whether occupied openly or by stealth; and everyone knows the sudden flop which greets the ear, when one enters a room tenanted only by Jack, while his somewhat flustered expression as he hurriedly dumps himself on the mat in front of the fire, trying at the same time to look as innocent as possible, deceives nobody.

To continue the parenthesis, has anyone ever noticed that the exact centre of the fireplace belongs exclusively by length of custom, and also that of possession, to the family dog? There is no doubt whatever on this point in *his* mind, and one of the crosses of his life, is the perpetual effort required on his part, to impart and impress this fact on his family, who are forever arguing the point.

And here let me put in a plea for the poor fellow. There are all sorts of petty and annoying ideas, from his point of view, in connection with this, his most favourite position. Many very kind masters and mistresses think the fire will make him blind, and apart from wanting the coveted position themselves, they really believe it injurious in one way or another, and they draw him away, and make him take up a chilly position in the rear. Now this theory is only a superstition. The fire will not hurt him. It will be noticed that if it is very bright, Jack sits in front of it with his eyes nearly closed, and the pleasant glow of warmth does poor Jack as much good as it does his master. I am sure one of the first questions dogs ask each other on introduction is, " Hallo ! What sort of fenders do they keep at your place ? " The fence-like Queen Anne variety, whereby he is in the unpleasant position of receiving an intense glow on his head and chest, and a cold draught for his feet, is anathema to the canine species. A nice low curb, over which he can spread a chilly pair of paws, is what the family friend desires.

After this digression let me revert to our household guardian, ensconced for the night in a snug bed in the hall, with head exposed, and ears ever at half-prick, even as he dozes. The family are asleep upstairs, and how well he knows that on him lies the responsibility of the safety of his friends and their home—*his* home ! Jack's head is lying on his front paws, and hazy impressions are floating through his mind—pleasant remembrances of tasty bones lying buried in various secret spots in the garden, a drowsy resolve to settle on the morrow if possible, once and for all, a lifelong dispute with an impudent baggage of a cat in the next street, a feeling of annoyance that the new cook stints him in house scraps amongst his biscuits, and a determination to " go sick " until his mistress sees this is remedied.

Suddenly a strange footfall on the lonely road, and stopping at his gate ! Instantly the head is erect, eyes wide open in the darkness, ears strained. Steady now ! No silly panic ; it may be passing on. Hallo ! Is that the creak of the gate? A moment's tense listening, when a slight scrunch of gravel on the path is heard.

Jack is rising to his feet now, every hair on his back standing straight up on end. Already he is beginning to growl, but curbs himself till he follows further developments. He will make certain first, before arousing the family, and he knows his power in reserve. A tense stillness for a second or two, and then a slight rustling noise in the bushes under the dining-room window—a sharp click of a catch. . . . Instantly Jack gives tongue! There is no hesitation now, and he sends up a roar, that not only awakens his master, but can be heard at the other end of the road. The gist of the roar is, "Come down at once! There is someone trying to get in at the dining-room window. Undo my chain, and let me get at him!"

Paterfamilias tumbles downstairs, and lets Jack free, who tears off to the window, determined to pin his man. By this time, however, the burglar will probably have decamped, if he is wise. If, however, the house is in a lonely position, and the burglar is of an exceptionally adventurous disposition, he may try conclusions with Jack, who is not in the least daunted, but spends the next few minutes selecting a suitable holding-on spot on the burglar's anatomy. This is very hindering to Mr. Sykes, and, moreover, gives paterfamilias time to get on some clothes and look out his weapons.

The situation is not a pleasant one for the intruder. He feels he has made a mistake. A big fellow such as he could have tackled paterfamilias, but this adjectived dog thrown in is more than he bargained for. He decides to clear as quickly as he can, circumstances permitting! It is probable, however, that, by this time, a message has been carried to the police, by some fleet-footed inmate of the house, or by telephone, and with the up-to-date police patrol system now in force, a ring of telephone messages, whereby all the roads are watched, makes escape difficult and risky.

This sketch of what might happen under such given circumstances is not exaggerated, but is a picture of what is taking place in many places all over the country.

Another moment of peril to a household can take shape in the visit of a burly tramp after paterfamilias has left the house for his business. Madam, passing through the hall, may see the man standing on the front doorstep, or he may make his approach to the kitchen entrance to the maids. In either case his requests are made in a menacing tone, and if they are not acceded to by the women, worse may follow, unless——! "Here, Jack, where are you?" "Coming, coming!" infers Jack, who has been having a little relaxation in the nursery upstairs, having been included in a game of Zoological Gardens by the young folk. Before that other Jack, with the surname of Robinson, can be invoked, our Jack is downstairs, and proceeds in an exceedingly businesslike way to superintend the tramp's departure, and who leaves with one sentiment uppermost in his mind, which is that he is sorry he spoke!

Not long since, an elderly lady told me that her sister answered the front door bell, and found just such a man on the step. He demanded money in angry tones, and when she hurriedly drew back and tried to close the door, he thrust it back, and knocked the poor old lady senseless, and tore off her rings and jewellery. There was no Jack in the house and the man knew it!

As a matter of fact, the likelihood of such a happening ever taking place, or, indeed, burglary of any sort, is immensely decreased by the inclusion of just such a canine friend as I have described. Burglars do not like being bitten, and they generally take means to find out what they are up against before starting to "crack a crib."

A good watch-dog is one of the best preventatives of these crimes.

It is a mistake to suppose that it spoils the watch-dog to make a pet of him. That is to say, in the right sense. The more a dog loves his people the more they can make use of him. When people ask me how to treat sick dogs, I always ask them to suppose they are nursing one of the babies of the family, and act accordingly. In the same way I believe in training dogs along the same lines on which we bring up our children, namely, through control of their affections, and by convincing them that the necessary discipline is invoked as part of their legitimate work, and in their own interests.

The more Jack is made the "pal" and confidant of the

family, therefore, the greater will be his devotion towards them, and the more acute his intelligence. But he must also, like the rest of the family, be taught to keep hours, obey orders, and generally comport himself as a responsible individual, with a stake in the family life and an ideal to live up to.

Does this seem an exaggerated estimate of doggie capability? Not at all. Anyone who procures the right sort of dog to start with, then proceeds to recognise and cultivate the individuality and personality in him, will very soon find out all sorts of unsuspected attributes, amongst which is a very strong sense of right and wrong—an acutely sensitive conscience. This individuality in the dog must be addressed and cultivated, and anyone who has done so knows how a dog so treated will respond, what devoted service and intelligent co-operation will be the result.

Commonsense will naturally ensure, that when Jack goes off duty in the morning, he must be immediately allowed a run out-of-doors under supervision before coming in to await the convenience of the family for a morning promenade.

GUARDING COUNTRY HOUSES

It is sometimes not sufficient to have only one watch-dog when the house is large and rambling, and may have a plethora of doors and windows on the ground floor. In a neighbourhood where there has perhaps been an epidemic of burglaries it is better to have two dogs indoors, one chained up in the front part of the house and one at the back. If it is not desired to keep both of them indoors all the time, it is quite easy to have them kept out of doors during the day, and bring them in to their respective positions at night. Some people will keep one dog indoors, and the other one outside; but a dog outside is not so useful as when he is inside.

It is sometimes desired to leave a dog outside to "roam the grounds." I do not recommend this. In practice it is not as satisfactory as it sounds very often. For one thing, there is a risk of a deliberate intention on the part of some evil wisher, to put poisoned meat down at nightfall, where the dog may find it, with disastrous results. It is not always easy, either, to confine the animal to the exact boundaries of his own grounds. Also perfectly authorised persons, and yet who may not be known to the dog, run the risk of being held up on their way to the house. Besides, the dog might be inspecting one side of the grounds while a burglar, watching his opportunity, may make his approach from the opposite side, so from every point of view it is better to keep the dog under some form of control when on duty, and best of all, to have him indoors.

GUARDING LOCK-UP SHOPS AND BUSINESS PREMISES

There are, however, exceptions to the above rule. In the case of lock-up shops and similar premises it is better for the dog to be left loose inside, so that it can have the run of the building.

This was a method largely adopted during the war, in relation to the canteens at many of the large camps in this country. At Bulford, there had been very serious raids on some of the canteens. At night, some watch-dogs from the War Dog School were posted nightly in the buildings. The intelligence department of the raiders was evidently not in good working order, as they failed to hear that these sharp-toothed sentries had been instituted. The unpleasant discovery was made shortly after, and was heralded in the silence of the night by a tremendous din of scuffling, barks, shouts—and then silence! A broken window, pieces of torn trouser, etc., were discovered next morning in the canteen, and the sentry dogs were observed to be carrying their tails exceptionally gaily and with a very self-satisfied expression. Everything inside was intact, and it was the last attempt made on the premises.

Sometimes the dogs were used thus by themselves, but in other cases, where the place they were guarding was very important or secret, human sentries were posted as well, and it was found that they were very greatly aided in their work by the presence of the dogs, as the latter always gave them warning of danger long before they heard anything themselves. Also on dark or stormy nights, when guarding was eerie work, and nerves were apt to be on edge and every sound seemed magnified a thousandfold, the discrimination of the dogs was of great assistance. At such times the rustle of the wind in loose shavings, the creak of a bough or even a falling leaf may assume alarming proportions to the sentry, who can see nothing in the darkness, and who stands in strained apprehension that the sound proceeds from the stealthy approach of an enemy. The strain would be almost unbearable were it not eased by the fact that the sentry dogs were lying down quietly, which they certainly would not be doing had the sound proceeded from a human being's approach. Owing to their acute hearing and scenting powers a dog is able to sense the real cause of a sound very much better than we can.

GUARDING STACK-YARDS AND WOOD-YARDS, ETC.

Where it is desired to safeguard stack-yards, wood-yards, etc., or any yards where valuable property is stored, and where there is no night-watchman, the dog can be left loose, but it is necessary that the place should be enclosed, so that it cannot get out. There must also be a kennel placed for it so that on inclement nights it has shelter. Before the workmen go to work in the morning the animal must have been previously chained up, otherwise there may be casualties!

Sometimes it is not convenient or possible to enclose this sort of property, and yet it is desired to employ a dog or dogs to guard it. The best method then is to put each animal on a running wire, long enough to cross the most vulnerable spots. A kennel can be placed at the middle of the wire for sheltering purposes, and the dog is attached by a lead and running ring to the overhead wire.

PATROL DOGS FOR NIGHT-WATCHMEN

A night-watchman without a dog is deprived of more than half his usefulness, and wherever such men are employed they should always be provided with a good guard-dog. Some people think that the man would be likely to leave the watching to the dog, and to go to sleep himself. Well, it is extremely probable that this sort of character would sleep in any case, and even so, at all events the dog is on guard. But given a conscientious man, his protective value is immensely increased by the vitalising and discriminating presence of the dog at his side, and also his own safety in the event of assault and in the *prevention* of assault. In his case he may keep his charge on the lead, if he wishes, whereby he can detect by the demeanour of the dog whether danger is near. This he should certainly do if the dog and he are not fully acquainted with each other. He can patrol the property with the animal, which will both hear and scent out any intruders.

When the watchman is accustomed to the dog, and is moreover, a good man to handle it, he can, if he wishes, let it loose to investigate the immediate neighbourhood, but he must never let it get beyond the distance from which a low whistle will recall it. He should make a friend and companion of it, as it will work far better if it is attached to him and regards him as its master. In the event of an alarm he can urge the dog on to the attack, or he can call it and put it on the lead, and proceed to investigate the cause himself, accompanied by his canine companion.

GUARD DOGS FOR GAMEKEEPERS

In these days, when the rights of property are so constantly assaulted by a certain section of society, no landlord should permit his keepers to go about without a dog to shield them in the event of attack while the men are on duty.

Recently I was speaking to a keeper who carried out his work both by day and night without any dog to protect him, and on my remarking that it would be a safeguard to him to have one, he was rather inclined to question the necessity, maintaining that he could well defend himself. Within a very short time he was attacked on a Sunday afternoon by three ruffians who grievously injured him.

The same week an attack took place on a parcels' office

in a railway-station. The stationmaster's dog defended the position, and the attackers, of whom there were three, tried to shoot it. It dashed from one to the other so rapidly, biting and impeding them, that they could not hit it. In the meantime the station staff was aroused, and the further development of the situation rested with them. This incident shows how a dog can hinder the intention of the attacking party until further help arrives. Furthermore, if a keeper is known to have a good sharp dog always with him, able and willing to give a nasty bite, he will not be so liable to molestation. He should keep it with him both on day and night duty, and it should be trained to work both loose and on the chain.

There is a tendency among gamekeepers and night-watchmen to think that half the value of the dog as a guard is lost if taken out on the lead. This is a mistake. There are times, more especially at night, when it is a great advantage to have it so close to one that every movement and tension on the animal's part can be noted. In very thick, enclosed surroundings it is effectual to keep the dog thus, and every now and then stand absolutely still, and while listening himself, the man should note the demeanour of the dog. He will often obtain a clue from it which he himself would not have noticed, and so avoid either an ambush or else the escape of some unauthorised visitor.

This hint is based on valuable experience gained with sentry dogs in the army. Many a column, marching through dense scrub or jungle, has been saved from annihilation by the timely warning given by the sentry dogs, marching ahead with the scouting party, who were given directions to keep the dogs by their side on the lead, and, while listening themselves, to give constant heed to the behaviour of the sentry dogs, which, by their greater sense of hearing and the additional sense of scent, would be likely to detect any enemy in the vicinity, before anyone else could do so.

The more intelligence applied to the management of a patrol dog, the better will be the results obtained.

In the chapter on man-tracking, I show also how game-keepers can be safeguarded and their work facilitated by the use of tracking dogs.

GUARDING A POULTRY-FARM OR ORCHARD

Now that poultry-farming and fruit-growing have been so commercialised, and a man may sometimes sink several thousand pounds in such a venture, it is necessary that his valuable stock should be preserved, and, unfortunately, this is not always very easy to do, especially near large towns.

One of the best preservatives is a system of dog-service, which must be taken quite seriously, and which will give excellent results if a little trouble is given to the matter.

In this case, the area to be guarded should be encircled, or nearly so, by a guard of watch-dogs on running wires. The wire should be about fifty yards long, and should be attached at each end to a post standing about two feet out of the ground. A kennel may be placed beside the wire, about the middle. Where the owner has been very greatly harassed by thieves, and when the territory is not very large, I have known him provide himself with sufficient dogs to entirely surround his property, so that each animal's wire just met the other—an impregnable fortress!

When, however, the place is very widespread, this is not always feasible, and in that case he must arrange the dogs so that they are within good hearing distance of each other all round. They very soon get to understand what they are there for, and one gives notice to the other in the most obliging fashion. Anyone who has a number of animals together knows how greatly the trainer's work is assisted by the cordial co-operation he obtains from his pupils. The "old stagers" are proud of their knowledge and attainments, and are only too anxious to display their prowess for the benefit of the enquiring and well-meaning but frequently blundering novices.

At the War Dog School I had an entire valley set aside for the training of this class of dog, which was found extremely useful for the protection of munition dumps and all sorts of places where isolation from intruders was vital. Their kennels and wires were placed on each side of the valley, on the top of the slopes, and the dogs were enabled to see the surrounding country to great advantage. Each dog would be from one hundred to two hundred yards apart.

It was absolutely impossible to approach any part of the valley undetected by night or day. The best-trained dogs were placed at the most vulnerable points, and also at those posts which commanded the most extensive views.

I have often observed the tests made with strangers or men disguised. The nearest outpost dog would suddenly seem to be arrested, gazing with fixed attention at the far-off approach of the stranger, who would be using every endeavour to creep up under cover, and as unnoticed as possible. Then it would run hurriedly down its wire to its neighbour, and request his immediate presence and attention.

Number Two would then rush out to the end of his wire, and both would consult together as to possibilities of danger. They would then agree that the matter wanted looking into, and would bark. At this sound Number Three, who might be a fairly new arrival and not quite alive to his duties, and had been reposing in comfort in his kennel, would run along his wire in a state of bewilderment, gazing wildly in all directions for the foe until directed by his more highly-trained brother to the right quarter. Number Three now thinks he had better let off a bark, too, as the incident certainly looks suspicious. By this time all the other sentinels are thoroughly aroused, and on the *qui vive,* and are running up and down their wires, calling out to each other their views on the outrageous impudence of any stranger daring to enter their valley, and adjuring each other to rouse up and put the attempt down with a strong hand immediately.

I have frequently found also that the dogs trained like this become very interested in their work, and that if they, by any chance, escape from their wires at night, they do not attempt to stray away, but remain close at hand.

WATCH-DOG AS A LADY'S GUARD

One of the most necessary functions of the watch-dog just now is to attend on the ladies of the house, and on their walks abroad, more especially if these are taken in lonely places. The dog need not be savage, but it must be of sufficient intelligence to defend its mistress in the event of interference, and, moreover, must be of sufficient size to raise doubts in anyone's mind as to the wisdom of risking the animal's wrath. A small terrier is not much use, and I particularly recommend the Airedale for the duty.

The dog need not be kept in to heel all the time, but it should not be allowed to stray too far away, or to hunt *en route*. When any suspicious-looking person is seen approaching, it should be called in to heel, and a very good effect is produced by putting the animal on the lead at such a time. No one likes to interfere with a dog on a chain beside its owner, and the action conveys the idea, also, that it would be wise not to do so! A lady friend of mine completely intimidated two surly molesting ruffians, whom she met on a lonely road, by carefully, and with great display, leashing up a large dog she had with her. As a matter of fact, this particular animal was not suited for his job at all, being a most chicken-hearted fellow who would not have hurt a fly, but the tramps thought her efforts were with a view to prevent their speedy annihilation, and were duly impressed, edging past her at the extreme limit of the path.

As a matter of fact, any dog, as a rule, will be very unwilling to allow a stranger to touch its owner, when kept beside her on the lead, and I have explained already that a dog confined thus is always much more on guard than when loose.

A man's guard should be managed in much the same manner, and the same rules which govern the keeper's dog can be applied to it when the master is traversing dark roads at night. When it is very dark it is better to keep the animal quite close to one.

WATCH-DOGS FOR CHILDREN

The nursery should also be safeguarded in like manner when on walks along the countryside. Many domestics who have not been accustomed to dogs are at first vehement in their protestations that they detest the animals, and could not possibly be troubled with them. I have found, however, in nearly every case, provided the right sort of dog is found, that nurse is very soon induced to change her opinion from the fact of the security she feels by Jack's stalwart co-operation in the guardianship of her beloved babies, and also by the pleasure his companionship gives the children. She generally winds up by becoming the dog's most devoted slave!

ALL CHILDREN SHOULD BE BROUGHT UP WITH DOGS

The animal selected for the nursery should be carefully chosen so that no real cause for objection on the nurse's part exists, and if this is done and she still declines to accept Jack's presence with the children, I advise that the dog should be preferred to the lady, and that she should be given notice to quit forthwith.

The fact is, dogs are an education in themselves for the youngsters. They bring out all that is best in the human character—kindness and humanity, consideration and true affection. Furthermore, a child who has never been brought up with animals—dogs, especially—is in after-life greatly handicapped. They sometimes suffer agonies of nervousness, and when too late, realise what they have missed.

I remember taking a party of country youngsters into my kennels and watching them tumbling about amongst the dogs with all the delight and interest of bairns to whom dogs and horses were perpetual friends. One fine boy, however, seemed strangely abstracted, and I soon noticed he was going deathly pale, so quickly proposed an adjournment. I heard afterwards through a friend that this lad had had a cranky old nurse as a young child who refused to let him have animals about him, and, the parents weakly acquiescing, the result was that the poor boy endured tortures from a timidity towards dogs, etc., he was quite unable to conquer.

Children should be allowed to caress and fondle their dog, but no teasing or treatment in any way distressing to the animal should be tolerated. The best disciplinarian in this case is very often Jack himself! Provided he is a dog free from guile (as our Jack is certain to be), so that he is neither savage nor treacherous, a growl as a warning to the child does a great deal of good, and need not be in any way checked by the elders.

The following episode took place in connection with a little friend of mine which illustrates this. Myrtle enters in tears and extreme self-pity. "Uncle, Jack growled at me. Boo hoo!" Uncle, quite unmoved, "And what were you *doing* to Jack?" Myrtle, suddenly recalled to introspection and to the path of truth and justice, stops howling, and says slowly and in a tone conveying immense self-revelation, "I was *teasing* him." Nothing further was said on either side, and the incident was closed. This young woman is now growing up, but she tells me the lesson in self-control and truth has remained with her all her life.

Another occasion brought out a sense of justice in a young child from another standpoint. A little lad, who certainly had not been starved, fell with some violence on the nursery dog. Poor Jack—the dog—was really for a moment in severe pain, and in his distress gave his little master quite a nip. Loud howls were the consequence from our laddie, and mother, who as a rule never fussed about things unnecessarily, thought it as well to administer a good slapping to Jack to teach him self-control in emergencies. More howls—from Jack this time. The little master, however, on hearing this, instantly ceased his own din, and flung himself in between. "Oh, mummy, how could poor Jack help it when I hurt him so!" All trace of self-pity had gone, and the two friends, dog and boy, finished the evening in close embrace.

A great many people are obsessed with a fear that animals bring dirt and even disease into the nursery, and for that reason exclude one of the best influences in a child's life. This is a very great mistake. So fatal, in fact, do I regard such action that I would almost go the length of advocating a dirty dog rather than none! But as a matter of fact, there is no need for the family friend to be anything except sweet and clean, provided a little ordinary care in his toilet is used. He is *worth* it.

A great deal of the slackness in keeping a dog in a clean, wholesome condition is due to the anticipation of the tremendous amount of labour this is supposed to involve. As a matter of fact, under proper management, the process is extremely simple, and need not take any time. Reference to a later chapter on the grooming and care of the watch-dog will describe how this can be carried out with complete simplicity.

The nursery dog should have its face washed every morning with a soapy sponge, and a bath once a week. Its teeth should be cleaned with a toothbrush dipped in Vim once a week, and it should have a tooth-comb run through the coat every day. This can be made a duty for the children to carry out under supervision. It is good discipline for them, and teaches them a sense of dainty cleanliness and neatness in their pets.

A good terrier is the best dog for a child, as they are alert and full of fun, and are very reliable as a rule.

CHAPTER IV

The Choice of a Watch-dog

"In man, true friendship I long strove to find
But missed my aim;
At length I found it in my dog most kind.
Man! blush for shame."
—*Verse on a dog's collar.*

THE oldest races of dog existing in this country are those of the hound breeds. These are mentioned in very early history, and were used for many purposes, but mostly in connection with the chase. The next in order in point of antiquity come the mastiffs. These, it may be stated, are the oldest of all the watch-dogs. They did their work well in those far-off days, when they were looked upon as part of the establishment to which they belonged, and were absolutely necessary adjuncts.

At that time the natural ferocity of their nature was greatly appreciated, and was assiduously cultivated. Queen Elizabeth's physician, Dr. Caius, wrote about these dogs: "An huge dogge, stubborn, eager, burthenous of body, and therefore of but little swiftness, terrible and fearful to behold." The size and spirit of this breed began to decline as the years rolled on, and the inhabitants of our islands became less savage towards each other. The gradual enrolment of an efficient police force also contributed to internal peace, and so reduced the necessity for such extremely pugnacious household guardians

Fine specimens were still maintained, however, at the great castles and houses up and down the land, many of the strains having been in the families for generations.

There was one special revival of the breed about a hundred years ago, and this effort no doubt saved it from extinction. The animals bred at that time were magnificent specimens, large and powerful, but, while maintaining the true guarding instinct, they were not as ferocious as were those of early history. Still, they could always give a good account of themselves, and, unless kept well under control were apt sometimes to land their owners in trouble by too-vigorous attack on unauthorised persons. Up till the time just before the war there were still some fine strains in the country, and very respectable classes, both in quality and numbers, were entered at some of our classic shows.

The exigencies of wartime, alas ! wrought great havoc among all these large breeds, on account of the difficulty of feeding and exercising them. The War Dog School was able to save a good many fine specimens, as they were sent by their owners for guarding purposes, and were thus fed during this strenuous period. They eventually went back to private owners at the end, and in many cases are being bred from, so that one hopes this old national breed will be kept extant. They may, however, at the present day, be regarded more as curiosities, and as examples of bygone ages. The ferocious spirit has died away and they are mostly of a lazy and sluggish temperament, but at times if anything rouses them they can blaze forth with terrific vehemence, and their great weight and size renders them a serious menace in attack. A friend purchased a very ancient baronial castle recently, with battlements, drawbridge, and moat, entire. To complete the idea of antiquity he secured a fine mastiff to act as guard to the castle court. It is to be hoped he has dressed it up in the correct spiked collar, and that there are a few " varlets " standing about to restrain it in the event of its taking a sudden distaste to a visitor !

Mastiffs, however, are too sluggish and lazy to be good house-watchers. They are not alert enough, and in the case referred to my friend has taken the precaution to provide himself *as well* with a good Airedale.

AIREDALES FOR GUARDING

Perhaps the reason for the excellent all-round working value of this dog is on account of the careful and well-

Training the Dog to Pursue in Face of Revolver Fire.

p. 50.

thought-out manner in which the breed was manufactured, and the sterling qualities of each type of ancestor which was brought with use. It originally sprang from the old-fashioned Scottish terrier, not the Aberdeens of the present day, but the old-fashioned terrier of the Border hills and dales—a stout, hearty little fellow, with very rough grey or tan coat, fairly long in the leg, and of a medium size. The type varied in details, but as a whole it was pretty much the same, and certainly was so as regards quaintness of character, sagacity and dauntless courage. From him spring also, besides the Airedale, the modern Aberdeen, Skye and Dandie Dinmont.

The first cross for the subsequent development of the Airedale was with the bull-terrier, and this, I think, was a mistake, as no greater courage was required than that possessed by the Scotch terrier, and the evident admission of the bull-terrier cross is that which all trainers of the Airedale have of recent years been working hard to eliminate. At one time, a generation or so ago, the working men of the Midlands, and especially of the Aire Valley, exulted in this cross as an excellent production for the dog fights in which they delighted. The pugnacious tenacity of the bull-terrier nature was useful. After this, in order to encourage the working qualities in water, another cross was made with the otter hound, and this was a very advantageous, sound one.

The combination of the qualities of the old Scotch terrier and this hound confirmed and accentuated in a remarkable degree the good characteristics of the breed. This type also began to stabilise, the rich red-tan and the black saddles of many of the otter hounds, and has been especially cultivated, and the result has become a dog combining all the best instincts of both breeds.

The definite advantage to be gained in using the Airedale as a watch-dog is, that in it one obtains the alertness and general companionableness of the terrier species, and also the size of a comparatively large dog. This last is most important, as it renders it an extremely difficult matter for a burglar to treat a dog of such weight with indifference, even supposing he is willing to brave the mere watching powers of the animal. He cannot easily kick it aside, and once it gets a hold of him, it is difficult to shake off.

For several generations now this dog, which became definitely the Airedale, has been used, more especially for guarding purposes. The peculiarly faithful and sagacious nature of the breed, combined with its adaptability to every circumstance where it may be required, whether it be the farmer's yard, the factory, or a lady's drawing-room, makes it very useful indeed. Its quickness of hearing, its courage and discrimination are capable of keeping our families in perfect safety. It has, therefore, by this time, the *tradition of guarding in its nature,* and one frequently notices this instinct developing when the puppies are still toddling about the dam. It is amusing to observe the most forward ones stand up on their legs and emit sharp little barks at what they consider an intrusion, till they rush to their mother for further instructions.

Any reproach the breed may once have had as to quarrelsomeness with other dogs, due to the bull-terrier ancestry, is now, by judicious training, being eliminated. In my own kennels, as many as fifteen Airedales go out exercising together, racing and chasing and thoroughly enjoying themselves, and they are trained to refrain from attacking each other. At the same time, they are not cowards, and any one of them, if insulted by a strange dog, will hold his ground, and keep his tail up. They are devoted to children, and make excellent nursery companions, and it is a wonderful combination of character, in which a baby can fondle one of them and receive affectionate caresses in return, and yet a burglar's reception is a row of molars! As guards for ladies they are remarkably valuable, and are easily controlled and disciplined.

I have owned and trained at one time or other, nearly every kind of dog suitable for guarding work, and will discuss some of these further in this chapter, but as the result of all my work of years it is my considered judgment, that for all-round watching and guarding work, the most reliable dog in size and character is the AIREDALE TERRIER. This conclusion has been reached, not only from experience in my private kennels, but also from that gained during the time I was Commandant of the War Dog School, during which time hundreds of dogs of all breeds passed through my hands for training.

TRAINING AN AIREDALE TO SAVE LIFE.

TRAINING IN OBEDIENCE.

(*See page* 83.)

In discussing other breeds for use in the home against unauthorised intruders of all sorts, a sincere mead of praise may be accorded all the smaller terriers, such as the fox, Scotch or Aberdeen, Irish, Yorkshire, Welsh, etc. In these are obtainable everything that is required as regards pluck, fidelity, intelligence, and alertness. The only drawback is that they are not sufficiently powerful to be a sufficient deterrent to a really determined ruffian, and while they are efficient in giving the necessary warning, they cannot, to any extent, give any further assistance.

The bull terrier is a fine animal, and can render a good account of himself in a struggle, but he is too excitable, is not a very suitable dog for the women and children of the family to manage. The same may be said as a whole of the bull-dog. The modern bull-dog nature is a curious mixture of sluggishness and suddenly-aroused wrath, which at times is rather more than the average householder requires. This criticism applies in an equal degree to the mastiff, and also to the bull-mastiff. The mastiff is, in any case, too big for indoors, and when thoroughly aroused is an extremely dangerous animal, and makes the punishing business too much his own affair. The Great Dane has the same disadvantage. The bull-mastiff, while not so large, and quite suitable for indoors, can also be too vehement for average purposes, and takes a male to control him. He has his uses, however, when a man is faced by an exceptionally dangerous and lonely situation at home or abroad. Absolutely undaunted in attack, and with this reputation alone carrying added value, this is a fine breed for special circumstances.

Retrievers are frequently met with as guards, and make quite good house dogs. The curly-coated ones are the best watches, but they are sometimes not quite reliable in character; especially is this so as they increase in years. The flat-coated variety are usually not sharp enough. This remark also applies to all the spaniels and setters. They have their uses in the field and elsewhere, and are delightful companions, but when the protection of the home, as a vital need, has to be considered, they are not sufficiently determined. Collies, and all the sheep-dog varieties, are quick and alert at giving warning, but are highly strung and nervous, and are apt to retire in the attack. They are also not always quite reliable with the youngsters in the house, if teased, but many of the old-fashioned collies with the broad heads are quite trustworthy.

The hounds (and bloodhounds) are not suitable for house-guards as a rule. They are animals of extraordinary concentration along certain lines, and seem unable to expand outside these. There are, however, exceptions. I will discuss the tracking qualities of the bloodhound as an asset in the guardianship of the home in a later chapter. Of all the hounds, the most intelligent as a companion is the otter hound, but he is not sufficiently alert for a guard.

I do not propose to discuss any of the foreign breeds. There are individual specimens among them, no doubt, which prove useful inmates of the family, but the fact remains that they are aliens, and as in the human family, so in the dog—the national and racial characteristics of each country are invariably reflected, and not less so in this most intimate associate of man. The mind of the master becomes mirrored in that of his dog. That this is so I have shown forth fully in a later chapter in this book. I am sure that my readers will agree with me, that we cannot do better than to stand for British characteristics, both in man and beast. Apart from this, it is up to the public to support the British breeder in his efforts to keep the national breeds going, after the struggle of the war. Furthermore, there are no dogs in the world which can compare with the British in reliability and courage.

If I were to define a combination of breeds, whereby the home defence of a family could be rendered absolutely secure at night time, I would suggest a bull-mastiff or an Airedale on a patrol wire out of doors, an Airedale chained indoors in the hall, and another Airedale or a small terrier on the upper floor. As an extra touch, a bloodhound kept round at the stables, and ready to put on a trail. It is certain that any family thus protected may, if they wish, leave their valuables displayed, and their doors and windows wide open, without any danger of intrusion. This combination might be called guardianship-de-luxe, but even without this display a house is well guarded by one good Airedale dog indoors, or posted at a vulnerable spot without. (See chapter on Kennelling.)

Another point which must be taken into consideration when choosing the family watch-dog is that of expense. While it is true that all good dogs of true breed (which implies accentuation of the desired characteristics), and which are well trained to their work, are not to be cheaply obtained since the war, it is necessary that our suitable watch-dogs should be bred in sufficient numbers to bring them within the reach of the average householder, seeing that large numbers are now required. All the large breeds, under which heading come the mastiffs, Newfoundlands, St. Bernards, Great Danes Irish wolfhounds and deerhounds, are scarce and costly, and they cost a good deal to feed. They are of necessity, therefore, for the few. Airedales are being bred in large numbers now, and are not expensive to keep, so that in this particular also they are useful dogs.

DOGS FOR HOT CLIMATES

Many of the terriers adapt themselves well to hot climates. Fox-terriers are good if a small dog is preferred, and if a more powerful animal is needed I can recommend an Airedale, as this breed is excellent both in the Tropics and in the Far North. Bull-terriers can be relied on to "carry on" in warm places of the earth. These two last breeds are excellent protectors for masters whose duties take them in dangerous places. I have sent many bull-mastiffs abroad for this purpose also, but on the whole prefer the Airedale to any other breed, on account of its hardihood under trying conditions, and its alertness.

CHAPTER V

How to Purchase a Dog

" But the poor dog, in life the firmest friend,
The first to welcome, the foremost to defend,
Whose honest heart is still his master's own,
Who labours, fights, loves, breathes for him alone."
—BYRON.

HAVING decided on the most suitable breed, the next thing is to obtain a good specimen. To the novice this is a rather difficult matter. He may know little or nothing about dogs, and also may be painfully aware that the purchase is attended by many pitfalls for the uninitiated.

As a matter of fact a truly ignorant person is often in a safer position than one who knows just a little, and who exemplifies the maxim that "a little knowledge is a dangerous thing." The latter person frequently resents advice, and prefers to rely on his own judgment, both as regards place of purchase, and of the article purchased, whereas a man who admits ignorance generally goes to some friend who is a real authority and takes his advice, or he decides to buy from some well-known and high-class kennel whose name is one of good repute, and to place himself in the hands of the principal there.

The many periodicals which deal with the interests of dogs and other live stock are full of advertisements of every kind of dog for sale, but it is very confusing to a novice to distinguish, amongst the quantities offered, which would be the best for him to select. The dog-shops also do not offer much safeguard, as, except in the high-class ones, it is difficult to be certain of the origin of the wares, nor do they know the dog's character. The best advice, therefore, to give just such a would-be purchaser, is to let him enquire for the name of a reputable breeder of such breed as he has selected, and go to the one mentioned, telling him his full requirements and putting himself in the recommended person's hands. If the breeder has a well-known reputation of years to sustain, he will not be likely to endanger it by shifty dealing, but he will watch over the interests of the customer, and will do his utmost for him to ensure good value. Unless he had made a practice of doing this, he could not have maintained the good name of his stock during the passing years.

Nearly all the big breeders advertise regularly in the various dog papers and magazines, and it is therefore easy to find their addresses. It is true that there are also many good dogs advertised singly by private individuals, that is to say, who do not make dog-rearing a serious occupation, but it is rather difficult for the novice to distinguish the wheat from the tares, or, in other words, to pick out those dogs which genuinely represent the value and qualifications offered.

The best-known breeder is therefore the safest for him. He will, however, have to pay more probably, but he will have the satisfaction of knowing that the stock purchased will be good, also that the statements as to character and disposition will be accurate.

In the event of the transaction from any cause not turning out satisfactorily, most high-class breeders are always willing to meet the situation in a friendly and accommodating spirit, and to adjust any mishap which may have occurred. This standard is the reason of the higher charges. The maintenance of everything in such a kennel will be high, and the fact that the attitude towards a purchaser is one of sincere intention, entails a large amount of wastage in stock, in order to put out for sale only that which may be of first-class health and character.

Only those who have tried to run a good-sized head of stock know what a number of specimens have to be put aside, either temporarily or permanently, from one cause or another, as unfit for sale, because they happen not to conform to the high standard set up by the owner. This means a serious leakage and expense, and has to be considered in the charges, as naturally a commercial enterprise cannot be carried on except at a profit, and in these days very few people can afford to run a large kennel as a hobby, or even a small one, for that matter. It must be made to cover its expenses, at all events.

Having decided on a breed, and having been recommended to a good high-class vendor, therefore, the next thing is to consider the selection of the actual animal. Is it to be a puppy, a half-grown, or an adult? There are many considerations to be taken into account, but it may be said that expense is the chief, or rather the amount of purchase money which it is possible to lay down. A puppy will be cheaper, but in the long run the money spent on the upbringing will total the cost of a fully-grown dog, and, furthermore, there is always the risk of losing the pup through one of the numerous canine illnesses which may attack it during growth. As a whole, it is better for a novice to purchase a fully-grown dog, if possible, unless he really has enough knowledge of dogs to rear a puppy successfully, and also to select one which will turn out a good dog, in which case, however, with such judgment he would be, I expect, no longer a novice.

It must be remembered that one can only judge of a puppy's ultimate appearance and character by inference, whereas with a dog which has attained full growth the purchaser can see what he is getting as regards appearance, and to a certain extent can also gather what the animal's character is likely to be. The grown dog will, however, be the most expensive.

On the other hand, some people may prefer a puppy for other reasons as well as the cheaper cost. It is amusing and interesting rearing a puppy, watching it develop and teaching it oneself, and where there are children a young thing like this gives great entertainment. On the other hand, a good deal of attention has to be administered, and this takes time, and is a certain amount of trouble. A good plan is to state the exact circumstances of the case, and ask the vendor's advice as to the resultant purchase. This is another reason why it is best to go to a really reliable breeder, whose suggestions can be received with credence, and whose experience qualifies him to point out the best animal for the purpose.

For very young and especially for nervous children, a puppy is very often the best, as the smaller size of their pet gives them confidence. Where there are other dogs, and especially if these be of a quarrelsome nature, where there are cats, and where there are sheep and chickens close round the place of abode it is better to choose a puppy, as in the midst of all these temptations a young adult might occasionally lapse until disciplined, whereas a puppy will grow up into the necessary amalgamation of interests, especially those of the cats, without undue mishap.

A very good age for an environment such as this, and where a quite young puppy is not desired, is a young animal of the age of six months or thereabout. This is an excellent age to purchase a dog. They are very adaptable, and yet they are sufficiently grown to be easily fed and to be more or less independent. They will not have attained their full growth, nor will they in all probability have had distemper, but they will be so far grown, that the ultimate size and quality of points can be pretty accurately judged. They are at this age more expensive than a pup just leaving the mother, but not so much so as a young adult or a fully-trained dog. At this age, too, the really experienced breeder will be able to prognosticate pretty accurately the ultimate characteristics with which the adult animal will be permanently endued.

As a matter of fact, the expert can judge fairly accurately what the various characteristics will be even of the young pups which are just able to play around their dam. When they begin to feed themselves it is easy to note those of strong constitution and character, as they toss their weaker brethren away from the bowl and with determination seek their own nourishment. The way they stand on their legs, their alertness and desire for play, their quarrelsomeness round the bowl—all these are so many manifestations of character, which are reflections of what the later development will be, more or less. But at six to eight months of age, this character-reading is, of course, still easier.

On the other hand, many people prefer to see exactly what they are getting straight away: that is to say, to purchase the completely developed animal. A good age, therefore, for this requirement is a dog of from one year to eighteen months old. This is a very delightful age, and is quite an adaptable one. As each dog, however, has a definite character of its own, as does a human being, it is as well to choose one with a nature already developed along the lines one wishes according to one's requirements. At this age the dog will have been sufficiently trained to have quite a clear understanding of its duties, but no dog can be considered absolutely fully trained much under two years. It may understand what is required of it quite well, but it will not have had the necessary disciplining to be stabilised until two years of age. But from a year old onwards, the points will be fully developed and the dog will have attained practically its full size, although it will fill out and grow heavier as it grows older. The sort of disposition will be fully apparent, or will be at all events to the breeder of the dog, so that he will be in a position to advise as to which one will be the most suitable.

With regard to the older dogs, the finished article, both as regards appearance and character, stands ready to hand. The only thing to remember here is, that the outstanding characteristics will be intensified as the dog grows older, and it is, therefore, as well to be careful in one's choice. Thus if a dog is selected on account of it sharp disposition, it will certainly not show any diminution of this characteristic as it grows older, but will, in all probability, increase in this respect and might under certain conditions become savage. As, however, such a dog is very often desired in areas liable to attack, this intensification of character would be no disadvantage.

Where a nice mild dog, with perhaps a bark or two in it is required, an animal displaying such a disposition at two years of age will not be likely to alter much. Any special training which the dog may have received can be considered complete at that period. It will either be very good, or it will be untrainable beyond a certain standard.

Having discussed the age, the next thing to be considered will be the points. Without going into the fashions governing each breed, there are certain broad rules which should be observed when choosing a dog. To take the large and varied family of terriers, the head qualities are the first to look for in each breed. In fox, Irish, Scotch, Airedale,

Skye, and, in fact, almost all terriers, a long narrow head, good foreface, small, well-carried ears, and nice dark eyes should be looked for. A good terrier expression, which implies a smart, alert air of extreme intelligence. Colour is also important, where there is any question of tan, which should be as rich and red as possible, and well defined. This does not necessarily mean that a fox-terrier need be all white, or evenly marked. A common error among novices is to suppose that a fox-terrier, with an evenly-marked head, is better than one with uneven patches. It may be so, but not necessarily on account of this. It is shape and size, which count much more in the value of such a terrier. Another common mistake is to suppose that black Scotch or Aberdeen terriers are better than the brindles in point of value. This is not so. Shape and size is here again the chief factor, and while a pale-coloured dog will certainly be at a disadvantage for the present fashion, still, a good heather or dark brindle dog of fine shape and correct size will take precedence of a black dog faulty in the other respects.

Quality of coat is important, and should be of a wiry, hard tendency on the body in all terriers, this being of much greater weather-resisting tendency than a soft coat. Feet and legs are also important, and should in every case be straight with close toes, and well stood upon. In all hound breeds the foregoing qualities are also necessary, but high quality of feet and legs is of paramount importance, and great attention should be paid to this last question in connection with all the very big breeds. When choosing a puppy of a big breed, say a Great Dane, Irish wolfhound or deerhound, or similar sized dogs, pick one with big bone. This will ensure a good-sized dog, but also see that the pup is well grown and strong for its age, as there is always the risk of the legs bending in the growth.

I have mentioned the importance of quality of coat and in different breeds there are special points to be looked for from this point of view.

A prolific soft silky topknot in the dandie dinmont, along with a large domed head—that delightfully quaint little terrier, which is not nearly sufficiently bred just now —in contradistinction to the wiry jacket along the saddle.

In the long-haired varieties of the larger breeds a good promise of a fine thick second coat (if it is a pup that is being selected). The toy dogs have all their various specialities, from the long, silky coat of the Yorkshire terrier and Maltese, to the fine thick fur of the Pekinese and the Pomeranian.

Weight, of course, enters very greatly into these small breeds, and the smaller specimens are greatly sought after. The best way to ensure a fine pup from any breed is to select it in the first place by its pedigree. Well-bred parents, which have themselves lived up to their reputation, will probably have satisfactory progeny.

A lady was extremely annoyed because the judge in the show-ring merely glanced at her dog and then waved it out of the ring. Afterwards she went to him and protested, saying, " Just see what a beautiful pedigree he has ! " The judge's reply was, " What a pity you did not bring the pedigree and leave the dog at home ! "

This story illustrates the fact that a pedigree dog need not necessarily turn out a perfect specimen. Still, the chances are, that if the ancestors are pure-bred dogs, you will not have an animal you are ashamed to show to your friends, and, as a matter of fact, your pup may turn out a very fine winning dog.

It is a common theory that mongrels are more intelligent than pure-bred dogs, but this is a fallacy. The qualities which one is looking for should, as a matter of fact, be ensured in a pedigree dog, whose ancestors have for generations been specially bred for that particular purpose, and the reason that such dogs are sometimes not so intelligent as others, is because, on account of their value, they have been pampered and kept more or less in isolation. Nowadays, however, people understand this better, and make a point of developing the special instinct in their dogs, by judicious training, and they also cultivate the general intelligence to a much greater extent.

To illustrate this point, I would quote from " British War Dogs " a passage which speaks of a collie-dog which was trained as a messenger, and did good service during the war. It was working in the Ypres sector, and in one of the advances the report made to me is as follows :

" The first message to come through was brought by the dog 'Roman.' He brought through a request for reinforcements in men and ammunition, thereby saving a nasty situation. . . ."

This dog was a pure-bred collie with show points.

It can safely be said that this dog alone saved hundreds of lives.

The mongrel is only sometimes more intelligent than some particular pure-bred dog because the former has probably been allowed to develop its own character by necessity, whereas the aristocratic and too-carefully-kept animal has had his mental training neglected.

A man offered me his dog during the war for training for messenger work in France. He sent it along with the remark : " I am sending you my dog Sam. He has always found his own grub, and has plenty of sense." Sam arrived and was a mongrel lurcher—very intelligent he proved to be, and his fine independent nature was disciplined along certain lines of service, and a very useful and life-saving animal was the result ; but this standard was also attained by other dogs of very blue blood indeed, and which had never had anything except a carefully-nurtured existence. In some cases, these more aristocratic dogs required rather more care in handling, and took longer in training, as they were often highly strung, but I cannot say that my experience has shown that mongrels are, in themselves, in any way more intelligent innately than pure-bred dogs, if the latter are given the same chances of development.

When selecting a puppy the purchaser should enquire the characteristics specially showing in the different members of the litter, and the breeder will certainly be aware of the more plucky ones or those of more timid tendencies, and will be in a position to advise.

In a grown dog, of course, his advice on the point of training and character is of great importance, and after I have stated plainly the requirements the purchaser will be well advised to allow himself to be influenced considerably by what the vendor has to say of the various tempers and the suitability of each dog he is being shown. The prospective owners who persist in selecting a certain animal because it reminds them of some defunct favourite, or because they " like his face," and against the warning that that particular dog is not so suitable for their purpose as another, have only themselves to blame if the deal is not a success. Where the purchase is made by correspondence, the requirements should all be clearly stated, and the sort of environment the dog will have. Much depends on this. It should be stated if ladies and children are to have the handling of the animal, if it is to live in or out of doors, and if it has to associate with any other sort of live stock.

It is much better, if possible, to visit a kennel and make a selection from a number of the same breed, but if this cannot be done, and the dog has to be sent by rail, do not be unnecessarily suspicious if the vendor refuses to send on approval. The best class of kennels do not send their dogs on approval, but the statements and description of any dog from owners of such kennels can be accepted as trustworthy. It is, of course, necessary to be sure of the exact status of the kennel in question.

In the event of a puppy or adult dog arriving with signs of illness, the vendor should be immediately wired to with the information, and asking for advice as to what he wishes done. In most cases he (the vendor) will ask for it to be returned to him immediately, as people prefer to nurse their own dogs to health, and in the event of the purchaser intending to repudiate the purchase, it is only fair to give the dog's previous owner the chance to remedy the error in his own way, and not to take it upon himself to send it to a veterinary surgeon, without permission to do so. Neither need any undue resentment in every case be accorded to the vendor, as, especially in the case of puppies, a sudden chill caught at starting can be very rapidly developed by the excitement of the journey, and an animal showing not the slightest sign of indisposition when packed up can, by sheer nervousness, combined with chill, work itself up into a serious condition in a few hours. A quiet rest, and warm surroundings, will in all probability effect a cure, but if this does not bring the desired effect, it is better to notify the vendor as directed.

A drink of warm milk on arrival is a very good thing, as it is warming and also soothing, and very often a dog in a highly nervous condition will take this, and thus check an incipient indisposition, when it will not look at more solid food—and puppies should, of course, be given warm, soft, milky food at once on arrival. After a dog or puppy has been kept for a week, the responsibility should rest with the purchaser, as by that time it would not be fair to return it, or to suggest doing so.

CHAPTER VI

Training Dogs

" For there an old man sat serene,
. . . . .
It was a comfort too, to see
Those dogs that from him ne'er would rove,
And always eyed him reverently
With glances of depending love.
They know not of the eminence
Which marks him to my reasoning sense ;
They know but that he is a man,
And still to them is kind, and glads them all he can.

What joy to watch in lower creature,
Such dawning of a moral nature,
And how (the rule all things obey),
They look to a higher mind to be their law and stay."
—*Sir Walter Scott and his Dogs.* By HALLAM.

THOSE persons who desire to instruct the growing thought of the young in a successful and harmonious manner will usually, if they are wise, study the metaphysical aspect of the subject. This is also true advice with regard to the training of all animals, and in proportion as the instructor does this will he be successful or the reverse. A close study of the relationship of man to the animal kingdom through the ages discloses many interesting facts and salutary lessons. It reveals the fact that wherever, and in whatever, man recognises the presence of good, cherishing and cultivating it, the object of this care, from that time, becomes useful and harmless. This applies, as anyone can see, to the vegetable kingdom, in which all carefully cultivated species immediately excel the properties of the wild varieties. And it also, with equal truth, applies to the animals.

Had man at all times recognised this, and realised his

tremendous responsibility towards the animal kingdom, we should not now have large numbers of savage, dangerous animals, nor vast collections of timid—nay, terrified—creatures. Where man has set foot in newly-explored territory, seldom or never trodden, the animals are tame, and advance to meet him with charming confidence, which is only dispelled when they find their trust is betrayed.

In confirmation of this conviction that this sense of fear in the animals for man must have been acquired, and is not in any way natural, I may quote Mr. Darwin, who says : " I have already discussed the hereditary tameness of our domestic animals. From what follows I have no doubt that the fear of man has always first to be acquired in a state of nature, and that under domesticity it is nearly lost. In all the few archipelagoes and islands inhabited by man, of which I have been able to find an early account, the native animals were entirely void of fear of man. I have ascertained this in six cases, in the most distant part of the world, and with birds and in animals of the most different kinds.

"At the Galapagos Islands I pushed a hawk off a tree with the muzzle of my gun, and the little birds drank water out of a vessel which I held in my hand. These wolf-like foxes were here as fearless of man as were the birds, and the sailors in Byron's voyage, mistaking their curiosity for fierceness, ran into the water to avoid them. In all old civilised countries, the wariness and fear of even young foxes and wolves are well known.

"At the Galapagos Islands the great land lizards were extremely tame, so that I could pull them by the tail, whereas in other parts of the world large lizards are wary enough. The aquatic lizard of the same genus lives on the coast, is adapted to swim and to dive perfectly, and feeds on submerged algæ. No doubt it must be exposed to danger from sharks, and consequently, though quite tame on the land, I could not drive them into the water, and when I threw them in they always swam directly back to the shore. See what a contrast to all the amphibious animals in Europe which, when disturbed by the most dangerous animal, man, instinctively and instantly take to the water !

"The tameness of the birds in the Falkland Islands is particularly interesting because most of the very same species, more especially the larger birds, are excessively wild in Tierra del Fuego, where for generations they have been persecuted by the savages. Both at these islands, and at the Galapagos, it is particularly noteworthy, as I have shown in my journal, by the comparison of the several accounts up to the time when we visited these islands, that the birds are gradually getting less and less tame, and it is surprising, considering the degree of persecution which they have occasionally suffered during the last one or two centuries, that they have not become wilder ; it shows that the fear of man is not too soon acquired."

The French naturalist, Gaede, says : "It is with the Bible in the hand that we must enter into the great temple of Nature to understand the voice of the Creator."

If this method of research had been more frequently followed by students of nature in the past, there would not be to-day such a host of theories in connection with creation which lead up to a certain point, but are incapable of any definite conclusion, because most of them are based on faulty premise.

The instruction in Genesis, in the first chapter, on the subject of nourishment for both man and beast is as follows :

"Behold, I have given you every herb bearing seed, which is upon the face of all the earth, and every tree, in the which is the fruit of the tree yielding seed, and to you it shall be for meat. And to every beast of the earth, and to every fowl of the air, and to everything that creepeth upon the earth, wherein there is life, I have given every green herb for meat, and it was so."

The dominion over the fish of the sea, and over the fowl of the air, and over every living thing that moveth upon the earth, could not have been, therefore, based upon that system of compulsion and slaughter to which man has reduced the original mandate. "God saw everything that he had made and behold! it was very good." Therefore the power of the dominion must have been one of love.

This strange and terrible misunderstanding of the loving intention of the Great Creator of all things is announced later in Genesis :

"And the fear of you and the dread of you shall be upon every beast of the earth, and upon every fowl of the air, upon all that moveth upon the earth, and upon all the fishes of the sea; into your hand are they delivered."

But this degraded concept of man's duty towards the animal kingdom only came after that debased condition of mind which is known as the fall of man had become manifest. It would seem, therefore, as though man will have to alter this attitude, and return once more to his original understanding, in which the animals are given into his care to receive love and protection. Until his mental outlook on this particular point is adjusted, just so much proportionally is he excluding himself from that state of mind which is called heaven, and from which he will continue to exclude himself until he does justice to the rest of creation. Milton says:

> "Discord first
> Daughter of Sin, among the irrational
> Death introduced, through fierce antipathy:
> Beast now with beast 'gan war, and fowl with fowl,
> And fish with fish; to graze the herb all leaving.
> Devoured each other; nor stood much in awe
> Of man, but fled him, or with count'nance grim
> Glared on him passing. These were from without
> The growing miseries which Adam saw."

How different is the picture of creation as shown forth in the first chapter of Genesis, when love reigned supreme between man and beast, and when that understanding must have obtained which is graphically described in the Book of Wisdom (Apocrypha):

"God made not death, neither hath He pleasure in the destruction of the living. For he created all things, that they might have their being; and the generations of the world were healthful; and there is no poison of destruction in them, nor the kingdom of death upon the earth."

It would be as well if this generation awoke to the great obligation placed upon it of bringing this happy condition to pass once more. That it will have to be done sooner or later there is no question of doubt, and God's immutable laws, which grind "exceeding small," will, metaphorically speaking, reduce to "powder" that mental attitude which resists the mandate.

Love for and the protection of animals, should be taught in all schools, and the churches might easily take a more energetic attitude on this point than they have done in the past.

It will be remembered that the Covenant was made with the animal creation as well as with man, and reads in Genesis :

" And God said, This is the token of the covenant which I make between Me and you, and *every living creature. . . .* And I will remember my Covenant which is between Me and you, *and every living creature of all flesh. . . .*"

The egotistical point of view which man has adopted, in allotting to himself the promises of the Bible, and of leaving the animal kingdom without them, is indefensible. Some of the greatest thinkers on this subject uphold the standard of the animal kingdom, and I may quote Professor Romanes —the great authority on animal instinct. He says :

" Just as the theologians tell us, and logically enough, that if there is a Divine mind, the best, and, indeed, only conception we can form of it, is that which is formed on the analogy, however imperfect, supplied by the human mind ; so with inverted anthropomorphism we must apply a similar consideration to the animal mind. . . . And this consideration, it is needless to point out, has a special validity to the evolutionist, inasmuch as upon his theory there must be a psychological, no less than a physiological, continuity extending throughout the length and breadth of the animal kingdom."

Addison, when writing on the subject of instinct, says : " I look upon instinct as upon the principle of gravitation in bodies, which is not to be explained by any known qualities inherent in the bodies themselves, nor from any laws of mechanism, but as an immediate impression from the first Mover, and the Divine energy acting in the creatures."

The above illuminating statement is especially interesting when we notice that one of the definitions of the word "instinct" means "urged from within," and yet another explanation is "animated," derived from *anima*, soul.

The description of the animal kingdom pictured by Isaiah is certainly a state which has previously existed :

" The wolf also shall dwell with the lamb, and the leopard shall lie down with the kid ; the calf and the young lion and the fatling together ; and a little child shall lead them.

" And the cow and the bear shall feed ; their young ones shall lie down together ; and the lion shall eat straw like the ox ;

" And the sucking child shall play on the hole of the asp ; and the weaned child shall put his hand on the cockatrice den.

" They shall not hurt nor destroy in all my holy mountain ; for the earth shall be full of the knowledge of the Lord, as the waters cover the sea."

This prophecy as to the return of this harmonious understanding between man and beast has not yet been fulfilled, but in the insistence by man for more humane treatment for all animals, one sees the gleam of the dawn, and one knows that, as thought in this direction progresses, as it is certain to do, the entire prophecy will be completely fulfilled.

There is no doubt that as mankind becomes more humane and lovable to his brother-man as well as to the animal creation, the animals themselves will become less ferocious and less timid. This may seem difficult to credit to anyone who has not studied the subject, but even a cursory examination will reveal the fact that all animals, dogs especially, reflect the mentality of those with whom they associate. This can be seen in the dogs of different nations. The bull-dog and the fox-terrier may be said to represent the tenacious and also the sociable qualities of the English race, the dandie dinmont and the Scotch terrier the independent and argumentative characteristics of the Scotch, and the Irish terrier partakes of a remarkable degree of the impulsiveness and relish for " a bit of a shcrap " of his master. The underlying ferocity in the Prussian character is often reflected by the Great Dane, the favourite breed of the German students, and, until well tamed by long residence in this country, is always capable of unexpected outbursts of anger and uncertainty of temper. German sheep-dogs (or Alsatians, as they are called for trade purposes) are much the same in this respect.

When travelling in Norway and Sweden I have been struck with the sedate and aloof demeanour of the dogs, which so closely resembles the human inhabitants of these countries. The very puppies disport themselves in a more dignified manner than is usually seen elsewhere. The gay insouciance of the French is well represented in the poodle, the inscrutability of the Chinese in the chow, the wild and lawless spirit of the mountainous races of middle Europe in the savage sheep-dogs of these regions, and so on, in varying degrees all over the world one can see that the dog, the closest associate of man, partakes of his master's qualities.

Coming down to individuals, this is even more apparent, and one can almost judge the character of any person by noticing the sort of dog they keep, or, to put it the other way, the dog has been selected and trained according to the tastes of the master or mistress, and reflects these attributes of mind whatever they may be. Thus, at opposite ends of the scale, one gets the keeper's night dog, and the timid and circumscribed little lap-dog of the old lady. In pondering this matter, therefore, it is perfectly apparent that the dog, owing to this intimate association with man, very closely assimilates the characteristics of the governing human race.

The following leading article cut from the *Times* very graphically illustrates and confirms the above observations.

"THE TELL-TALE DOG

" The national sheep-dog trials, which were held recently at Lowther Castle, may serve to remind ' all proper men ' who acknowledge their descent from the original inhabitant of Mr. Kipling's Just So Cave, that their first friend remains a singularly adaptable creature, and, in many respects, a mirror in which they may see themselves reflected. Whoever goes to a cat show, though he may observe there a wide variety of form and fur, carries away with him always an impression of having encountered but one immutable cat, endlessly looking out at him from a thousand feline eyes. Cats that are well treated may have an outward composure, and cats that are ill treated a contrasted furtiveness ; but, in good fortune and in bad, they are in truth the same cat. Domestic we may call them, but even on the hearthrug and beside the saucer they are aloof from our ways, sharing, it seems, none of our thoughts and having borrowed throughout the ages no part of our personality. It is, therefore, never possible to judge a household by its cat. Dogs, on the contrary, are eloquent of their masters. If we may imagine an earth from which all the human inhabitants were suddenly spirited away, and into which a Martian explorer simultaneously entered, there is little doubt that dogs could show us to him, almost as if we ourselves were still living and moving on earth, in all our dignity and all our impudence.

" Sometimes dogs are restrained portraits, sometimes the fiercest of satires. A sheep-dog has exactly a shepherd's air of having to work hard and anxiously for his living ; he has his master's shyness in company, his deep concentration in repose, his resource and unflagging energy in action. If two mastiffs are employed, one to guard valuable possessions from thieves, the other as a companion of children, the first bears in its poise and gait the fierce, possessive pride of ownership, and the second becomes as mild and gentle as an old nurse behind a perambulator.

" The public parks are delightfully full of people who go about with four-legged replicas of themselves upon a leash. The likeness is often remarkable enough to win a smile even in the case of men who obscure it sometimes by their uniform habits of dress ; but all the world may instantly know a woman by her dog. If she is by nature of tweed and heather, she will own no canine trifle of silk and scent. If she is selfish and pampered, her dog will yap at every disturbance of its leisured comfort, will fume and fret as she scolds and complains, and will be saved, as she is, from the outward troubles of life, not because it is wise, but because it seldom ventures far from the shelter of its comfortable basket.

" Our Martian explorer would, moreover, as he pursued his travels, receive more than one hint of world politics, for dogs not only absorb the characters of their individual masters, but exhibit the idiosyncrasies of nations. Among sheep-dogs alone, England, Scotland and Wales are divided with true racial distinctness, and a glance into the faces of the dogs we have imported from China proves them to be decorative aliens in this land of setters and terriers. The observant traveller would discover, in every kennel throughout the world, more and more data for the problems of human psychology, so many, indeed, that he might at last return with relief to the imperturbable and international cat, who ' walks by himself and to whom all places are alike.' When ' he goes out to the Wet Wild Woods, waving his wild tail and walking by his wild lone,' he has his private mystery, but it is not, as the First Friend's is, the mystery of humanity itself."

It may be asked what has all this to do with the training of dogs ? The answer is, a great deal, for the study of the metaphysical aspect of the subject, that is to say, the research into character-training, which is really mind-training, assists one very greatly in the education of animals and enables one to perceive the soul in the creature.

As I will show, the most successful results are obtained when the dog is taught to rely on this intuitive prompting from within, rather than on any material guides it may find without, and it can perhaps be understood how important it is for the trainer to comprehend the original psychology of the dog.

It is a great compliment to man that when he does find the soul of anything, and uses it well, how wonderful is the response ! It may be said that, as a whole, this happy state has, to a great extent, been reached in regard to the dog, which, as I have shown, is so closely in touch with the mind of his master, and we are beginning to perceive that many characteristics which we have hitherto considered as belonging exclusively to human beings, and far above the animals, are really as much within the possession of our dogs as of ourselves.

Admitting, therefore, that the dog is capable of reflecting and manifesting the attributes of mind by teaching it (and expecting to see the result of this teaching) the highest qualities in man, such as honesty, reliability, endurance, patience—in fact, the qualities of soul—the trainer starts his work, cleared of many limitations that have been held over dogs and, indeed, over the entire animal kingdom, but which are now, thank God, rapidly breaking down.

The whole basis of the training of the dog rests in recognising and cultivating certain qualities of mind in the animal. These are, among others, fidelity, courage, honour, endurance. Hearing, sight and scent are also all trained and accentuated, but these last attributes must have their origin in the first mentioned instincts in order to obtain successful results.

George Jesse, in writing on this aspect of the dog's character, touches a note which I think wonderfully discerning as to the attitude of the dog to man :

"It has been well remarked, that the poets of various lands, and different ages, have delighted in commemorating the virtues of this favourite animal, as though they recognised in his devotion to man something of the love and obedience with which man should look up to his Heavenly Father and Almighty God."

It always seems to me as if the dog turns to us as though, in the meantime, all he knows about God must come to him through us.

I have very seldom, indeed as regards British breeds, known a really treacherous dog: that is to say, one that will bite the hand that cares for it. So rare, indeed, has this been as to prove that such a condition of mind in the dog is entirely abnormal, and, as a matter of fact, I have always been of the opinion that such animals were insane.

A sense of right and wrong, or conscience, is very strongly developed in dogs, and the moral sense has to be carefully brought out in the dog, as it has to do so much of its work entirely on its own initiative. But it is safe to say that if you can get a dog to understand a certain duty as a trust, it will rarely fail you. In fact, especially in relation to guarding duties, the dog will often rather lay down life itself than betray its trust. When training dogs for messenger work during the war the sense of honour had to be very carefully brought out in the creatures. Its work lay through so much distraction and when it was far away from its keeper. Many temptations had to be met and overcome, and sad were the falls from honourable conduct before our dispatch-carrying friend learned to listen to the prompting of the higher sense. Appetising food was the most serious temptation, and for this reason messenger dogs had to be very well fed so that the allurement of the road was less likely to trouble them.

I have seen many amusing instances during this moral education of the dispatch-carrier. On one occasion a collie found a workman's dinner, neatly done up in a cotton handkerchief, under a hedge. He was nearing home and going along with a steady swing. The delightful scent of the repast was too much for his half-trained sense of honour, and he stopped to examine it. Feeling uneasy in his mind, however, he did not care to delay to eat it there, and seizing the bundle by the knot, bore it away. He arrived at the training post with a curious expression, which desired to convey the information that although he realised he had not acted in an absolutely straightforward manner, at all events he had lost no time on the road.

I have sometimes watched a gentlemanly house dog sitting expectantly beside the tea-table, keeping his head self-consciously turned away from the lower shelves of the tea-basket, on a level with his nose, when the smell of the dainties became rather more attractive than he could conveniently endure.

This sense of honour in dogs can be cultivated in many directions. The "Ettrick shepherd," Hogg, points this out when telling of one of his collies, trained to accompany him to the hills to manage the sheep. "If coming hungry from the hills and getting into the milk house, he (the collie) would most likely think of nothing else than filling his belly with the cream," while another dog, perhaps a relative of this same one, which had been trained to remain at home, as the friend and guardian of the shepherd's family and property, is bred to far higher principles of honour in this direction. "I have known such a dog lay night and day among from ten to twenty pails full of milk and never once break the cream of one of them with the tip of his tongue, nor would he suffer cat, rat, or any other creature to touch it."

The sense of honour in the guard dog is often very wonderful, and it may be said that the basis of the training rests chiefly on this instinct. I have heard people deride a dog said to be a very determined guard, because they have met this dog on the road and it has allowed them to pat its head. But the dog really exhibited greater intelligence than the person, because it was not at the time on duty, and did not consider it necessary to obstruct anyone who had no evil intent, and who had every right to be there. Give this same dog its bit of territory to protect, and its attitude towards the stranger will be very different, and "Halt!" will be the meaning conveyed in no uncertain manner.

A good trainer will always remember that his training should be adjusted so that love, justice, honour, truth, will be reflected all through the daily lesson. A dog should never be tricked or deceived. There are few human beings who feel such treatment as acutely as the dog. At the same time, it can be trained to thoroughly appreciate and enjoy a joke and friendly "ragging." If one hits a dog quite lightly in anger it resents it, but if one is having a joke, one can play a tune with a stick on the dog's back and hit it relatively much harder, and it will enter into the fun with great zest, and stand to be hit until the ditty is finished, when it will bound round one in high delight at participating in the joke.

Obedience and discipline, based on reason, are the result of the cultivation of the highest qualities of mind. Both can be attained by compulsion, but the only discipline in which I place any real reliance is that which is based on spontaneous qualities of good in the dog's mind, such as love for its master, honour, justice, etc.

It is an interesting fact that the story with which we are all familiar of Gelert, the famous dog of Wales, whose grave is still carefully tended to this day, on account of his brave and faithful defence of the child from the wolf, is found in varying forms in the folk-lore of most widely-separated countries and races.

The following clipping from the *Times* of December 18th, 1919, illustrates the development of discipline in a dog, based on its love and trust in its master's judgment and ruling:

"For days past every morning has brought fresh news

of wrecks on the coasts of Nova Scotia, and along the Gulf of Saint Lawrence, ships having been driven ashore in terrific gales, accompanied by blinding storms of snow, on barren, rocky coasts, far from human habitation. From Newfoundland this morning comes the story of the wreck of a coasting steamer on a terrible coast. Ninety-two passengers and crew were saved by the intelligence of a Newfoundland dog belonging to one of the crew. The ship had gone ashore on a reef of jagged rocks, and it was impossible to get a boat out to her in the boiling sea. Finally, a light line was tied round the dog, which obeyed his master's signs and swam ashore, making it possible to rig a block and tackle, by means of which all the souls in the ship were brought to safety. A baby of eighteen months was taken ashore in a mail-bag."

If discipline is inculcated on the right lines, so that reason is cultivated simultaneously, it will be found that an understanding is born into a dog's mind that orders should be obeyed for their own sake, and therefore its training in discipline should be along those lines, in the first place, which the dog is most easily able to comprehend.

To illustrate this I may mention the case of a young dog I had great faith in as a dispatch-carrier. It was a collie, with a strain of spaniel, and it displayed extreme intelligence and affection. While joyfully adapting itself to all its duties, it unfortunately had the greatest dislike to any sounds of firing or passing near any explosions. I had arranged a test one day, where Rob was asked to run down a trench on each side of which were exploding powder-flashes. Nothing would induce him to do it, and the promise of the most delicate dainties had no effect whatever. He had been brought to this pitch of training gradually, but this final test, which it was essential he should pass, seemed to be one he would never be able to attain.

I, however, remembered someone for whom Rob seemed to have conceived a very special affection. This person stood at the other end of the trench, and in his desire to reach the object of his love, Rob cautiously, and with many qualms, stepped gingerly past the danger zones, needless to say, to be greatly rewarded and caressed by his friend.

After this first test there was no further trouble, and he became accustomed to run down the trench between the powder-flashes with complete nonchalance. After a time his special friend was replaced by one of the ordinary staff, and Rob understood that this test was part of a system of duty, and must be disconnected from any personal element.

This ability to reason out things in connection with their work, and to realise that the rules must be obeyed for their own sake, as part of the very high mission with which the war-dogs, as trained for the British army, were entrusted, was borne out in France when a dog's keeper was wounded, or removed from his own particular charge. It at once "carried on" with another keeper, accepting the change, no doubt with deep regret, but as a necessity due to circumstances.

A wonderful instance of this sense of discipline is narrated, concerning a collie, by the poet Hogg, in the "Shepherd's Calendar." In this case the strict observance of what the conscientious animal conceived to be its duty overcame even the maternal instinct.

A collie belonged to a man named Steele, who was in the habit of consigning sheep to her charge without supervision. "On one occasion," says Hogg, "whether Steele remained behind or took another road, I know not: but on arriving home late in the evening, he was astonished to hear that his faithful animal had never made its appearance with the drove. He and his son, or servant, instantly prepared to set out by different paths in search of her; but in their going out into the streets, there was she coming with the drove, not one missing, and, marvellous to relate, she was carrying a young pup in her mouth. She had been taken in travail on the hills, and how the poor beast had contrived to manage her drove in her state of suffering is beyond human calculation, for her road lay through sheep the whole day. Her master's heart smote him when he saw what she had suffered and effected, but she, nothing daunted, and having deposited her young one in a place of safety, again set out full speed to the hills, and brought another, and another, till she brought her whole litter, one by one, but the last one was dead."

It will be observed how cleverly the collie must have

reasoned out the needs of her flock, and also of her puppies.

A wonderfully clever dandie dinmont, belonging to my family, in a long life of absolutely human intelligence, on one occasion, by utilising his reasoning powers, saved what might have been a very serious disaster. He appeared late at night upstairs in one of the bedrooms, and by his extremely agitated demeanour induced one of the family to accompany him downstairs. Here it was found that a lamp had been left burning, and the wick had in some manner fallen down into the oil, so that the entire lamp was a mass of flame.

A sense of justice is to be found, too, in a high degree in some dogs, and is easily affronted. From man it feels such affronts severely, but also from its own comrades.

I remember an amusing instance of this in the case of a young dandie dinmont of ten months, who accompanied me for a walk. As we approached a certain gate a fox-terrier rushed out and attacked the dandie savagely, although the latter was not encroaching on the preserves of the fox-terrier, but was trotting innocently down the middle of the road. The dandie carried a very fine silver topknot, which seemed especially to irritate the fox-terrier, who concentrated his energies on this ornament, and shook poor dandie in a most brutal manner. Dandie put up a good fight and managed to shake off his assailant, but being only a young thing was obviously somewhat shaken in his nerves, and much affronted altogether.

On arrival at home, we were met at our gate by the pup's elder brother, and in canine language the whole story was poured out. Both dandies manifested intense indignation, bouncing about the garden with stiffened fur and tails, and gurgling loudly to each other.

Foreseeing it would be much better to have the matter settled once and for all, as soon as possible I started out again, accompanied with both dandies. As we approached the gate of the enemy's residence both dandies became much excited, and the elder started ahead, giving directions evidently to his brother to follow behind. He arrived at the gate and stood stiffly to attention. At that moment a whirlwind of white fur hurled itself under the gate. The conflict was short but sharp, and presently a sorry-looking fox-terrier limped back to its home. After that there was a definite understanding, and while no friendship was attempted between the three, it was admitted that the roadway was right of way.

I have also seen a strong instance of justice and honourable dealing manifested by messenger-dogs under training. When two or three dogs arrive at the post together and receive a reward, I have seen one dog take its piece of meat from the ground and step back, and watch the other competitor receive its reward, which would be frequently placed on the ground. There was no attempt to snatch it, and there was evidently a distinct understanding that it was a definite reward for good work done, and, therefore, to interfere would be a most unsportsmanlike act. At any other time when feeding a group of dogs with scraps, there would not be this withholding, but a lively scramble would ensue, sometimes with exciting results.

It may be summed up that, in inculcating any form of training, reason must be convinced. Reason is best reached through the dog's affections. It can readily be understood, therefore, that whipping and ill-usage will not attain this end. On the contrary, the attention of the pupil should be attracted at the outset, and all through the training, by the principle of reward for good service. Thus, whatever the duties it is desired to teach should be done by kindness. The best reward is, of course, some food of which the dog is particularly fond. A small piece of meat is always acceptable, but for all ordinary purposes a sweet biscuit (not dog-biscuit) is easy to carry in the pocket, and will always be received with delight.

TEACHING OBEDIENCE

This system of training by reward can be applied to various necessities. Thus if a puppy or young dog does not seem to be learning obedience very satisfactorily it can be called, and if it does not come, persist, until it does so. Then pat it and reward it with a tiny piece of biscuit. It will soon learn to associate obeying with its master's approval and something pleasant.

This method is an excellent one to follow in the case of a dog with disobedient ways and bad habits. Simply checking such an animal and perhaps striking it does not really train it. What is required is to place *a fresh impression* in the dog's mind, and a new thought of approval, which is conveyed through the presentation of a little reward, will bring out a different attitude.

TEACHING A DOG TO FOLLOW

This is practically the first lesson which a dog has to learn. It has been explained elsewhere that the basis on which the true and practical relationship between dog and master is founded is that of affection one for the other. On the part of the dog it will be devotion. Some dogs are by nature much more obedient than others. Spaniels, and other sporting dogs, are all much more amenable to strict discipline than most other breeds. The reason is simple. For generations they have been trained for certain work which is done at word of command, and always under the eye of the master. While strict obedience is necessary, and a clear understanding of what is required of it, the initiative is in the first place with the master, who gives the orders, and the animal carries them out under his eye. They are taught to turn to him for direction in all things.

Other breeds are sometimes swayed by strong influences, which counteract the word of command. All hounds, for instance, are greatly under the domination of their sense of scent, and an individual of any of the hound species can never be trained to the state of perfection of control, in dropping to hand, and obedience in general, to which sporting dogs will attain.

A hound on the trail is completely lost to any sense except that of determination to run its quarry to earth.

Most of the terriers have been kept as house pets, and companions, and as such have developed independence of thought, and have been encouraged to do so, as tending towards the growth of amusing originality in the animal.

While the desire to obey can be inculcated by training and by affectionate treatment, the tendency towards a more independent attitude of thought and behaviour is common to most dogs, which are kept more or less as pets and companions. It is one thing, however, to allow a dog plenty of freedom of action and another to tolerate disobedience.

One of the best methods of teaching discipline in the first place, is to train the dog to lie down at word of command. This has a very steadying effect on a young animal. Give it a lesson every day, but not too long at a time, and always reward it with a piece of biscuit.

The next thing is to teach it to answer the whistle or call. A good method of teaching this lesson quickly is to make a game of it. Let one person take the dog away and hold it while the owner whistles and calls to it. It can then be immediately released, and must be rewarded with a pat and a piece of biscuit on coming up. The next stage is for the dog to be held in leash out of sight of the master, but within sound of his voice, and to be released in the same manner. This exercise is to be repeated until the lesson is thoroughly learnt. It is one which will be entered into by the pupil with great zest. When it understands, if it disobeys and does not come to the whistle, when out walking, it is a good plan to hold the dog by the collar and whistle and scold it for not coming, and if the offence has been very flagrant to add a smack as well. It should by this time connect the whistle with immediate return, and it will know quite well that it has not done its duty. All sorts of variations in this lesson in obedience can be practised, and a dog well trained from the start in this respect will be found to be capable of many little tricks and duties, which will make it not only very intelligent, but also much happier.

Anything which increases the tie between it and its master will make for the greater happiness of both.

Unreasoning discipline, especially for young things, is not desirable, and has a bad effect. It is not natural for a young dog to be always walking into heel and not to be allowed a scamper. If the lesson, as indicated above, is well taught on the basis of affection and reward, it will not be difficult to apply this teaching to the daily walks and duties of the dog. It will soon learn to enjoy itself within limits, and to come when it hears the call or whistle.

With a young dog, or a new one, it is always a good plan

to carry sweet biscuits in the pocket when out walking. The knowledge that something good to eat is available attracts the dog's mind towards its owner, which is always a good attitude to inculcate from the start. This may be cupboard-love, certainly, in the first place, but will merge into something better. This form of training is so much better and more thorough than that based on frequent scoldings and thrashings. When the dog has shown great fortitude in the face of temptation to disobey, it should always be rewarded with biscuit. A code of words should be thought out, and the same ones used for each action or duty. All tricks should be taught in this way, and leaping over a stick, walking on the hind legs, etc., etc., will be entered into as a delightful joke if carried on under this system.

STOPPING A DOG CHASING MOTOR-BICYCLES

Many dogs have a bad habit of chasing motor-bicycles. This is an exceedingly dangerous trick, and must be stopped at all costs. The best way to do so is to take the animal out on a lead, and make a point of going where motor-bicycles pass. If a friend can bring one along for the experiment so much the better. As the bicycle rushes past, the dog should be severely scolded if it jumps after it, and the lead should be strongly held. Next time the bicycle can pass less fast, and the lead can trail on the ground, or be loosely held, and the dog should be cautioned by the voice all the time. Whenever it begins to pay attention, and refrains from noticing the temptation, immediately offer it a piece of biscuit as a reward for good behaviour, and continue this lesson until the dog's trend of mind is altered.

There are many other forms of disobedience and indiscipline, which can be corrected in the same way. This does not mean that physical correction can be eliminated altogether, and, in fact, a good smack when required should not be withheld, when dealing with a dog which thoroughly *knows* what you want it to do, and does not intend obeying, but the training should not rest there, and should always be continued along the lines of approval as well. Beating with a stick is a mistake. The stick is sometimes necessary, where a number of large dogs are together, in case of fights, but as a means of correction, the hand or the flick of a dog-lash is far the best.

HOW TO STOP A DOG CHASING SHEEP

The only occasion where really severe whipping might be permitted is on the *first* occasion of the dog chasing sheep. It is so vital that it should realise then and there the awfulness of its crime, that such a punishment will come as a great and necessary shock to a dog, accustomed to nothing but kindness, and it is likely to have a very arresting effect. But it would be unfair to it to leave the lesson at that. In the first place, it may have commenced the chase in a sheer spirit of fun, and without realising the magnitude of the offence. One of the best ways to break in a dog there and then to sheep, is to take it right in amongst a flock and train it by leading it about on a check string, curbing and scolding whenever the dog looks at the sheep. Then drop the lead on the ground, keeping the foot ready to step on the end and check a rush on the part of the dog. Proceed with this until the lesson is thoroughly understood, and then use the biscuit as a reward, when the temptation is met and denied.

Another method of training a dog to sheep is to board it with a shepherd, and let it go daily with him on a lead, until it has got quite accustomed to them. The shepherd's own dogs will also help in inculcating the lesson.

It will be understood from all this, that what is really required is that the dog's intelligence should be trained. Most of its faults will arise in the first place from ignorance of the result of its actions, and of what is required of it. Gentleness of handling, therefore, is most important, otherwise the poor animal only becomes bewildered. In the old days before this was so well understood as it is now, the training of both horses and dogs was attended by much cruelty. Sporting dogs were especially severely handled, and many a good animal was ruined by being bullied by a brutal gamekeeper, who had not a quarter of the delicate sensibility of the animal he was attempting to train.

Again, let it be reiterated that many dogs seem disobedient because they do not sufficiently understand what is required of them, and a little patience and rewarding will remedy this.

HOW TO TRAIN A DOG TO BE CLEAN INDOORS

This training can begin with the young pup, and if the latter is to live straight away indoors on leaving the mother, a good way is to provide it with a box with high sides over which it cannot clamber. This box should have a nice little bed of hay in the bottom, which can easily be changed when needed. The puppy can be put to sleep at night in the box, and also during the day, but when it is thought that it requires to go out of doors, immediately lift it out and put it outside. In this way the little thing learns manners very soon, and I have known some puppies never make a mistake indoors under this system. Older dogs can be trained in the same way, by chaining them up when indoors, and putting them out to run loose outside every now and then. They very soon get to understand, and this is an excellent way to ensure cleanliness at night. Only, in the case of the adult dog indoors all night, as I have pointed out elsewhere, it should not be fed at eventide, as it makes it too much of a strain for the dog to wait all night before going out of doors. With the quite young things, a good deal of consideration is required, as they have to go out pretty often.

The idea to be inculcated, and which they quickly respond to by being kept quiet when in doors, is, that being put out of doors for purposes of exercise has also the object of relieving nature. They soon learn to connect the one with the other.

TRAINING A DOG NOT TO CHASE POULTRY

With the young dog this vice generally begins, as with sheep chasing, in a spirit of fun. A good method is to fasten it up in the poultry-yard or pen. The fact of being right in amongst the poultry takes away a good deal of the novelty, and the desire to chase is frequently eliminated by this lesson without further trouble. If this is not sufficient, however, the lesson must be continued, and a check lead to trail on the ground and a good dog-lash to flick the culprit if necessary will be the next step. A little patience, and the offender will soon understand.

TRAINING A DOG NOT TO CHASE GAME

The training against this vice must commence when the instructions in obedience and discipline are first inculcated. The tie between master and dog should always be such that the latter never feels happy if separated for any length of time, but one thing must be carefully guarded against, and it is that the young dog does not come under the influence of another dog whose delight it is to form an expedition to the nearest coverts and act as instructor to the budding idea. This deleterious influence is very often the way in which the vice is taught to a dog which would otherwise never have thought of it. If, however, the animal's affections have been captured and it has also been trained in obedience, it will not be nearly so likely to go off on hunting expeditions, as it will never wish to be too far from its owner. Therefore it will be seen that the true method of control in the first place is through the creature's devotion.

The next thing is to teach it to walk in the coverts, and behave in a reasonable way. As long as it keeps its attention always fixed on its master's whereabouts, and comes out at once on the sound of the whistle, a little run through the bushes is not considered a crime for a young animal, but this permission must be very carefully conceded, and prompt obedience to the whistle is necessary, or an alternative smacking will follow. If this can be done it is better and kinder than compelling a young thing to walk close into heel all the time during the walk, as that is rather unkind. It is natural for it to enjoy a scamper, which does no harm, and it is better to allow this and to concentrate on teaching obedience to the whistle, and to the necessity for keeping in touch.

I have known dogs play about along the sides of the road among the rabbit-holes, but never once to lose touch with the master during the whole course of the walk. A head is poked out from the bushes every few minutes so as to see where he is, showing that the primary instinct of discipline by affection has been properly instilled, and is stronger than the desire to chase. Walking into heel must certainly be taught, so that when it is considered necessary to control the animal in this way it will understand, and it will respond all the better if such control is administered reasonably.

When, however, the dog has perhaps come into the owner's possession after it has reached years of discretion, and has not been taught self-control already in respect to game, a different attitude may have to be taken towards it. Here, except in certain cases where the affection between dog and master becomes unusually spontaneous, *there will not* be the same draw between the two as there would be in the case of a youngster, which had grown up at his side, and although it may grow just as devoted as time goes on, care will need to be taken at the outset, to guard the pupil from temptation, which it might find too strong to resist. It should be taken in the first place into the plantations on a lead, or if it is sufficiently obedient to follow without this, any attempt to bolt away into the bushes must be at once stopped by word of command and a flick of the whip. A check lead is here a good safeguard, if the creature's obedience is still in doubt, as it is most important at the start that the pupil should be prevented from having a real good chase on its own. It has to learn that the enticing sounds and scents of the woods cannot be enquired into except under the will and wish of the master. The check lead, which may be allowed to trail, need not be more than a long piece of string, which will allow the dog sufficient liberty to stroll on each side of the path, and ahead a little way, but which can be stepped on whenever a sign of indiscipline is shown.

As recommended elsewhere, the process of correction through coercion must always be accompanied by the inducement of reward, and a sweet biscuit carried in the pocket is a great assistance in rewarding resistance to temptation and obedience to call or whistle. A form of training such as this, and carried out by the owner with concentration for a time, will repay, and is worth much more to the dog, than several weeks spent with a gamekeeper, whose assistance might have to be called in, if the first lessons are neglected.

The lesson to be inculcated is, that the dog can go out in the woods with its master, and enjoy a pleasant run as long as it replies immediately to call, and does not stray unduly. A warning voice, a check lead, and a biscuit are the methods to employ.

HOW TO TEACH DOGS NOT TO WALK ON THE ROADWAY

In these days of motors it is extremely dangerous for a dog to walk on the roadway, and a little training will soon teach it to keep to the path. Keep one particular phrase especially for teaching this lesson, such as, " Don't go on the road," " Off the road ! " or " Keep near." Whenever it shows the inclination to step into the road shout this sharply, and insist on it coming back on to the path. Emphasise the order with a flick of the whip, if necessary. In a very short time this lesson is understood. The reason for the same phrase being always used is because in quiet country places it may not be necessary to keep the animal too closely on the side path, and it will be all the more likely to obey the order when the real necessity arises, if it is allowed a reasonable amount of liberty when this is safe. Hearing the same order given, however, will teach it that these words mean that that particular form of obedience is required, and it will obey. After a time many dogs become quite inured to walking on the footpath, and seem to understand the order is for their protection.

It is observable also that town dogs, nowadays, are much more respectful to the motor-horn than they used to be. When the dog has crossed the road for some reason, and a motor is seen rapidly approaching, it is better not to call the creature back, as if it hesitates it may cross too late and be run over. The best way is to cross over the road oneself and stay by until the danger is past. Then fetch the dog over and apply the instructing words.

HOW TO TEACH A DOG NOT TO FIGHT

The best way to break the young dog of this very annoying form of bad temper is to bring it up with other dogs older in years than itself. In a large kennel a youngster which may be introduced with its head unduly " swollen " will very soon find that it will have to take " a back seat," if it indulges in a domineering attitude towards the older dogs. I have known young fellows such as this, which were on the road to become downright fighting dogs, become quite toned down and amenable, after associating in the daily exercising ground with a group of others. It very soon found that rude and provocative remarks did not pay! There are certain breeds which are more prone to fighting than others, but nowadays when the high value of such stock makes specialised attention worth while, this bad trait is being bred and trained out of them. All round, it may be said, that dogs are being trained to be much more gentlemanly.

When there are no older dogs to restrain the growing bumptiousness of the youngster, it is well to introduce it as much as possible to other dogs elsewhere, and let it play with them. A walk in Hyde Park brings it in contact with many canine natures, cantankerous and otherwise, and it must learn to associate amicably with them all, or be whipped. If a few smart lessons do not teach what is required, or if the animal has been spoilt, and has attained an age where it is not likely to respond to training, it may be necessary to take it out muzzled. It is far better to let the dog run about untrammelled as far as possible, but with a muzzle on, rather than keep it chained up all the time. Nor is it fair to other peoples' property to let a fighting dog vent its spleen on inoffensive animals. Furthermore, it is an excellent method for breaking it from this bad habit, as after it has had the experience of receiving the result of insolence made by it to other dogs, while in a muzzled state, it decides to refrain from such behaviour in future. In a case like this, the muzzle should be put on the first thing in the morning, if the dog is going out of doors, and it is, of course, most important that it should be of a sufficiently large size for the dog to be able to open its mouth. In fact, it must be as comfortable as possible consistent with safety. After a time no resentment will be shown to having the muzzle put on, and habit will be inculcated without undue discomfort. It has been found that this treatment has the effect in many cases of completely curing, or greatly diminishing, this vice, and the muzzle can then be dispensed with almost, if not altogether.

HOW TO TEACH A PUPPY OR YOUNG DOG TO GUARD

Where a very special need for a good guard dog is required—that is to say, where the locality is dangerous to one's person, or where very valuable property requires guarding—it is as well to select a dog from a breed which has been more especially adapted for this purpose, both by tradition and instinct. I have touched on this elsewhere, and have specified the best dogs for the purpose. But if one does not happen to have one of these, it is possible by judicious management and training to inculcate even into some other breeds quite a good idea of this protective instinct.

The greatest help is afforded in the training of a young animal if it can associate with another older dog which is already a good watch and guard. They are very quick to imitate and emulate each other, and this influence can even commence before the pups have left the mother, if the latter is a good watch. On hearing an unaccustomed sound she will bark, and it is amusing to watch the youngsters, if they are old enough to do so, advance with puppy yelps to the attack. One or two amongst them will probably be better at this than the others, and, while some amongst them may show actual nervousness and retreat. The indications are as straws which show the way the wind blows, and the nature of each animal can be gauged, even at this age, by the observant.

In the chapter on Training I have enlarged on the necessity for reaching out to the inner nature of the dog, cultivating and protecting its fine sensibility, while all the time nculcating the desired duties. If this is done, the affection of the dog will quite naturally develop, and it is on this basis that the lessons in guarding must be commenced. The first few months of the pup's life can therefore be chiefly occupied with mutual attachment. It can be taught to associate mastership with a definite person. In the little saunters, (no young growing pup should be taken long walks), it can be taught to follow and to lie beside its master when he sits down. This is a very good moment to teach it to take notice and bark at any approaching person, by very gently hissing and saying, "Who is it?" The youngster will very quickly learn its lesson, that it must give warning of strange footsteps. The same sort of training can be accorded when it is indoors, by hissing when strangers approach.

Obedience must at the same time be gently taught, so that the tendencies developing can be controlled. Judicious calculation is necessary, as to how much encouragement is wise in urging the pup, as much depends on the natural instinct it may possess in this respect. Some have it very strongly, and if it were too much brought out the pup might manifest too suspicious tendencies, and become too savage as it grew older. It is sometimes a great nuisance when a dog rushes out and attacks all and sundry, who may come to the house, and if it is only required that the training is to inculcate, discriminatively, watching qualities, carefulness in training is needed. For this sort of requirement a dog, which has to be a companion running loose about the place, alert but not savage, is to be desired.

It is a complaint sometimes that the house dog takes a dislike to certain persons coming regularly to the house, such as the postman or tradesmen's boys, while at the same time they are quite well-behaved with other visitors. This shows lack of discrimination on the dog's part, but it can be overcome, by presenting the particular person with a biscuit or two, to feed the dog with on approaching the house. A little trouble taken in this way soon teaches it that it has made a mistake. Many an otherwise excellent and valuable animal has been sacrificed, owing to lack of understanding that a little persuasion is all that is needed to readjust the situation.

Keeping a young dog continuously on the chain is one of the most certain ways of spoiling its temper. This does not mean that it is a bad thing ever to chain up a dog. On the contrary, when it is not convenient to have it under supervision, this method of control for a short time is to be recommended, but when this restriction is overdone the results are, in a sensitive dog, disastrous. At the same time, putting it on duty on the chain at night is an excellent way to encourage the watching and guarding instinct as soon as the pup reaches an age when it can understand the use of a collar and chain. This age may be about six months, but eight to ten months old is the best age to begin any serious training in guard work. Up till this time the endeavour should be confined only to encouraging and preparing this tendency. It will, however, be some months afterwards before the young dog will be considered fully trained in this respect, especially if serious personal guarding is required.

All the various side items of the guard work can be proceeded with at the same time. For instance, if the dog is required to accompany its mistress or master as a protection on lonely roads, it is well to begin this instruction seriously about the age of a year. The dusk is the best time, and the animal will learn quicker if it is kept on the lead. Stand still in a quiet lane or lonely spot at night, or when dusk is drawing on, and watch the dog's demeanour towards the various sounds. Especially note its attitude to approaching footsteps. Judiciously encourage it to give warning, and as far as possible confine this warning to growling, by checking any tendency towards barking. By keeping a curb on too noisy a warning, the dog will understand on another occasion, when perhaps it is desired that an unpleasant-looking customer should be given a good fright, that it can give tongue freely, and in some dogs of the right disposition this angry warning can be still further encouraged into attack, if need be.

The faults of a guard dog may be summed up briefly in that they are either too savage, or they do not display the watching tendency sufficiently. If the dog displaying either of these failings is not too old, it can usually be corrected, or at least improved, by changing its environment for a time. This may be rather a trouble, but it is the quickest way, and where the dog is in any way prized, it is well worth while. In the case of the dog which has become too sharp for the owner's requirement, it should be transferred to such a dwelling where it will be in a position to see plenty of people passing by, and where it can be left loose. Thus, supposing it has been living at a country house, or somewhere in a more or less isolated position, and perhaps chained up, it should be boarded out in a town, or at a cottage in a village, and left loose, so that it becomes accustomed to plenty of people round about, and knows they must not be interfered with.

On the other hand, a dog sluggish in watching power may be encouraged by sending it to an isolated place. A shepherd is a very good person to help one here. He will be usually quite pleased for a fee to take the dog with him. His own dogs are nearly always good watchers, and they will encourage the pupil to note strangers coming near, and the isolated position of such a teacher is always helpful in bringing out alertness in the dog. It is not possible to make a good watch of every dog. In fact in some cases nothing that one can do will produce this, but the lines indicated are those along which the quickest results can be obtained. After a course of training the dog can be brought back to its home again.

HOW TO TRAIN A DOG TO DO TRICKS

The correct method of training is by reward and encouragement, and the tricks should be entered into as an amusing game. Under this aspect the dog will readily respond, and my own experience has always been that such diversions have always been thoroughly enjoyed by both pupil and master. Some people imagine that the animal is starved beforehand, and performs under the goad of starvation. This is, of course, nonsense. Such cruelty may be practised by stupid trainers, but is certainly not necessary, as a dog will learn to walk on its hind legs, turn somersaults, do sums, etc., etc., just after a hearty meal, for the sheer pleasure of entering into a game with its master, even without a reward; but no healthy, normal dog thinks lightly of ginger-snaps or a piece of sugar, and will do a good deal for either.

I have never been able to understand how it could be possible to teach a dog anything by coercion. It would certainly show fear, which would give the whole training away. If it does not show fear while working, it has not been ill-treated. For this reason I think it very advisable to restrict the training of many wild animals and timid animals, such as monkeys. They *do* show fear, and one does not receive any sense of co-operation in their case. Dogs are different. The tie between them and man is so close, that what interests one, interests the other also, which is a very wonderful fact.

Teaching a dog to lie down, when told to do so, is a very useful method of disciplining, and should be taught while the dog is young; that is to say, about a year old. This lesson has a very settling effect on its character, and is the preliminary to many other lessons where obedience is required.

The dog should be pressed down to the ground with the hand and held there till told to rise, and should then be rewarded with a tit-bit, and this lesson can be continued daily until it has learnt to lie down itself, at word of command, and without being touched. Vary the length of time of lying down, and on no account over-do the lesson, so as to tire the dog and make it bored. Little and often is better. After a time teach it to remain lying down while the owner goes out of sight, and the best way to teach this is to give it something to guard—a coat or a pair of gloves. Never forget the reward for good service, and never strike the dog, but indicate by the voice what is required.

TRAINING A DOG TO CARRY A MESSAGE

The principle of messenger-service as described in another chapter, as taught to dogs in the Great War, can be adapted to civilian needs if need be, and if co-operation with another person can be secured. One of the quickest ways of teaching this is on the retrieving principle.

Where it is desired to send a dog on a message, or to fetch a small parcel from the local village, it can be taken to the shop, which we will suppose may be the post-office. Before starting out give it something to hold in its mouth, a stick or parcel. Most dogs can readily be taught to carry an object with a little practice, and they are particularly fond of carrying a basket by the handle. If at first, however, the dog refuses to carry anything in its mouth, tie the object to its collar, seeing that it does not hang down low enough to impede its legs. It must now accompany its master, and the shopman or someone in charge of the shop or post-office must be asked to accept the basket and reward the dog, which the owner can, if need be, slip over to him for presentation. If this training is persisted in, and the same words used each time, the dog will soon get to associate the whole train of action with those words, and will carry on later independently of its master.

After receiving the basket the shopman can insert something in it, give it back to the dog and wave it away, saying, "Go home!" This lesson can be taught, if desired, in the first place at home, by sending it to and fro between two people at increasing distances, and using the same words every time. After a time the dog will associate its actions with the words, and then the commands can be used under different conditions. By doing this gradually the pupil will be found to adapt itself to what is desired.

Another method for the preliminary training for this messenger work is to throw an article, and teach the dog to bring it back. This can be done at greater and greater distances, until the article is placed out of sight, and the dog has to search for it and retrieve it. The words of command should always be adhered to. I have known these exercises develop into very useful work with an intelligent dog, and one was trained to go to the hat-stand and pick out its master's cap, from among many others, and bring it to wherever he was; another went regularly for the evening paper, fetching it from the local post-office. Another was even trusted with the morning incoming mail from the post-office, which was placed in a bag on its collar. One very clever animal used to stop at the baker's every day regularly, *en route* for home, and receive a bun. In seeking the co-operation of the dog in such daily duties, there is nothing but good. It rejoices in the invitation to take an executive part in its master's avocations. A sense of importance and responsibility is at once imparted and joyfully accepted.

CHAPTER VII

How to Feed your Dog

"Come my auld towsy trusty friend,
What gars ye look sae dung wi wae ?
D'ye think my favours at an end,
Because thy head is turning gray ?

Although thy strength begins to fail,
It's best was spent in serving me,
An' can I grudge thy wee bit meal,
Some comfort in thy age to gie ?

For He who fed the ravens young
Let's naething pass He dis na see ;
He'll judge o' right an wrang,
An' aye provide for you an me."
—*Address to his old dog "Hector."* HOGG.

IT is as well to remember when you are considering the best method of feeding your dog, that it is just like yourself, in so far that it also, dislikes monotony of diet. A great deal of canine illness, skin trouble, etc., is due to a too-monotonous bill of fare. At the same time, it is not always easy for the average dog-owner just to know how a correct and yet varied form of nourishment can be achieved. Dog-biscuits, which can be obtained in so many excellent brands, are extremely useful as a stand-by for a foundation for the daily principal meal, but where only one dog is kept, or one or two small ones, bread is usually more appreciated. Where biscuits are used these should be soaked, and the *bon bouche* of the meal is contained in a nice basin of mixed house-scraps which have accumulated in the previous twenty-four hours in the kitchen. These scraps may consist of meat, fish, the remains of puddings, the scrapings of saucepans, pieces of bread, a few pieces of potatoes, etc., etc., and they should be well mixed with the soaked biscuits, and the whole should have some nice gravy, or soup, or milk, or all three thrown over it.

This mixture makes a nice tasty dinner, which your dog will thoroughly enjoy. When bread is used, the soaking will not be necessary, as long as there is enough milk or soup to thoroughly moisten it. I am frequently asked if vegetables should be given. The reply is, that there is no harm in doing so, but that dogs do not, as a rule, care for them, and eat round them, so that their presence in the mixture must not be at the expense of another ingredient, which would be more relished. Bones also should not be given in this bowl of food, but a meaty bone of good size is an excellent thing for a dog to gnaw at, *after* it has partaken of its legitimate meal.

Chicken, rabbit and game bones are dangerous, as they splinter, and they should therefore be avoided. As to the quantity of food a dog should eat, a very safe policy to pursue is to give it as much at this principal meal as it can eat, and then remove anything left over. Some dogs have bigger appetites than others, and in some cases it will be found that an adult dog does quite well on one good meal in the twenty-four hours, provided this is given always at the same time, and is made plentiful and also as tempting as I have described. I think, however, that it is a good plan to offer a second meal of a very light nature in between the principal time of feeding. Thus if the dog is fed early in the day, let it have a drink of milk at tea-time, and a few bits of dry dog biscuits or sweet biscuits (of which dogs are often very fond), as a contrast to the soft food of the principal meal, or if it is fed in the evening, let it have a few scraps at breakfast-time.

Dogs fed in this manner will be found to keep good health, and never to grow too fat, and therefore they also will retain their youth and vigour until a green old age. Skin troubles will also be infrequent, or will not appear at all, and at the same time the owner can feel that his dog is well nourished and is happy in its menu.

It is quite a mistake to think that meat is bad to give. In a certain proportion, mixed with other ingredients as

Mr. Lloyd George's Guardian for Stormy Times.

p. 98.

described, it is excellent, and gives zest to the meal as does nothing else. I also have a great belief in milk, and dogs are very fond of it. Where there are signs of too great accumulations of fat or bad breath, which are frequently put down to meat or milk-eating, it is quite certain the real cause is not this, but is probably because the meals are not regularly given, and the dog is fed at odd times, and its digestion becomes upset in consequence.

It must be remembered that the canine process of digestion is much slower than that of the human being, and a good meal takes about nine hours to digest. Therefore it can be understood, that frequent scrappy bits of food given to it, will very soon upset a dog's digestion, with all the subsequent results following on. It is much better that a dog's feeding should be in the hands of one person, who will know what it should have, and see that the proper hours are kept. This last point is one of the most important, and is the secret of good health. The household cook very often has the task of feeding the family dog, and is an excellent person for the job, as she controls the sources of supply; but there is always the regrettable temptation to use the dog as a convenient incinerator, or dust-bin—a convenient receptacle for odds and ends at any given moment.

A good method is for the house dog to be fed by its master or mistress at luncheon-time in the dining-room. A convenient mix-up from the table can be put into its own special bowl, brought in from the kitchen, and already reinforced, if desired, with a collection placed in it by the cook. In this way, the owner can see exactly what the dog gets, and can alter the diet at any time that seems necessary.

Where dogs are kept out of doors, the feeding has usually to be deputed to one of the servants, but one definite person should be put in charge, so that correct diet and hours can be insured. The food can be the same—that is to say, soaked dog-biscuits or bread, mixed with house scraps and milk or gravy.

Where the household is small or for other reasons there may not be enough mixed scraps to ensure a sufficiently appetising mixture, it may, in that case, be necessary to procure other forms of food to assist the menu. It is generally easy to buy cheap pieces of chilled beef from the butcher. Boiled down, these will make excellent soup and stew, which, mixed with dog-biscuits or bread, will make a cheap, and very tasty dinner for a hungry dog. There are also certain forms of dried milk on the market which, mixed with warm water, are excellent, for pouring over the bowl of food, where cows' milk cannot always be given. Most dog-biscuits contain a certain proportion of meat, but no brand that I know of contains sufficient, without additional meat from the larder. Fish-heads boiled down are excellent for a change of diet, and mixed with bread.

Where there are a number of outside dogs, especially if they be of large size, the feeding arrangements will, of course, assume important proportions, but, nevertheless, although the actual ingredients may have to be altered, the principles laid down already must be followed: that is to say, the dogs must have sufficient variety, they must have sufficient meat and other aids to appetite.

For a large number of kennel dogs, a useful addition to the out-of-door larder is that food called "greaves," a hard cake composed of fat and meat. This article of diet for dogs is largely used by gamekeepers, for sporting dogs. It necessitates cooking, but a large pot or boiler, in which dog-biscuits and greaves are cooked in equal proportions, covered over with water, will turn out a very much appreciated dish for all dogs. They all like this, and although it would not do to give it as an unvarying diet, still, it will be found to be a good stock repast. As a variety to this, where there are a large number of dogs and when sufficient cows' milk may not be obtained, I would especially recommend the dried milk, which goes a good deal further than the former, and is also much enjoyed by dogs when poured over the biscuits.

The same care as to regularity of hours must govern the feeding of kennel dogs, and they should all be fed regularly at the same time. In the case of the older dogs, one good meal in the twenty-four hours, is generally found sufficient, but the half-grown ones, and young adults require another meal within that time.

It is necessary also to notice if all the dogs have eaten their dinner properly, as, if they are off their food, it is advisable to offer another feed, before twenty-four hours have passed, and something different should be given.

The water jacketed boilers are very useful, where large quantities of food have to be cooked, and when one of these is available, an excellent substitute for the biscuits is Scotch oatmeal, well cooked with butcher's offal, or horse-flesh. Hound-meal, cooked in the same way, is also excellent.

In using these boilers, care must be taken that the jacket is always full of water, as otherwise they very easily become burnt out.

Horse-flesh is a very good food where it can be obtained fresh, but it is dangerous to depend on this too much, as at certain times in the year, the summer-time especially, it is very difficult to get. Cooked with some farinaceous substance, it makes one of the most satisfactory and nourishing canine repasts available.

The foregoing remarks on food can be applied to all breeds of dogs. It has been generally thought that toy dogs should be, as regards their food at all events, a class apart, and as a result of this idea, their food is often the subject of quite unnecessary fuss. I think that nowadays wilful cruelty directed against dogs, at all events, is practically extinct, or is getting happily very rare. There is still, however, a large amount of treatment which, while intended to express the owner's most earnest solicitude, is really productive of extreme discomfort, if not actual hardship to a dog.

It is a fact, that toy dogs, if treated as healthy, hardy and intelligent animals, will respond and develop extremely sporting and attractive personalities, with good healthy appetites. They should be fed as directed ; that is to say, one large meal, as much as they can eat at the time, and then a smaller meal in between. In the case of these small dogs it is, of course, very easy to vary the diet, and a portion of chopped-up chicken, mixed in with the chief meal, is a nice change from the meat. They should on no account be fed oftener than this, nor should food or milk be left standing about for them. Their movements should be unrestricted, and they should be expected to behave like sensible, self-reliant animals.

I have seen a sensibly brought up Pekinese leading the

way to the local rabbit-burrow, and followed by one or two of the family terriers, and after a glorious morning scraping, returning with the others to a large and satisfactory meal. A suspicion that a rat might be discovered round by the stables had him out again in the afternoon, and the only inducement to desist in the chase, was the invitation to accompany his mistress on the front seat of the motor, and act as a self-constituted guard dog along with the Airedale, while she was paying calls.

The idea that, because a dog is small, it therefore differs in temperament and needs radically different treatment from the larger breeds, is a great mistake. There are fundamental laws which govern all living creatures, and apply particularly to young growing things. Warm and dry surroundings, good and varied nourishment, fresh water to drink, sufficient freedom and exercise, regular hours. If these fundamentals are recognised, there need not, and should not be, any difference in the application of them to any specific breed of dog. Their application, with very definite effort, in no way implies pampering, but, on the contrary, is all in line with commonsense. It is when restriction, or excess of these rules is allowed, that they can be transformed into actual abuses.

The elderly lady's dog, with its perpetually supervised and restricted time-tables of life, with too frequent meals thrust upon it, and the bowl of cream left standing always within reach, the lack of natural freedom, is really a victim of persistent cruelty, all the more difficult to cope with, because actuated by sincere affection for the pet. When this treatment also involves fussy ideas as to what is considered correct food for the unfortunate animal, the cruelty is intensified. Thus some people think their dogs should never have a drop of milk, others that they should never touch meat.

I have seen an unappetising mess of dry rice mixed with green vegetables offered each day to a dog, and have listened to the bemoaning of the owner on account of the poor appetite displayed by the feeder for what she considered was a scientifically-thought-out meal. The suggestion that some nice stew mixed with the rice would be appreciated was coldly received.

Another small dog I know, turns with disgust from an almost perpetual diet of raw meat, and can one wonder!

All these fads as to feeding are a great mistake. Dogs should be regarded much in the same light as healthy, normal children, and treated accordingly.

This fetish as to green vegetables, is another fad with which dogs are often pestered by their owners. Dogs do not like vegetables. They do not even care for potatoes particularly, unless well mixed with gravy. They will generally eat carefully round any vegetables that may be left uncut up, and it is a great mistake to inflict too much of this on the resisting feeder. The meals require to be *relished,* in order to be really nourishing and beneficial.

Care should be taken where there is more than one dog, when bones are handed out. Especially is this necessary where there are a number of large dogs, as very severe mutilation is the result, sometimes, of quarrels over a bone.

Fresh, clean drinking water is an important point. It is often not recognised how much the dog's health depends on a good supply of fresh water.

THE TIMES OF FEEDING

The question of the right time to feed your dog must be regulated to a great extent by the sort of duties which are expected from it.

Where watching powers are required for the night hours, it is certainly essential that the chief meal should not be too late in the day. For this work the dog requires to be alert, and digestion should have taken place; therefore it is better to feed before or about midday. With a night-watchman's dog, or sentry dogs, where alertness is of surpassing importance, it is better to feed when going off duty in the morning, a good hearty meal which the dog can digest quietly, while resting during the day.

But even the household dog is better to be fed not later than midday, as cleanliness of habit is thus made easier for it during the long hours of the night. It will have had time to digest its food and exercise itself afterwards, before being confined indoors till next morning.

The only dogs which can legitimately be fed during the evening hours, are those whose capabilities are called upon very vigorously during the day-time, such as dogs used for sport, or where a relay of watch-dogs is required for guarding valuable places. This sort of duty was often required, officially, during the war, when vital interests were at stake, and perpetual watch was necessary. In this case a succession of guard dogs was arranged. Those on duty during the day were fed in the evening, and rested at night, while those who carried on the guarding work at night were fed on coming off duty in the morning, and rested all day. Thus the dogs were in each case rested and well fed, and yet alert for responsible duties, and with undimmed hearing and scenting capabilities.

CHAPTER VIII

Exercise and Grooming

" It has been well remarked that the poets of various lands and different ages have delighted in commemorating the virtues of this favourite animal, as though they recognised in his devotion to man something of the love and obedience with which man should look up to his Heavenly Father and Almighty Friend."—JESSE.

THE bounding energy of our dog is one of its chief attractions, and those who do not provide themselves with a good doggy " pal," are unaware of the stimulating and cheering influence they are missing in their daily life. We, who have this privilege, however, must not neglect it, but must see that sufficient freedom and exercise are obtainable to minister to this natural love of movement of the animal's nature. There is no need for the dog to be on the run all day, but it is necessary that it should have a certain amount of exercise, and certainly a great deal of freedom of movement. There is a good deal of distinction in these two phrases. For instance, if a dog has a country home, and has the freedom of a nice garden to wander in, it will need much less walking exercise than will a town dog, or a dog which for some reason or other is kept in a kennel, or on the chain for considerable periods. It will enjoy a walk very much, and should be taken out as frequently as possible and given a good walk, but the fact that it is always at large makes a great difference, and the exercising does not assume such importance.

An intelligent dog generally makes little duties for itself in connection with the routine of the establishment, and keeps on the trot most of the time. It is not always possible, however, to leave a dog loose all day about the place. Until a dog is perfectly trained and obedient, too much freedom without supervision is apt to spoil its character, and it is better to confine a young dog during the time its master cannot attend to it, rather than let it deteriorate by getting into straying habits.

In other cases, dogs of certain temperament develop cross-grained tendencies as they grow in age, which makes it unsafe to allow them to remain at large unsupervised. These dogs are nevertheless of great value very often for this very reason. They are usefully employed as guard dogs for either inside or out, and are useful where perhaps the younger and milder animal would not be of any use. They have to be kennelled or kept indoors until their master, or some member of the household, can take them out.

The town dog also cannot always be at large. In the old days, when dogs were much more plentiful and quantities of half-bred animals of no particular value from a monetary point of view abounded, these ran about the streets of London and elsewhere in happy liberty, and thoroughly enjoyed themselves. In those happy days the dogs of South Kensington and other parts had regular beats every morning, and I have seen numerous sagacious-looking animals trotting off in a businesslike way to the end of their different terraces on being let out in the morning. There they would forgather by appointment with other happy little pals, and the contingent, joined *en route* by other recruits, would march up to the park for a morning scamper on their own, returning for breakfast in an hour's time or so. As many as seven dogs have been counted advancing up a broad thoroughfare like Queensgate, the cohort having been recruited from the various streets adjoining.

Nowadays, unfortunately, dogs are much scarcer. They are generally purely bred, and as a matter of fact, owing to their diminution in number, all dogs are of value monetarily. This commercial value makes the dog-thief's trade a prosperous one, and it is not possible to allow one's dog abroad in the manner just described. It would run a great risk of being stolen, so that this convenient method, whereby the animal exercised itself, cannot be permitted. A dog which is kept loose indoors always has a certain freedom of action even in town, and does not feel so confined as a dog which is kept in a kennel, but under whatever circumstances of confinement an animal is kept, it must get, one way or another, a good walk every day, and preferably two.

The amount of exercise required depends upon the breed. Short-legged dogs need less than those whose legs cover the ground quickly, and relatively the exercise required by a small-sized animal or toy, would be very different from that needed by the larger breeds, or some of the active terriers. Some dogs, such as dandie dinmonts, Sealyhams and Scottish terriers, especially where these have short or bent legs, do not care for long walks but prefer freedom to "potter." The characteristics with regard to the necessity for exercise of each breed must be taken into account, and it must be understood that, while it is not necessary that a dog need be running loose all day, and in fact it is sometimes not desirable, a sense of *lack* of freedom and exercise, is extremely bad for a dog, both physically and mentally. Many a dog's disposition is spoilt by mismanagement under this heading.

Dogs of uncertain disposition cannot be left at large with safety, and in their case the exercise must be given on the lead, or else an enclosed portion of the grounds must be used as an exercising-ground. A walled garden is useful for this purpose, as there the dog can have its liberty and run about, but cannot do any harm to anyone. It is kind, however, to give the animal a walk on the roads, even if it has to go on the lead, as it will always be a pleasure for it to accompany its master, and dogs thoroughly enjoy seeing what is going on in the world, outside their own domain. If this cannot be done by the master, a servant should be deputed to exercise it. One thing is certain, and it is that the dog must not be left on the chain all day without exercise.

Dogs living in towns can be given much more exercise than they would ordinarily have, if they were trained to go about with their owners wherever the latter go. Now that it is permissible to take them on buses and in tubes, it is a very good thing to teach them to follow nicely on the lead, to sit down immediately close to one in trains, and to mount omnibus stairs quickly, and board trains without any fuss. In crowded thoroughfares it is always safer to have the dog on the lead, not only because the crowds are apt to confuse it, and thereby cause it to lose sight of the owner, but also because the dog-thief is always on the prowl, and can easily confiscate a dog which is running loose in a crowded street, even if it is close behind one.

A small girl was exercising her fox-terrier down Oxford Street on a rather invisible lead, and a dog-thief, not seeing the lead, made a lunge at the animal and caught it up in his arms and was proceeding to bolt down a side-street. The child, however, held on to the end of the lead, with the result that the dog was hurriedly dropped, and the thief fled off as hard as he could. She would never have known where the dog went, had it not been for the lead.

Where shopping is intended, and it is found that shop rules do not allow the entrance of the dog, it is not well to leave it chained at the shop door for long, if the animal is a handsome one, as here again there is always risk of theft, and as far as possible it is better to carry it under the arm when in the shop, or, if permitted, to take it in on the lead.

A well-trained dog will sit down quite quietly and give no trouble. I have found it possible to train a country bumpkin dog brought into London for the first time, to go everywhere with his master, in tubes, buses and taxicabs, shops and private houses, and behave nicely, without causing any trouble whatever, in about a week. At first it was nervous and did not enjoy the expeditions much. It was afraid of being stepped on in the crowds, disliked boarding trains and buses, and was in a state of tension most of the time. After that period, however, it had adapted itself to the situation, as its desire to accompany the master outweighed all fears, and in the end enjoyed itself immensely, negotiating the crowds and vehicles, as to the manner born. It was a little trouble at first, but this was repaid later on as the creature's companionship was amusing.

It is possible to hire the services of people who make a speciality of exercising dogs, and one can hear of these through the advertisements in the daily papers, and the dog press. But care must be taken only to allow the dog to be taken out by someone, who is in every way qualified to safely undertake the task.

MOTORING

One of the greatest pleasures in dog-life is to be taken for a motor-drive. It is difficult to analyse just exactly what it is that contributes the extreme satisfaction displayed during this form of travelling. An immense complacency, and serene and complete enjoyment is manifested. The sensitive nose is obtruded in the breeze, and evidently a sense of intense exhilaration is experienced, but the crux of the enjoyment is reached when a pedestrian dog is passed on the road. Even if actual vituperation is refrained from, it is impossible for the motor "nut" to disguise the feeling of enormous superiority, with which the plebian animal, padding along on its own feet, fills him. The increased height of the motor, also, gives him a greatly lengthened vision, from when he is himself on the ground. This adds to his experience and his appreciation of things in general, and is extremely good for his mind. Altogether motoring is extremely good for dogs, as giving them great pleasure, and also for making them more intelligent. In cold weather, however, they must wear a coat or have the rug put round them.

REMARKS ON GROOMING AND WASHING YOUR DOG

Great care should be taken with the washing of puppies. It is better not to wash them at all, unless really necessary, while they are very young. If the mother has been well kept, and the bedding of the litter irreproachable, the pups should be in good clean condition. Certainly later on when they begin to get about, and roll over each other they are apt to become soiled, but a good brushing and combing will generally rectify this, and they must be regularly groomed in this manner.

Where a bath is necessary, however, this can be given with safety as long as great care is taken in the drying. A special shampoo soap has been invented of extraordinarily healthful and cleansing qualities, and which is also exceedingly good for the skin, besides being different from the usual dog soaps in that it has an extremely pleasing odour.

The puppy should be placed in a bath of warm water into which the elbow can be comfortably placed. Some of the shampoo should be poured into the water, until it is rather cloudy, and the pup should then be well sponged with this all over. Then pour some shampoo out of the bottle on to the wet coat and rub well in ; rinse in clean warm water. Dry carefully in towels. If this can be done on a warm, sunny day, a scamper in the sunshine afterwards is advisable, until quite dry. If it is winter, the pup must dry in front of the fire, and then be taken for a run, when quite dry, with a coat on.

The procedure is the same with adult dogs of all breeds. In the case of a large dog, a good-sized bath is required for the animal to stand in, while the preliminary sponging is given of the shampoo water. Then pour a plentiful supply of the shampoo mixture on to the coat, and thoroughly lather the whole body, and rinse well.

Where a bath is not available, the dog can stand outside and the shampoo made up in a pail and sponged over. Dry as already directed. At all costs the adult dog or pup must be clean, and it is not that baths are bad for them, on the contrary, a weekly bath, or even oftener, is in no way deleterious, as long as protection from chill is guarded against.

For long-haired dogs a comb with medium and fine sections should be used, and a good stiff brush. The comb should go right through the under coat. A thoroughly good brushing is generally enough for dogs of close and wiry coat, but a comb should always be run through the coat along the back. A chamois leather is very good to use, as a finish for fine silky skin and fur. A stripping comb is useful at times when the outer coat has overgrown and is spoiling the outline the dog should have. The combs have short fine teeth, and catch the long loose fur and pull it away.

The points in each breed which it is desired to emphasise should always be borne in mind, when the grooming is in process. The correct line must be carefully preserved. Thus in the rough-haired terrier breeds, the eyebrows, whiskers and beard, should be carefully preserved and cultivated, while the fur on the cheeks and ears must be kept free from long hair, so as to accentuate the other points.

The top of the head, except in cases where top-knots are required, should be kept smooth. The legs should be nicely trimmed from long, untidy hair, and only along the saddle is a good coat allowed ; but even here if a dog carries too heavy a coat, attention will have to be paid, and it will have to be trimmed down.

The appearance to be attained is a smart, well-set-up, glossy impression, and a dog with a quantity of ragged-looking hair, which blurs the good points of the animal, can never reach this standard.

In the smooth-haired varieties, a good brushing with a fine but strong-bristled brush, will keep the fur in good condition, but a fine tooth-comb is also advisable, as it keeps the skin clean and free from parasites.

The teeth should be kept clean by being well brushed with a toothbrush dipped in the shampoo soap and Vim.

In summer-time, when fleas are troublesome, a fine tooth-comb dipped in paraffin, and run through the coat will extract them all. Pay particular attention to the root of the tail.

CHAPTER IX

A Dog on its Travels

" Therefore to this dog will I,
Tenderly not scornfully,
Render praise and favour :
With my hand upon his head,
To my benediction said,
Therefore and forever.

And because he loves me so,
Better than his kind will do
Often, man or woman,
Give I back more love again
Than dogs often take of men,
Leaning from my Human."

To my Dog " Flush." ELIZABETH BARRETT BROWNING.

THE method of sending a dog on a journey differs according to the distance it has to traverse, but under all circumstances it should leave in a fully-fed condition.

In order to ensure this, its ordinary meal should be given to it before leaving, and should be added to with an extra bowl of tit-bits, or a good drink of milk, and it should also be offered a drink of water. It will thus be amply fortified to stand a journey of fully twenty-four hours, if necessary, without any particular strain, and if any mishaps or delay should happen *en route*, would even then be in quite a position to put up with a longer fast, without actual danger.

HOW DOGS SHOULD TRAVEL

It may be said, that as a rule, it is better that a dog should travel in a box. It is safer, because it is thus protected from draughts, and from the risk of boxes falling on it in the van. Food and even water can also be inserted in the box for consumption on the journey.

The box should be of proportions, that the dog, of whatever size it is, should be able to stand up and turn round easily inside, and it should be ventilated *according to the season.* A great deal of unnecessary suffering is caused the animal by insufficient care in this last respect. Thus, when the cutting blasts of winter are whirling down the platforms, the slats of the travelling box should be sufficient to ensure a plentiful supply of air, but should not be so large as to allow the inmate to become chilled. In summer, however, plenty of ventilation is necessary, and in very hot, sultry weather extra care will have to be taken in this respect. In fact, it is only under such conditions that it is almost safer to send the dog on a collar and chain.

When travelling this way a dog can be given water *en route,* which the railway men are generally very ready to do if it shows signs of thirst.

It is true that a muzzle is generally insisted on by the railway companies, but in an emergency this can be easily removed and replaced so that water can be given. In any case, a large enough muzzle through which the dog can drink is advisable, and it is most important that the muzzle should be easy and comfortable.

A label bearing the legend, " Please give me a drink," is sure to attract attention with consequent desired results, and I recently saw a dog travelling with an attractive verse of poetry attached to it, conveying the information of " Bruno's " long journey to his destination, his friendly and reliable disposition, and his earnest plea for kindly consideration in the shape of a drink.

These flights of fancy are, however, not advisable where the traveller is in its box, as it is unwise for strangers to tamper with the fastenings in order to insert the vessel of water. Either they might not close it sufficiently safely again and the dog might subsequently escape, or it might jump out on being opened up, and refuse to be caught again.

As a matter of fact, the greatest care should be taken before the box leaves to see that it is very securely fastened, as a dog away from its home sometimes develops great timidity, and will bolt immediately, if it gets a chance of escape.

A special dog travelling-box is the best kind of case to use as these are ventilated, or should be, all round the sides, so that if one or two sides are up against other boxes in the van, there is always ventilation still coming in from the other sides.

There are two disadvantages, however, to dog-boxes very often. One is that they are frequently not large enough for the larger breeds, and secondly, unless they are made on an approved plan of sliding shutters, which can be opened or shut as required, *as well* as the ventilating slats round the lid, they are difficult to ventilate sufficiently in hot weather.

A packing-case, which can be purchased from the grocer, makes quite a satisfactory travelling-box, and the advantage of this is that the wooden strips closing the box can be regulated according to the required ventilation, and holes can also be bored in the sides to ensure safety in this respect.

For the small breeds and for puppies, sugar, soap or tea boxes are good sizes, but large cases are required for the larger breeds, and it cannot be too emphatically stated that boxes should be very commodious for the dogs. Hay or straw litter is soft and comfortable, or an old blanket. The latter may be discarded at the end of the journey, but is useful in that any food supplied for the journey does not get covered up, as it is apt to be in the case of the hay or straw.

A good-sized bone, with meat on it, is a good thing to put in the box; a knuckle-bone for a small dog, and the bone of a leg or shoulder of mutton for the large breeds. With this to chew the traveller will spend its time quite happily for a long distance of the journey. The only drawback, to this form of nourishment in the box is, that in the case of dogs which are apt to be testy when in touch with their food (especially with bones), they are sometimes on guard over the bone on arrival at the end of their destination, and give the impression of bad temper towards what may be a new master, when really the dog may be perfectly good-tempered in an ordinary way, and many dogs are absolutely sweet-tempered in every other way, except when they are eating.

With such a dog it is best not to send it away with a bone in its box, but to confine the extra refreshment to bread-and-butter, or some broken biscuits.

In every case, however, it is important that food of some kind should be in the box, as such things occur as break-downs or missed connections and the delay is not of such serious consequences if extra nourishment is provided, which the dog can easily find for itself.

Hampers are not to be recommended. The wind sweeps right through them, and in this climate there are few days or nights when an animal in confinement can be left about on station platforms, with safety, in such an airy receptacle. Besides this, it is comparatively easy for a dog with a good strong jaw to eat its way out.

When sending a puppy on a journey the food question is an all-important one, and it is extremely necessary that it should have a large meal just before it starts. Some pieces of raw meat cut small and put into the box ensure a meal *en route,* which it can eat with relish.

The best time for starting dogs off on their journeys depends on the distance. Except for comparatively short journeys, it is generally better to look out a good evening train and let the dog do most of its journey at night. There are several reasons for this. First of all, the dog, having had its usual food and exercise during the day before it left, will travel better and more restfully at night. In summer-time it is cooler. If it misses a connection and is delayed anywhere it will not be so upsetting to the dog as if the lost hours were mostly from its active day hours.

A dog sent off by a reasonably early evening or afternoon train will generally reach its destination at most parts in England by midday next day, and not the slightest harm will accrue, even if it should not do so till later, provided the foregoing directions as to packing and feeding have been followed.

People often think that if they send the dog off early in the morning it will necessarily arrive at its journey's end the same evening, but it is very difficult to ensure this if a cross-country journey is in view, or even merely a change of lines. The railway companies do not always send them by the connections one anticipates, delays occur, and the dog is left lying overnight at some junction, or it only arrives late at night, when it is difficult to get it removed to the house.

In these days of depleted staffs and short hours it is sometimes very inconvenient having to send down to the station late at night. Of course, if the journey is a short one, and the dog can be certain to arrive that afternoon, it is better to let it start early in the morning, but otherwise the evening hours are the best for the start.

HOW TO GREET A NEW DOG ON ARRIVAL

The first thing to do when a new dog arrives is to take it to an enclosed place, from which under no circumstances it can escape if inclined to do so. If it is in a box have this carried into a room or stable, and shut the door firmly. Then proceed to open up, having a suitable collar and chain in readiness the moment the first gap in the lid opens. Do not open the lid wide and let the dog jump out, but insert your hand gently first and pat the animal, speaking to it at the same time. Fasten the collar and chain to it, while it is in the box, and then let it jump out while you have the end of the chain in your hand.

Negligence of these precautions sometimes results in the new arrival making a clean bolt, whenever the box is opened, as it must be remembered that many dogs are of a highly-sensitive nature, and; until they take to their new master and surroundings, they are in a high state of apprehension. This nervousness will sometimes make them apparently somewhat vicious and inclined to snap while they are in the box, and leather gloves should always be worn when unpacking a new dog which shows this tendency. Usually the dog is really not bad tempered at all, but is only afraid of being touched by a stranger. By speaking to it and handling it gently, but with a certain decision, while the collar is put on, it very soon gains confidence. In the event of a snap while this is being done, the gloves will protect the hands from anything serious.

Where the dog is so nervous and is of a size to render it really risky to handle even with gloves, an efficient method of abstraction is to open the box sufficiently to insert a rope with a running noose. By dangling this above the dog's head it is easy to drop it down so that it slips over the head, and then the noose draws tight enough to lift it out. When outside the box, and with the noose still attached, slip on the collar and chain, holding the noose drawn well up so that the dog cannot move its head to bite. It will be found that the moment the dog has on the collar and lead safely and is walking about, all desire to snap has gone and it will gradually settle down.

In the case of very highly-strung dogs, it sometimes takes them a week to a fortnight to really become at home in new surroundings, but with normal animals and where the new owners have the "right way" with them, they settle in two or three days and in some cases where the dog is of a friendly disposition and the new master reciprocal, a very devoted affection ensues from one to the other on sight. It must be remembered, however, that sometimes those dogs which are the most difficult to settle at first, turn out extremely well in the end. It is perhaps a devoted impression of a former master at home on the mind of a deeply sensitive and affectionate nature, which causes it to very greatly resent the substitution of a new environment. With a dog like this it takes some time to supplant the old affections, but when this is accomplished one has the benefit of an extremely faithful companion for oneself.

One of the most devoted and most humanly intelligent dogs I ever had tried to bite everyone it could reach on its first arrival and remained in an extremely *farouche* state of mind for quite a fortnight after. It had been extremely devoted to its former owner, and resented deeply being separated. I am glad to say, however, he settled down after a time and became an extremely happy dog and lived to the age of sixteen.

I do not suppose a dog like this ever really forgets its first master, or indeed any master on whom it sets its affections, and very wonderful instances of joyful remembrance and recognition long years after separation are common knowledge. I myself have known several such cases, and there is the famous one of the dog of Ulysses.

> " When wise Ulysses
> Arrived at last,
> Poor, old, disguised, alone,
> To all his friends and even his queen unknown
> The faithful dog alone his master knew.
> Him when he saw he rose and crawled to meet
> ('Twas all he could), and fawned and kissed his feet,
> Seized with dumb joy—
> Then, falling at his side,
> Owned his returning lord,
> Looked up, and died."

When the dog has been walked about a little out of doors, after its cramped position in the box (always remembering to still keep it on the lead), it can be brought indoors if it is to be a house dog. It is as well, however, not to take off the chain but to fasten the end to the leg of a table. In this way the new acquisition can be made friends with and encouraged and fed with no risk of it escaping, and it will also settle far quicker. For the first twenty-four hours at least it should be kept on the lead and taken from room to room as its new owner moves about the house, or takes it for a walk out of doors.

Some dogs settle much quicker than others, and much also depends on the amount of understanding accorded to it by its owner. Those who understand dogs have usually the capacity of conveying this sympathy by tone of voice and by touch, and the dog is quick to respond.

If the animal is to live out of doors, the same precaution should be adopted, that is to say, it should be kept carefully in a kennel with a run and the door safely closed and only exercised on the lead for at least two days.

It is almost needless to say that food and drink should at once be given it on arrival, but no great stress should be laid on the fact that it will very likely not touch either owing to excitement.

HOW TO ENCOURAGE A NEW DOG TO ACCEPT A NEW HOME

One of the first things to find out is the new friend's name. Hearing its name called by a stranger makes a very great impression on a dog, and is one of the first avenues of approach.

It is a good plan, too, for the sender, if he has not already conveyed the information by letter, to write the name on the address label on the box. This is helpful to the new master and also the dog likes to hear its name called on the journey by friendly porters. It conveys a sense of comradeship which cheers it up.

The next step will be to introduce the dog to its own particular resting place, so that it can "take possession" at once. In the case of an outside dog this will be a kennel, which should be filled with plenty of nice clean straw to induce it to creep in and rest. If it is to live indoors it should be provided with a nice bed somewhere out of a draught—a box with fairly low sides and with comfortable cushions inside makes a good bed. A packing case cut down, so that the sides are about seven inches deep, makes an excellent couch. It can be covered with some material nailed round the sides and the cushions can be of some washable cretonne.

The size of the box depends on that of the dog, but it should be large enough to enable the inmate to "loll" comfortably.

There are plenty of dog beds to buy, but, unless these baskets, as they always seem to be, are lined, they are not so good as the box. It seems somewhat of a mystery why so many articles for canine use are composed of wicker work, a most draughty and unsatisfactory form of material. It cannot be too strongly impressed that no animal should lie in a draught, and it must also be remembered that there is always a tendency to chilliness along the floor.

The dish of fresh drinking water should always be kept beside the bed so that it can be easy of access.

TRAVELLING LABELS

When sending a dog away by train the correct labelling and equipping is most important.

If the dog travels on collar and chain and muzzle, the first thing is to see that all these things are in good strong condition. The collar should be just so tight that the neck is firmly grasped and that the dog cannot, by jerking violently backwards, pull its head through. The catch must be firm. A frequent cause of breakdown in equipment and consequent escape *en route* is a faulty chain swivel or hook. The correct attachment is a good chain with strong links, and a good strong hook at each end.

It is an excellent plan to tie the last link of the chain next the collar to the collar buckle with a thick piece of string, so that, in the event of the hook giving, the string will still hold good. It is an extraordinary thing how people will send a dog worth a very large sum on a journey, and yet will hesitate to spend a few shillings on a good collar and chain to ensure safe transit. The real reason is generally because they are not sufficiently cognisant of the way a dog may behave, when it finds itself alone with strangers and among strange sights and sounds.

Some dogs are not perturbed to any extent and in fact are rather interested in seeing fresh faces and places, but others are in a highly nervous condition on leaving their home, and their whole attention is concentrated in an attempt to escape and return, so that they attempt biting through the lead (hence anything but metal chains are inadvisable), or pull their collar over their heads.

A dog's collar should always be a hole tighter than is ordinarily comfortable. *The strap must be loosened after the dog has made itself at home in its new home.*

The muzzle is better to be of the regulation wire type, and should be of a large size in relation to the dog's head, so that it can open its mouth to a quite reasonable extent inside. As the nervous tension generally induces panting, it is extremely cruel to send a dog away in a tight muzzle. Although the regulations regarding muzzling are fairly strict on the railway, still, when the dog to be dispatched is obviously an extremely genial and good-tempered animal, it is frequently allowed to start without the muzzle being actually adjusted, but hanging to the collar in case of emergency. In this case the only difficulty which may arise from the sender's point of view is that the dog may chew the labels. It is therefore advisable to tie on two labels, one to be attached to the handle of the chain, and one to the collar end.

Two labels are also safer, even when the dog travels in a box, as obliteration from various causes, or mutilation of a single label causes inconvenience and delay. The address on both labels should be very clearly written or, better still, in printed writing.

It should also be stated that a valuable dog or puppy, as the case may be, is inside, and the word 'Immediate' should be largely written. The dog's name should also be stated, and it is a good plan to include the name of the sender and his place of abode, so that, in case of any accident, he can be communicated with by the company.

CHAPTER X

Breeding Dogs and Rearing Pups

" This Dog hath so himself subdued,
That hunger cannot make him rude :
And his behaviour doth confess
True courage dwells with gentleness.

Few men to do such noble deeds have learned
Nor having done, could look so unconcerned."
—*Written by a lady in* 1669.

If it is desired to breed a litter the selection of the parents should be carried out with a view to the desired appearance in the progeny. Under all circumstances it is best value to obtain pure-bred pedigree stock. In these days the question of food is always a consideration, and a pedigree animal costs no more to feed than a mongrel. Furthermore, the former can generally fetch a price as can its offspring, and this desirable state of matters is a sufficient set off against the difference in purchase money in the first place, which will certainly be considerable of course. Apart from this, the fine appearance of a pure-bred dog is greatly to be appreciated, and, as I have already stated elsewhere, it is quite a mistake to imagine, as many people do, that pedigree stock is not so intelligent as that without such forebears.

Now pedigree dogs of good quality are sure to be expensive. During the war hundreds, nay thousands of dogs were killed off owing to shortage of food, and only those of the best type and breeding were preserved. This fact, in itself, put up the value of dog flesh considerably, but apart from this, although by this time breeding has replaced many empty kennels, still the numbers remain far behind pre-war times, and furthermore the standard has been kept high. If people keep dogs now, it pays better to keep only the best.

At the present time a fine, well-grown young dog with all its points up to show form, and of correct size and in fine health, fetches a good price, and if the same animal shows very unusual merit in any particular points, the price it can reach will be greater than that at which many horses are sold.

A nice companion dog, that is to say one, while showing all the necessary breeding of its pedigree ancestors, does not excel to any very noticeable extent in some of its points, can be purchased for a moderate price, but even so this will be a good deal higher than before the war.

If one is already in possession of a good dog, and desires a mate, consideration should be given to those qualities which are weak and should be sought for in excess in the mate to be selected. Thus, if it is a dog which errs on the side of coarseness, that is to say lack of finish in its points, a bitch should be chosen of refined and dainty type. If the dog is good in size, but lacks good head qualities, this can be adjusted through the dam for the progeny. In the same way, if one is in the possession of a bitch and desires to purchase a mate, or to send her to stud, the same discrimination should be exercised. As a general rule it is best to aim at size in the dog, and quality in the bitch, but it is impossible to lay down any hard and fast rule in this respect, but to make as judicious a combination as is possible, so that weak points may be counteracted. When nearing the time of parturition the bitch should be put to sleep each night in the place where she is expected to rear her puppies. With small breeds this is easy to select. A nice box with a pad of hay in it, placed in a warm, quiet place, will be suitable, but the box must be of very ample size to ensure against the mother crushing any pups, which might crawl behind her against the sides.

If the bitch is a good mother and the litter is not a large one, this is not so likely to happen, but if she is careless, or is becoming exhausted with the care of too large a litter, the pups are apt to get separated from her and accidents happen. If, however, there is a good space all round her, they can find their way back again to the others. In the large breeds the right sort of breeding and rearing place is not quite so easy. On no account should the bitch be allowed to have her litter in her kennel, as the area is too confined, but a quiet isolated shed or barn *with a wooden floor* is an excellent place. A good thick bed of straw or hay should be spread in the *middle* of the floor. This gives plenty of room for the pups to crawl all round her so that they cannot be easily lost or lain upon, which eventuality is especially common with the big heavy breeds.

Stables with their stone floors are not so suitable on account of this last point, which is bad for both mother and progeny. If the litter arrives in winter the heating question in such a place is also difficult, unless there are horses kept there, which heat up the atmosphere within. Unfortunately comparatively few people keep horses now, so that unless some artificial heating can be arranged, such a place is too cold in winter.

If the puppies are really valuable and it is desired to preserve all the litter, it is worth taking some trouble with them. Good pure-bred puppies can fetch from five to ten and fifteen guineas each, according to the rarity of the breed, and each one lost is a serious mishap.

Before the arrival of the litter the bitch should not be confined in any way, but should be allowed to move about freely, but if she is heavy in pup she should not be taken long walks too near the time. Her diet should be as usual, and one which she appreciates, but she should have additional milk given to her and she should be in good condition, but not too fat. While suckling it is not well to change her diet in any degree from that to which she is accustomed, but it should be added to by milk foods of various sorts.

A litter of five or six can usually be comfortably looked after by the bitch without much assistance, but if there are more than this she should certainly be assisted, both while the puppies are arriving and for some time afterwards, otherwise the weaker pups are apt to literally " go to the wall " and the mother becomes exhausted from the drain upon her. If help is given her, however, there is no reason to be apprehensive with regard to the number of puppies, no matter whether they number eight or ten.

I have had successful litters of eleven well-reared pups and a healthy mother. In such cases there are two methods of assisting the mother. A foster mother can be procured to help to nourish the pups, or they must have extra nourishment supplied them through a feeding bottle. If the former plan is adopted a foster mother of suitable size according to the breed in question must be procured. A certain amount of tact must be used when introducing the alien pups to this mother. First of all she must be given an equally nice warm bed to the important lady she has come to relieve. One puppy only must be slipped in at a time amongst her own pups. It is as well to do this as far as possible without her notice, say, when she is up feeding, and the new puppy should be rubbed against the others to acquire the same scent. She will then take it into her care equally with her own. Her own pups can be extracted, one by one, as the new ones are inserted, if it is not desired to keep them. All dogs are, however, of value in these days, even if not pure bred, so that if her own can be kept as well, without injuring the chances of the more valuable specimens, it should be done. Foster mothers can be obtained by wire usually, and are advertised as available in the dog papers. But, unfortunately, they are much more difficult to obtain than formerly.

All foster mothers should be sent with some of their own pups. If a foster mother is not used and the litter is a large one, the first puppies to arrive should be taken one or two at a time while the rest are arriving, and kept in a warm basket in front of the fire. A baby's feeding bottle filled with blood-warm milk should be applied to the puppies lips every now and then. Until all the litter have arrived, the mother should only be left one or two puppies, sufficient to interest her. After they have all been born, the rest can be put back beside her for the night, after having been fed with the feeding bottle. In the morning they should all be given a drink from the bottle of warm milk, and, for a time, the strongest pups can be removed to the warm basket, which should be covered with a piece of flannel. This gives the smaller, weaker ones a chance to get a good feed from the mother. By encouraging these weaker pups in this way, it is possible to rear the whole litter, when otherwise they would be pushed aside by the stronger ones. Just at first, none of them must be removed for too long from the mother, but each pup should be watched to see if they are feeding well with her. Until they are rather older, some of the weak pups will be found to get more nourishment from the bottle, especially if care is taken to see that the teat of this is not too large and that the holes in it allow the milk to flow easily. Even if the litter is not very large it is an excellent plan to assist the feeding in this manner, especially where the weakly ones are concerned. The pups should be taught to lap as soon as possible, especially in the case of a large litter; at from three weeks to a month old. The milky food presented should be warmed, and the puppies muzzles dipped in it. They will soon find out that extra nourishment is available and act accordingly.

At this age, and for some weeks after, it will be found that many of the half-digested milk foods on the market are excellent as an aid to, or substitute for the dam's milk. Where her milk supply is weak they should certainly be used.

Young bitches with their first litter require special consideration and help, both in respect of helping her with the food supply, and also with the general care of the pups. Many bitches, who subsequently become bad mothers, are induced to become so by neglect of such attention with the first litter, which has been too much of a strain for them. They were, in the first place, bewildered by such a charge and then bored, and this impression remains with them in subsequent experiences. Clean, fresh water should always be supplied for both mother and pups—the bedding frequently changed.

HOW TO REAR THE PUPS

The pups should be introduced to extraneous food from the mother at about three weeks of age, even if they have not previously been assisted with the bottle. The food supplied should, for at least a week, be rather fluid, and of the milky nature indicated above. After about a week, and when the little things are a month old, something more solid can be introduced into the milky mixture, porridge (well cooked), crumbled sweet biscuits, or ground rice pudding. When the pups are six weeks old they can be given quite a mixture of scraps, including a little finely chopped meat. To any of them which seem lagging a little, raw meat is good if cut small. They should be fed three times a day up till the age of eight weeks. All this time they are inbibing as well from the dam, and should be put to sleep with her at night. Cream is very good for them and a good spoonful for each pup, as a tonic after a meal, has excellent results.

Mention may here be made that if for any circumstance it is found during any portion of their upbringing that they have to sleep away, or be separated for any length of time from the mother, a hot water bottle, or preferably bag, is a useful thing for putting under the blanket in the box the separated pups are in. Care must be taken, however, that they do not creep under the folds on to the hot bag itself, or they would suffer.

At eight weeks of age they should be quite free from the bitch, as far as nourishment is concerned. They should then be fed three times daily. The first thing in the morning, at mid-day, and the last thing at night. If they are offered this nourishment they will not need anything more from the bitch, and it is better now to wean them from her entirely as otherwise she becomes too much drained. Always remember that the Baby Foods on the market are excellent, but as bitches' milk is richer in cream than cows' milk, cream should be added to the mixture.

In winter-time, however, it is advisable to let the pups sleep with her at night for warmth, unless they are being dispersed. Many puppies are sold at seven weeks, or even six weeks of age, but this is too young—no pup should leave the mother under eight weeks. Until this age it cannot have had time to become properly stabilised on ordinary fare and it also requires the warmth of its brothers and dam when sleeping.

A good mixed diet from now on can be given, of a nourishing and varied nature. No particular foods need be advocated beyond saying, that everything that comes from the dinner table of the master, if in mixed quantities and well-chopped up, is permissible. All farinaceous foods, fish, meat, gravy, etc., can be given and mixed with milk and bread and cream.

After a puppy is three months old, two good meals a day are sufficient, morning and evening, and should consist of the above mixture, as much as they can eat each time. The food basin should not be left after the meal has been taken. Wait till the pup has quite finished and then remove anything that remains. On no account, however, present the sour food later on. Each time the meal must be fresh and appetising. When about six months old the diet can be brought up more to the grown up dog standard by introducing dog biscuits into the feeding mixture, but on no account must the food be allowed to become monotonous.

Having discussed the feeding of the puppies, the next thing is to mention the question of warmth, as it is one of the most important points in the successful rearing of good dogs. The necessity of a warm, dry place for the first arrival of the litter has been mentioned. In summer-time this is easy to arrange, and indeed the subsequent rearing of the pups is altogether easier in the summer. But in winter, even if the first reception of the litter can be successfully carried out, as the pups grow up and need more space this is not always easy to arrange. An even temperature is what is so beneficial. A lesson can be learned from the mother bird sitting on a nest. For hardly a moment does the mother leave the nest uncovered, either when the young are still in the egg, or when they are hatched. When she finds it necessary to seek food for herself, the cock bird takes her place and keeps the young things warm. This careful consideration continues until the nestlings are fully fledged, which would correspond in a dog to about one year old, or nearly so, and in a human child to about seventeen or eighteen years of age. Human parents might also take note, as many a constitution is undermined and the seeds of future illness laid by insufficient warmth in their homes when children are growing up.

It will be found with both animals and human beings, that if the young things are given warm sunny surroundings, winter and summer, during growth, they will develop like healthy young plants and any hardening process, which may be necessary or desirable afterwards, will be attended with no bad results. A mistake is very frequently made by solicitous guardians to harden *during* growth. This should never be done. On the contrary, everything should be as easy and harmonious as possible at such a time. All the impressions received by the young things, both as regards their bodies and minds, should be happy and pleasant. Many a storm, both physical and mental, has been weathered in later years by the impression of peace and serenity and warm comfort instilled into the mind in those early growing years, when the impressions for good and for ill are received and remain for ever.

A well-known writer of Reminiscences remarks that, in looking back over a long life spent in unusually interesting and happy circumstances, those years when she was taken as a young child to a sunny villa on the shores of the Mediterranean during the winter months come back to her above everything else, with more insistent pleasure than any of her other experiences. She lives again in her remembrance those fragrant years, experiencing in memory a sense of the warm, scented air, the flowers and the sunshine.

It will certainly be found, therefore, that the adult dog will be far hardier and stronger if its growth has been attended with no obstructions and it should always rest warm both by day and night. With small breeds the young thing can be kept indoors, which will solve the question easily. And if this can be arranged for larger breeds it will be for the best in the end. The best way is to teach the puppy—whether singular or plural—to make its bed in a box, which should be placed in a warm spot. The sides of the box should be just so high that it cannot clamber over while it is young and until it has learnt house manners. The high-sided box is an excellent adjunct to train the inmate to nice ways of behaving. It should be put out to run about outside every now and then, and in winter it should have a little coat, put on while the pup is quite young and until its second coat has grown, while it is playing out of doors. When it comes indoors, the box is always handy to pop it into to rest and to prevent it chewing things. If a puppy gets plenty of freedom outside it does not need to be running about indoors all the time as well, but it is on the contrary good for it to rest. In winter-time, at night, it is good to put a coat on a pup if it is by itself. On leaving the litter it will miss the warmth of its brothers and sisters and this should be remembered. As the pup grows older, and has learnt nice house manners, the box with high sides can be discarded for one with lower sides, as described elsewhere, but a lead should always be attached to it, as it is often convenient to fasten the pup when a lesson in restraint is necessary.

RICKETS IN PUPPIES

The above complaint, which is shown by swollen joints and bent legs, is due to the non-observance of some of the foregoing directions, and can be caused by damp, and also ill-feeding—probably the latter. The mistake is often made in not assisting the bitch with the feeding of the pups soon enough, or else in not giving *sufficiently nourishing* food, while they are with her, and after weaning.

It is always necessary to remember that cows' milk is not sufficient nourishment in itself, being deficient in cream, as compared with that of the dam, and this defect needs making good by adding cream. Another mistake is to continue the soft sloppy food too long and monotonously, after weaning, without varying the meals sufficiently. When a pup seems tired of milky food give it a feed of cooked meat and gravy mixed with bread.

INDIGESTION IN PUPPIES

This is frequently shown by a swollen puffed-out appearance of the stomach though the rest of the body is thin and emaciated. The cause is that the food, while given plentifully, is not sufficiently nourishing. The poor little animal eats a quantity, but does not assimilate sufficient nourishment. Increase the fat values of the food, and offer cooked meat and gravy and bread as well.

WORMS IN PUPPIES

A great many bad symptoms, such as loss of flesh or appetite, are put down to the presence of worms in the pups, but mistakes in feeding are much more likely to be the cause. *Quality* as well as *quantity* must always be considered carefully, and this is frequently where the care

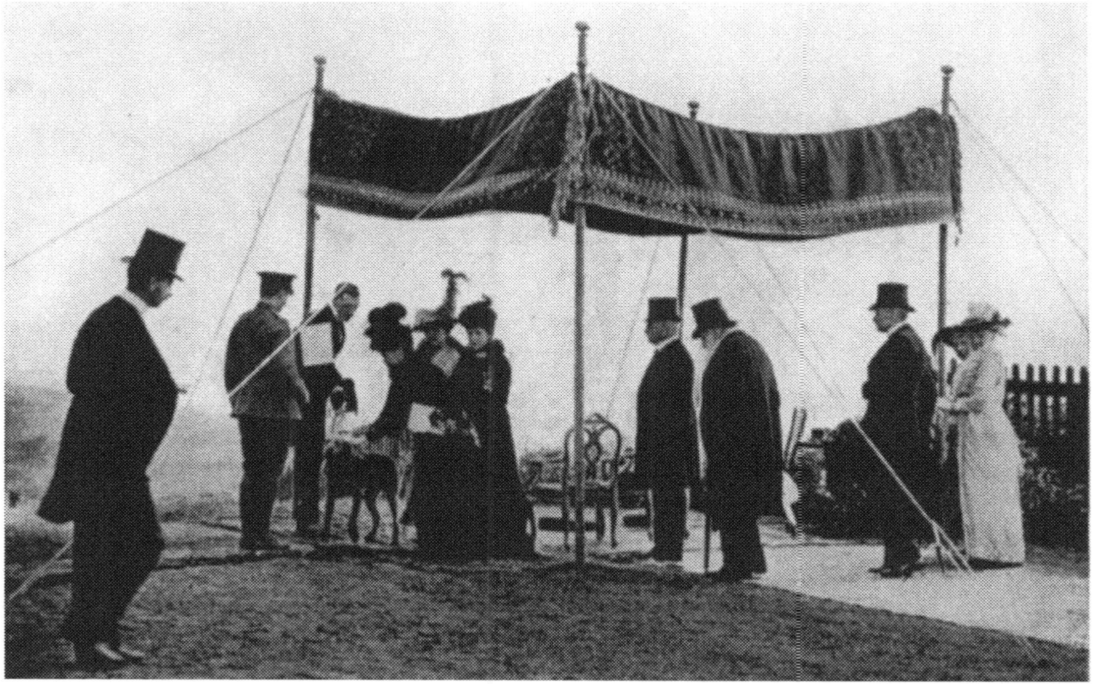

ROYAL INTEREST.

Queen Alexandra and the Empress of Russia inspecting Lieut.-Col. Richardson's Military Airedales.

p. 130.

of the pups falls short. Variety in diet is also extremely important, as they get sick to death of the daily milk pap which is frequently all they are offered. Therefore before jumping to the conclusion that the puppies have worms, on no other evidence than that they are out of sorts, first try a change of diet and make it more strengthening and richer. If, however, worms are actually seen in the discharge, then give a worm capsule according to directions on box.

All medicines are to be deprecated for young puppies as far as possible, and a vermifuge is always somewhat of a risk, so that if not certain that the worms are there, it is as well to try other methods of cure first.

If the food is clean, and properly cooked at each meal, the trouble should not arise.

CHAPTER XI

The Dog's Health

> "When wise Ulysses, from his native coast
> Long kept by wars and long by tempests tossed,
> Arrived at last, poor, old, disguised, alone,
> To all his friends, and even his Queen unknown;
> Changed as he was, with age and toil and cares,
> Furrowed his reverend face, and white his hairs,
> In his own palace forced to ask his bread,
> Scorned by those slaves his former bounty fed,
> Forgot of all his own domestic crew;
> The faithful dog alone his master knew.
>
> —Pope.

It is not proposed here to give a lengthy discussion on all the canine complaints. The object is more to show how to guard against these happenings, by pointing out those precautions which may be taken. Where a dog lives indoors, the care of its health is greatly simplified, for the reason that the great foe to all animals—damp and cold—can practically be eliminated: that is to say can be, if desired, and the necessity is understood by the master. This is not always done, however, and it is a common fault to put a dog to sleep in an insufficiently heated place, or in a draught. It should never be forgotten that the temperature along the floor is, in winter-time, sometimes very low, and that passages between doors are always more or less draughty. A dog in a well strawed kennel out of doors is sometimes warmer than one indoors, on account of the neglect to provide the latter with a warm, sheltered bed. For a young growing animal, this should especially be remembered, if a full standard of growth and health is required. A fully-grown and hardened dog can stand a good deal of exposure when necessary, without danger, but under ordinary circumstances even it should be made comfortable.

One of the chief causes of complaints in house dogs is overfeeding and feeding at irregular hours. A train of physical disabilities follow as a consequence.

SKIN COMPLAINTS—ECZEMA

It may be said that the state of a dog's skin and fur is a sort of indicator as to its health, and any stomachic disturbance very often is observable in some form of skin complaint. A chill after eating is sometimes the cause in the first place, or else a wrong diet or monotony of diet. Any of these three likelihoods should be considered, but in any case the diet should be altered to suit the case, and generally a light and nourishing milk-and-egg diet for a few days will help matters. The skin should also be dressed at the affected parts with a good skin lotion. It is a common mistake to jump to the conclusion that all skin complaints are mange. As a matter of fact this last complaint, which implies a parasite in the skin, is the least likely in a well-kept, well-groomed dog, with thoroughly clean surroundings, unless infected by a less well-attended animal. Some form of eczema, which is usually, as I have already said, due to stomachic disturbance, can be rectified best by altering the diet. It is far better to attack the first cause in this way, than by pouring down draughts of medicine, which only tinker at effects and furthermore are apt to still further upset the stomach. It is sometimes necessary to keep the skin dressed every other day, if the attack is a bad one, but the skin will dry up in a little time and the dressing will act also as a hair reviver. It sometimes happens that some animals have a tendency to eczema through the parents, which may have had this trouble in the system. In such a case it is apt to arise in the progeny, but it can be eliminated with proper management.

MANGE

Mange arises from a parasite imbedded under the outer skin. The fact that this insect found it possible to intrude itself thus implies a soft condition of the skin, and therefore a poor condition of the dog. The first thing is to dress the dog thoroughly with the skin lotion before-mentioned. Sprinkle this and brush well into the hair and skin. If put on in time one application may be sufficient, but otherwise it should be applied until the skin is dried up. At the same time the dog's diet should be enquired into, and a change should be made to suit any defect which may appear. It is usually a good plan to make the food rather lighter in quality for a day or two—not less nourishing, but more of a milky nature. This will relieve the system. No internal medicine need be given if this is done. It is always a mistake to resort to internal drugs.

It is sometimes found that no sooner does one patch of skin disease become cured than it breaks out elsewhere. It very frequently starts behind the shoulders and on the head, and travels right down the dog's body. This is very troublesome, but there is this to be said, that if such a bad attack is treated, as recommended above, very thoroughly, it is not likely to appear again in like manner. It would seem as though, in the very violence of the attack, the disease had expended itself. At the same time, where such an attack appears it may be that the dog is susceptible to this trouble, and until it has outgrown any weakness from which it may spring, it is as well to keep a good watch on the skin. The coat should be well-groomed always, and if the dog is seen to scratch at all the lotion should be applied. If treated in this way there is no need to be discouraged at all about the matter, as the trouble will die out.

FLEAS AND TICKS

Puppies are apt to be affected with skin eruptions.

These are due as often as not to stomachic disturbances during teething, or to little chills causing indigestion. Dress them in the same manner. The lotion advocated is also excellent for keeping the coats of dogs and puppies free from fleas and other insects. No dog can be happy and comfortable if troubled by these, and in summer weather it is a good plan to sprinkle a little of the lotion on the coat and brush well in every morning.

LICE

In the event of a parasite like the louse finding lodgement, this will require a very thorough dressing with the lotion. In this case the dog's skin should be well moistened all over its body. No portion should be excluded. It is better to be thoroughly rigorous about this in the first place, as it will be kinder in the end. The parasite is extremely impervious to ordinary forms of cleansnig solutions, and also causes the dog extreme irritation and discomfort. A second dressing should be given in ten days' time, so as to destroy any remaining lice. If properly applied two dressings should be sufficient, but for about a month afterwards the dog should be watched, and if it scratches at all search should be made at the spot. If any lice or their eggs be observed, a further dressing may be necessary. The best way to apply the remedy is on a summer day out of doors. Then take the dog for a scamper. It will not like the smell of the dressing, but this will not be so noticeable in the open air, and on the return the smell will have evaporated. In any case no notice should be taken of any objections. The lotion is distasteful only on account of the smell, and in no way effects the dog otherwise. The first effects will be a certain scurfiness of the skin, but this is desirable. The old cuticle will be removed and will peel off, leaving a healthy, clean animal. No fear need be apprehended as to the hair, which will grow thickly in a short time, as the lotion is excellent for encouraging hair growth.

If a nursing dam has been allowed to become infected with these pests the soft skin of the puppies will certainly give lodgement, and this would be very bad for their growth. They must therefore be carefully sponged over as well as the mother.

A daily comb with a fine tooth comb, and a weekly wash in summer is the best way of keeping the dog free from fleas, and is all that is needful as a rule.

These parasties, during the warmest period, elect as a host healthy dogs as well as weakly ones if they are allowed long enough immunity from interference, but are quite easily got rid of.

INTERNAL PARASITES

Internal parasites—tape worms, round worms, and various other worms—require an internal vermifuge, of which there are several excellent ones on the market. These should be administered according to directions. There must be commonsense used, however, with regard to this trouble in the dog. It is quite a common proceeding for an animal to be vigorously dosed for worms for the reason that it has been out of condition and off its food. This should not be done unless worms have actually been seen. If the dog has worms they will certainly be in evidence if they are watched for. If there are none visible, then the cause of the dog's ill-health is something else. But if worms are seen then certainly immediately proceed with the worm medicine.

The best method of giving this is to give the dog no food whatever after its principal meal at midday, or whatever time it has this. Then at the time next day at which it would ordinarily be receiving its meal, give the worm ball instead. This, falling in an empty stomach, will act very shortly. The dog should then be given a nice soft meal with some warm milk thrown over it. It is a good thing in certain cases to give another dose in a month's time.

Dogs fed much on uncooked meat are rather apt to entertain these parasites. But if the medicine is administered as directed above, there is nothing to be alarmed about, or to cause the owner or pet any inconvenience to speak of in the process of getting rid of them.

EAR TROUBLES

Ear canker is a cause of distress occasionally and is due generally to a chill. Great care should be taken not to do anything to the inner ear, if the trouble is located there. It is a mistake to pour in any strong remedies. A little warm salad oil is the only thing allowable if the dog seems in pain, but it is best to make a pad of wadding and dip this in warm water in which has been poured a little disinfectant. Gently rub the inner ear with this, using a circular motion. The dog will find it very soothing, and this can be done twice a day. At the same time always remember that the trouble should be attacked from within: that is to say, not with drugs, but through the diet. A change of diet is always advisable. The fact that the dog was amenable to the complaint shows a lowering of the system, which should be made good. A light nourishing meal twice a day instead of the one meal is sometimes a good alteration in the animal's dietary routine, and milk should enter into the scheme of nourishment considerably.

Where the canker attacks the flap of the ear, this sometimes is merely caused in the first place by an injury—it may be the result of a dog fight. If it takes the form of a slit at the edge of the ear it is rather troublesome to cure. With the small breeds the head can be sewn up in a cap for a few days, this is far the quicker and best method. The actual trouble is nothing in itself, the only difficulty is that the dog, feeling the little irritation, persists in shaking the ears, and this prevents healing. The cap, therefore, keeps the ears close to the head and in a few days the wound will have healed.

With the larger breeds it is sometimes difficult to get them to allow any form of cap to remain on, as their claws are sufficiently powerful to scratch it off, but if it can be managed, this is quite the quickest and most direct method of cure. It is not even necessary to apply any ointment as the ear will, under these circumstances, heal quite well. The cap should be made of strong canvas, or some such material, and will require to be tightly sewn on. If no cap can be used, it is best to leave the ear completely alone and not apply anything whatever. The application of any remedies, especially if they be of a caustic or astringent nature, will only attract the dog's attention to the ear, and cause it to shake its head more than ever. It is this perpetual shaking which is the chief cause of the continuation of the trouble, and no ointment will counteract the injury done by it. Therefore the only other alternative is to pay no attention. The dog will certainly shake its head, but it will not do so nearly so much as when dressing is applied, and after a time the wound will dry up.

WOUNDS

I have always found that wounds of all sorts heal far more quickly if merely cleansed with pure tepid water, and bound up with clean rags, than if any ointment or disinfectant is applied. The rags should be changed frequently in the case of bad wounds, and the injury should be kept very clean. If the wound is where the dog can lick it, it is quite a good plan to leave the bandage off after the bleeding has stopped, and let the dog keep the place clean itself. It must be confined until this injury is healed enough to ensure that the bleeding will not recommence, and after the first swelling has gone down.

A dog which has received an injury such as this will, at the same time, have suffered a considerable nervous shock, and a comforting drink of warm milk should be given with a lighter form of diet. Where a wound is a very severe one a stitch or two may be necessary by a veterinary surgeon, but in most cases these deep wounds are best left to heal from inwards, and if kept clean will do so quite quickly.

BROKEN BONES

Broken bones need the surgeon's hand, and here let it be said that the tendency where animals are concerned is far too easily to condemn the patient as incurable.

Many strong young animals, with prospects of happy years in front of them, are considered only fit for the lethal chamber if they have broken a leg, or other bone. This is quite a mistake. Where the dog is not too old, the bones join very readily and only need good setting and binding. The patient should be for some days confined in a box with hay in it, and sides high enough that it cannot clamber over. It will lie here very comfortably and it must be remembered that the shock it will have received at the time of the accident will be benefited by quiet repose. Even quite elderly dogs, if in good health, can be saved if the bone is properly set and bound.

I have seen dogs with broken legs running about completely cured in six or seven weeks' time.

With a valuable animal, or one greatly loved, it is well worth while taking every chance, and I have cured many dogs in my kennels that have been considered by veterinary surgeons as past help.

EYE TROUBLES

Great care should be taken when treating the eyes, not to put anything of an irritating nature near them. The best thing for inflammation of any kind is warm water, without anything in it whatever. Merely keep the eyes sponged with this.

In the event of any surgical operation being required, only a very expert veterinary surgeon should be consulted. If an occulist can be prevailed upon to accept the dog as a patient, this is the best method of all.

DOCTORS AS CONSULTANTS

In these days of extremely valuable and much prized dogs, many surgeons accept such as patients, charging fee for same; they need not, and in a great many cases do not feel any compunction in doing so. The benefit of such attendance is a high grade of skill, as the dog will be considered in the light of a human patient, and this view takes into consideration the animal's highly-nervous constitution. In their nature dogs are extremely highly strung, and are very like children and should be doctored as such. The acutely nervous system has to be greatly studied in all canine ailments.

Fortunately there are, nowadays, many very excellent and scientific veterinary surgeons who recognise this aspect of a dog's character and treat the case accordingly and in a different manner from a sheep or a cow, but I would earnestly ask for the co-operation of our physicians and surgeons, as their point of view would be extraordinarily valuable.

SORE FEET

It is a source of trouble with some dogs that they suffer from inflammation and pustules between the toes. Dogs which have been fed as directed in this book and which have been given plenty of exercise will not be so ready to develop this trouble, but when seeking for a cure, consideration should always be directed in the first place to the question of diet, and secondly of exercise. If the dog has been correctly fed, with varied food and at regular hours, and has received plenty of exercise, it will not suffer from this, and in any case this is the cure.

Nothing should be applied to the feet. The best remedy is the dog's tongue, which keeps the skin clean. Give plenty of exercise along the road and elsewhere, and a light, varied, but nourishing diet for a time, stopping all dog biscuits and substituting bread in the food mixture and supplying plenty of milk. The trouble will pass away in a short time, and even if it returns, too much should not be made of it.

DISTEMPER

This is one of the most dreaded complaints for our dogs. The fact that it is not properly understood is one of the reasons of the apprehension with which it is regarded, and it is on a par with influenza in human beings, in that there is no absolute preventative known for it, along the lines of medicine.

It is a disease which arises in the first place from cold and damp, and my observations induce me to conclude that a chill is the momentum which starts it. Young stock being especially sensitive to damp are particularly liable to it in consequence, and this is one of the reasons why I have emphasised so strongly the necessity for extreme care in respect to dry surroundings during growth. This does not mean that there should be any lack of air, on the contrary a fresh airy habitat is essential, but it must not be chilled air. An even temperature both night and day is to be aimed at and this is one of the best preventatives of distemper.

Perfect cleanliness of surroundings, and of the animal itself, and regular feeding along the lines laid down will also act as a deterrent.

I am frequently asked if it is absolutely necessary for a dog to get distemper. The answer is that it is not necessary, but the sensitiveness to cold and damp of the young things during growth, and until they are properly hardened, is so acute and it is so difficult to safeguard them from this, that they are extremely likely to get it. A dog living indoors can be much more readily protected, and, given such protection until something over a year (especially if it is the only dog), it may escape it altogether.

In most dogs there would seem to be a time of immunity from the complaint, as dogs over a certain age have been observed to associate constantly with those suffering from it, and yet take no harm. But no absolute rule can be laid down as to this, as I have frequently known quite elderly dogs develop it. I have also known cases of true distemper in the same dog, but this is not frequent and generally the first attack was a mild one.

When a dog attains the age of eighteen months it is much more able to put up a strong resistance to the complaint should it arise. At the same time the apprehension towards the complaint need not necessarily prevent the purchase of a puppy, as, with ordinary care and nursing and a definite understanding of the correct treatment, the young dog can be brought through it successfully without any undue disturbance.

It may be said that the attitude towards distemper in dogs should be the same as that towards a human being with influenza, more particularly a child. The symptoms of treatment are much the same. I have frequently found that this statement made to a dog owner who is a novice in the management of animals greatly relieves the outlook, as most people know very well how a child should be looked after. Young dogs and young children are in temperament and constitution much the same, and similar treatment in sickness and in health should be accorded to both.

I have not found inoculation of any benefit so far, and I do not recommend it.

Distemper is very infectious and transmission from one dog to another is a common source of trouble, but as it is necessary that one's pet takes its walks abroad, there is no use being unduly alarmed beforehand, but keep it in such a condition, that, in the event of the disease being caught, it will be in a fit state to resist it.

I have encountered people who kept their dogs in a sort of cloistered state, never taking them anywhere with them and never allowing them to play with strange dogs, for fear of infection. I am sure if their pets could speak they would express preference for the risk of a short life and a merry one, rather than a lonely, uninteresting succession of years even though free from the trouble.

There would seem to be two types of distemper. The first is more of the nature of a feverish cold, but the second is much more serious, as it is attended by complications in which the lungs, stomach or nervous system may be involved. The disease is in this way analogous to influenza in human beings, as it is never possible to say beforehand exactly which type the attack may be. The only thing to do is to care for the invalid in such a manner as will safeguard it against any form the illness may take.

A dog, which has been fed as directed in this book, will not be fussy or dainty in its appetite when in its normal health. It will not have been unhealthily fed, but will have a hearty appetite at meal time and will enjoy its food. The benefit of this will be discovered when it sickens, as it will not have been overcharged with dainties, but will appreciate the little tasty dishes presented to it during the illness. It is most important to keep the patient on its food at all costs.

Before proceeding with the treatment to be accorded, I will mention the first symptoms, as it is in the early observation of these that much subsequent trouble can be averted.

The first approach of the complaint will be heralded by a certain heaviness and a cessation from play. Sometimes a wateriness in the eye accompanies this from the start, but not necessarily so, though it will be sure to do so later. The surest indication of the dog's health, however, is the way it regards its food. If it seems out of sorts and heavy, but takes its dinner as usual, there is not likely to be much wrong with it as yet, but it should be watched nevertheless. A dog's nose is not always a sure indicator as is generally supposed. The nose may feel quite cold during the preliminary stages and yet the illness may be getting underway. A hot, dry nose will follow when the fever commences, but it is the stage before this that we wish to indicate first, as so much depends upon the early detection of the complaint. As long, however, as the dog continues to take its meals heartily it is not likely to have much the matter with it, and a chill may be the cause. In this case it is better to keep the dog quiet and warm until either the chill has passed off, or a further progress of the disease has manifested itself. The patient should be given a nice bed in a warm place, and fastened there. It can be allowed out to exercise itself every now and then for a short time, but not to run or lie about and it should be brought back and tied up. If it is winter-time a coat should be put on, unless the place where it lies is very warm. In any case the coat had better be put on at night, and when it goes out to relieve itself during the day.

The diet during this period should be of a lighter character, no meat. Milk pudding, and bread-and-milk, baby food, etc. No medicine should be given internally. If the diet is lightened as recommended, this will be all that is necessary to relieve the system. By dosing a dog there is risk of upsetting the stomach and putting it off its food, and the question of getting it to continue to take adequate nourishment is of the first importance. If a dog is cared for as thus directed during the early stages of the illness, it is possible to ward off distemper altogether, or to prevent it developing to any serious extent, and it is for this reason that it is so important to detect the early symptoms and take the necessary measures at once.

It must be remarked that there should be no hurry to discontinue the care which may have been accorded the patient in the first stage. Unnecessary haste to allow it to assume its ordinary mode of life may precipitate a worse condition, which could otherwise have been avoided. A quiet, warm, restful condition, with a regular light diet (that is to say, light in quality but as plentiful as the dog will consume twice a day), should be maintained for a fortnight to three weeks.

If the trouble has been allowed to go beyond this first stage without being treated in any way, or if, in spite of such care, it still continues to increase, the next symptoms will probably be a hot dry nose, with inflamed and watery eyes. It is impossible to say just exactly how long after the first stage these symptoms will appear. So much depends upon the care that has been taken of the dog when it is first seen to be out of sorts. The advice to a human being, when a feeling of chill and inertia comes to him, is to go to bed at once, and stay there till better. The same treatment should be accorded the canine patient, and "going to bed" is represented in the dog by its being chained up in its bed in a warm place, or being put to sleep inside its kennel with plenty of soft bedding and a coat on. I purposely reiterate the importance of doing this at the earliest stage and also to prolong this care *beyond* the time which might seem really necessary. It must also be remembered that the dog cannot tell of its first feelings of distemper. Three weeks is usually the time ascribed for the process of the disease, but a fortnight over this will not be too long to wait before relaxing the care of the animal.

I have not found, so far, after a very long experience, any medicine that in any way helps the patient, in fact the evidence is, that there is considerable risk of upsetting the digestion by administering any internal drug. The saving of the situation is contained in the possibility of the animal continuing to take nourishment through the crisis of the disease, and through convalescence. If this is accomplished there is no fear but that the patient will recover, and nothing therefore must be done which might put it off its food. A coat should be put on, and one of the *most important points is that the temperature of the place where the dog is kept, should not vary day or night.*

If such a thing is available (in the event of the disease being contracted during the winter or spring months), a conservatory makes an excellent hospital. There must not, of course, be many plants in it which require watering, as this would make the atmosphere moist, but the light and sun which will reach the dog will be good for it, especially during convalescence, without any risk of ill effects from cold winds. The place must, of course, be kept heated at night to ensure the evenness of the temperature being maintained, which should be about 70°. The patient must have a warm bed into which it can creep and it must only be allowed out of doors, for a few minutes at a time, to relieve nature.

If a conservatory is not available the best place to nurse a dog is an empty room indoors. Except in mid-summer, artificial heat will always be required, and the dog's box, in which is its bed, should be placed near the fire, where it can lie and drowse quietly until the crisis is past.

As looseness of the bowels is frequently one of the manifestations of the complaint, it is as well in the case of a room indoors being used to turn back the carpet and cover the floor with stout brown paper in case of accidents. This can be changed as required. Having provided for the dog's comfort in this way, the next thing to ensure recovery will be good nursing. This does not mean perpetually thrusting food at the patient, or giving medicine, but it does mean giving close attention to the heating, and also endeavouring twice during the twenty-four hours to ensure that a sufficient amount of nourishment should be imbibed. If the dog will take milk, and milk-and-egg food or baby food, all will be well, as this is certainly the best diet for it until the crisis is past. This should be given after breakfast and in the evening. And the patient can have as much as it wants each time. If it will only take a drink of milk at the feeding times, that will be sufficient during the worst period. Unfortunately the chief difficulty in distemper is that the appetite goes completely, and it is this fact which calls for skill in nursing and unremitting attention.

In the event of milk food being refused, something else must be offered. Fish is often taken when other things are ignored, and a kipper has saved many a dog's life. Meat may have to be offered, and sometimes a patient will take it raw when it will not take it cooked and vice versa, or a plate of mixed scraps may have to be offered, as in this there may be objects of attraction which the dog can pick out for itself. As far as possible it is better to confine the offer of food to twice a day, as it is disconcerting to the animal to be constantly bothered to eat, *and in no case should food be left beside it,* but if it has refused all food at one of the meal times it will be necessary to offer it something a little later.

A good nurse will induce a dog to eat, when another person less painstaking, or experienced, will fail. Thus a sick dog, which by the way will usually be sunk in the depths of self-pity and depression, will be greatly comforted sometimes if the food is offered in the hand. It will lap soft food out of the palm of the hand, or accept a proffered piece of meat thus, when it would listlessly pay no attention to the same if put on a plate in front of it. Again sometimes all efforts fail to get it to eat anything whatever until it has first been allowed out of doors to relieve nature. When it comes in it may then accept a little food. Where there is a total lack of appetite nothing whatever should be refused it, which the dog will swallow of its own accord. To keep it eating twice daily *voluntarily*, even if only a very little each time, is the great thing, and will ensure recovery in the end, and it is here that ingenuity has to be put forth.

If the dog takes nourishment in only very small quantities each time, it may be necessary to offer it food during the night so that too long a period in between the feeds does not ensue. In any case the firing must be kept up all through the night. It will thus be seen that a great deal will depend upon the nursing it receives, as to whether the dog recovers or not. The feeding should be voluntary on the part of the dog for as long as possible. *A very little nourishment taken at one time, of its own accord, is far more beneficial than considerably more which has to be poured down its throat*, and it is the various methods adopted to persuade it to eat something which entail intelligent and affectionate solicitude. For this reason it is better always to keep the sick animal at home, as very naturally it would not be possible for the attendance night and day, except in very exceptional veterinary establishments, to be sufficiently continuous.

In the event of the dog refusing all food whatsoever, it will have to have nourishment poured down its throat every now and then, until it turns the corner. A small amount only should be given it each time—about every three hours. The nourishment may consist of a beaten up egg—egg and milk beaten together—a little strong soup, or meat jelly. The best method of giving fluids is to hold up the dog's muzzle at a sloping angle with one hand, keeping its teeth closed. About a dessertspoonful or teaspoonful of fluid nourishment (according to the size of dog), should then be put into the pouch formed by the dog's cheek and gums. This will filter through the teeth on to the throat, and the upward position of the head will compel swallowing. Great care has to be taken not to pour too much at a given time, as there is always risk of choking, especially where the lungs are much affected. As many spoonfuls can be given as it is thought the dog needs, but it is better to feed it little and often (not oftener, however, than every two hours), than to give a great deal at one time. If properly managed the dog will not greatly resent nourishment given in this manner, but if it is overdone, or roughly done, there is risk of putting it off food altogether, and inducing nausea, which will end matters very quickly.

A coat must be worn from the beginning to the end of the complaint, as this protection over the back and chest frequently prevents congestion of the lungs and pneumonia. The breathing can be heard quite easily by putting the ear against the dog's ribs, and when it sounds laboured, hot compresses sometimes give relief laid on first on one side and then on the other of the breast. Medicated wadding can also be applied, and I still believe in linseed poultices for chest troubles.

Pneumonia is one of the chief dangers to be guarded against, and therefore the chest should be carefully watched and kept warm.

Diarrhœa is a usual accompaniment, but it is not wise to give any strong drug to stop this, at all events in the early stages, as it is very important to keep the bowels well open, and as the disease proceeds this trouble generally regulates itself after a little. If it is very severe a little port wine in which a few drops of augustura bitters have been poured is a good method for stopping it. About a teaspoonful after each meal.

The patient should be kept very quiet. If the nervous system seems very upset it is even a good thing to keep it in a twilight. There are cases of distemper where the brain is attacked, and darkness and warmth are helps to soothe the nerves.

A straightforward case of distemper, with no complications, will correspond to a very bad cold in a human being. The food of a lighter kind than usual will be taken, even though with difficulty, and in very greatly decreased quantity, but still it will be taken. The eyes and nose will discharge mucus, there will be a certain looseness of the bowels, but these conditions will gradually improve. Even if it seems quite well, comparatively, care should still be given to it, even after a month has elapsed. It should still be kept warm and quiet, although it can gradually go back to its ordinary forms and hours of feeding. When it is once more feeding as usual, and after a month's time, it can be exercised gently out of doors, but not for long. Over-exertion at this period sometimes brings on paralysis, and one cannot be too careful not to hurry matters at this stage. This complication is heralded by a certain unsteadiness in the dog's gait, and frequently develops after the patient is seemingly on the road to complete recovery. The dog must immediately be put " back to bed again ": that is to say, made to lie very quiet, and should be well fed up at once. It is possible to ward off the complaint if taken quickly, but there is no use disguising that it is a very serious complication, and is generally brought on by letting the invalid out too soon.

All through the illness the patient must be kept clean—with a very hairy dog it is sometimes a help to clip some of the hair away, so that the sponging can be more effectively carried out. The nose and muzzle must be sponged with warm water in which a little disinfectant is poured, it may be necessary to do this two or three times a day.

AFTER EFFECTS OF DISTEMPER

The lowering of the system, consequent to an attack of distemper, and the upset of other digestive organs sometimes produces conditions which need treatment after the illness itself is overcome.

Where the distemper is combined with such complications as pneumonia, or paralysis, or nervous affections, it is impossible to say exactly how long the actual disease will last, as so much depends on the strength the dog has left to throw off these extra difficulties.

Chorea is sometimes an after effect of a very bad case of distemper, when the dog's nervous system has been badly affected. It takes the form of twitching of the limbs or head, or a constant quivering. Nothing very much can be done for this, but as the dog gets older and stronger, the trouble may greatly decrease.

Loss of flesh.—If the attack is without outstanding complications, and the patient has been in good condition previously, there may not be much loss of flesh, but if the animal was not carrying much flesh at the commencement, it may become very thin as the disease progresses.

Tonics.—It has been explained that drugs given during the illness do very little good, if any, and are, as a matter of fact, apt to have a deleterious effect by upsetting the digestive organs. For much the same reason I do not advocate tonics during convalescence. The appetite will return naturally, as the disease is overcome, and it is a mistake to force things, but rather offer good, strong, nourishing and varied food for the purpose of nourishment and feeding up, and let the dog eat as much of this as it cares to. Twice a day will be sufficient for the meals, and nothing to be left beside it in between. It will gradually consume more and will put on flesh again. Fattening food such as cream has a beneficial effect.

Bad condition of coat.—The coat will most certainly fall out, but this will also grow nicely again with returning health; dressing with skin lotion now and then will help, and good brushing afterwards.

Skin affections.—Skin affections are frequent accompaniments of distemper, and are due to the lowered system. They are frequently manifested in the later stages, or during convalescence, and will pass away as the animal's condition improves. The skin may be treated with lotion as recommended under skin affections. A sharp lookout must be kept for parasites in the skin, as it will be in a soft, vulnerable condition for lodgment, and no animal can be happy and comfortable if worried by insects. Lice are difficult to distinguish unless the searcher knows what he is looking for. These little pests burrow in the dog's skin and leave a tiny point of body above the cuticle. Pale in colour and very invisible, they should be looked for under the sun's rays or a very strong light. If a dog is seen to persistently scratch at any given spot and no fleas can be seen, it should be very carefully examined in the sunlight, in case the trouble may be from these insects. A dressing with lotion will remove them, which ordinary washing will not do. (See treatment advocated elsewhere.)

Discoloration of eyes.—Another complication during, or subsequent to an attack of distemper, is a filmy condition of the eye-ball. Both eyes become affected sometimes, and then the animal cannot see, and the eyes resemble grey marbles. More frequently only one eye is affected, and the sight is unimpaired in the other. No undue apprehension need arise with regard to this discoloration, even though it appears, as it frequently does, when the complaint is, in other ways, nearly at an end. It will be found to gradually pass away quite naturally and the sight will be unimpaired. *On no account whatever should anything be put in the eye by way of cure.*

It may here be said that when washing the face and eyes during the whole course of the illness, nothing but plain warm water should be used, and nothing else should be used in connection with the eyes and ears, although a little disinfectant may be introduced into the water.

Jaundice and Stuttgart disease are other evidences of complications, and are observable by the condition of the patient's gums and lips. The general treatment for these complaints is the same as has already been advocated, except that the mouth will need attention, and should be kept well sponged with warm water, in which a few drops of disinfectant have been poured. In bad cases the jaws and lips become very sore, but, except sponging to keep them clean, nothing should be applied, and the trouble will pass away as the causative condition of the whole complaint wanes.

Condition after convalescence.—There is one great comfort with regard to distemper, and all the trouble it involves, it is in the knowledge that, after it is over, the dog will be very much stronger and hardier in its constitution. If it had not attained its full growth before the attack, this may be delayed for a time, but it will quickly make up for it afterwards, and will grow well. The coat will come on nicely, and the whole character of the animal will develop and improve. It will not be nearly so liable to chills or internal upsets, and provided a sensible and careful dieting is maintained, and the exercise and general interest of the dog's mind is cultivated, it may, barring accidents, live to a very green old age, with never any disease whatever attacking it again.

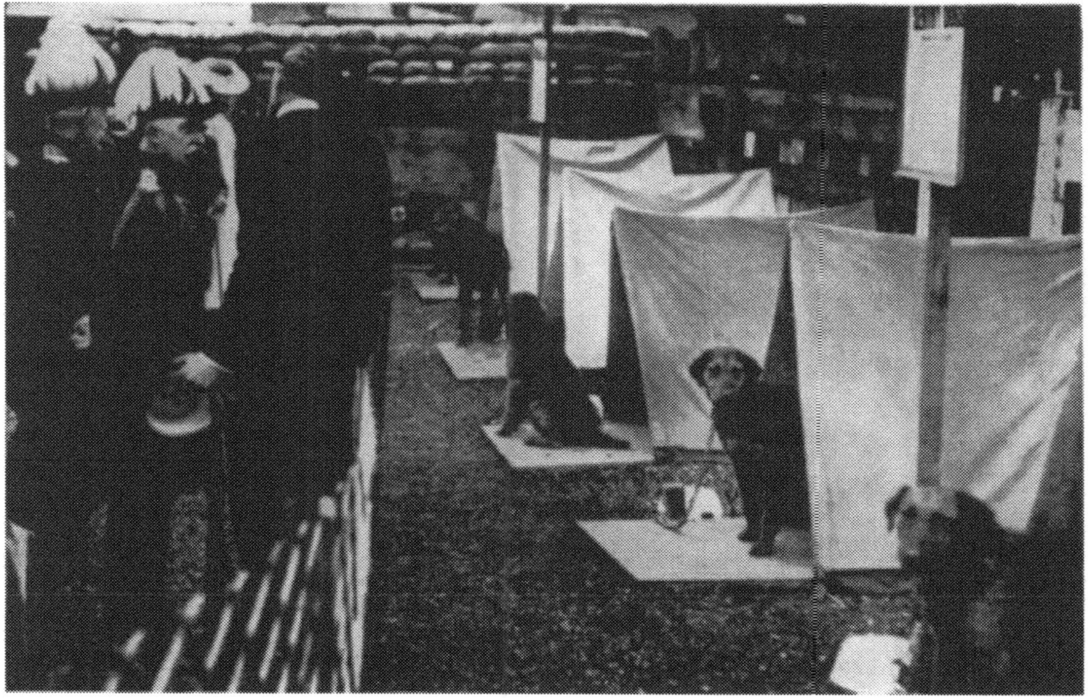

The Duke of Connaught Asks Questions.
Military dogs at Naval and Military Exhibition.

p. 150.

In giving these hints as to the management of the health of the dog, there has been no attempt to enter too fully into the exact claim of each disease. My endeavour has rather been to show how to prevent ill health, and keep one's animals healthy and youthful in mind and body. There is a variety of complaints, which could be mentioned, any of which the dog may *not* have, if the broad lines of direction herein laid down are followed.

The mind of a dog is very simple, and will be found to run chiefly on three things: its food, its opportunities for exercise, and its interest in its environment. Any manifestation of disease will be due to some cause hinging on one of these three points (accidents excepted), and if the master understands this he will know that adjustment must be sought along these lines, and the disease will abate and disappear. Another thing which must be constantly borne in mind, is the highly sensitive temperament; many complaints arise from a disturbance in the mental balance due to shock, anxiety, or over excitement. Quiet and rest therefore, are often very good, and it must be noticed when such treatment is required.

TEETH

Defective teeth are a cause of ill health, and of offensive breath in old dogs, and even with young ones attention should be given to the mouth, as much subsequent trouble can thereby be averted. If the teeth are allowed to become decayed, there is at once a difficulty in masticating food with consequent indigestion. It is a good plan to examine the teeth every week or so, and give them a good scrub with a tooth brush, kept for the purpose. The brush should be dipped in warm water with a few drops of disinfectant in it, and then apply a good sprinkling of Vim to the brush. The dog will not mind the brushing if it is done gently, and this treatment is a very excellent method of perserving the teeth and keeping them sweet and clean. In old age it is particularly important.

WARTS AND SKIN TROUBLE IN OLD AGE

Old dogs are frequently victims of warts and skin disease. The last is generally eczema, and must be cured in the first place through dietary, and in the second place by a skin dressing applied locally. I have generally found that this last trouble is due to the fact that the dog's food has been allowed to get too monotonous. As a change, the dog should be put on to a milk-and-fish diet and given plenty of exercise.

The simplest and safest way to get rid of warts is to tie a piece of strong linen thread round them. Leave the thread thus knotted, and each day or two, as the wart shrinks, apply a tighter thread. It will be found that, after a few days, the growth will come off. Quite large warts can be removed in this way, and without danger to the dog. The thread gives it no pain, as after the first tie all sensation speedily leaves the wart, as connection is cut off from the body.

RHEUMATISM

Stiffness in walking may arise from rheumatism. Investigations as to the sleeping accommodation and kennelling must be made. Damp bedding, sleeping or lying by day on stone flooring, even if covered by straw, draughty kennels or beds placed in passages along which the wind sweeps, can all be causes of this complaint. The cure is to remove the cause by seeing that dry and comfortable quarters are provided. The affected limbs may be rubbed with embrocation, if desired, but if the aggravating cause is removed and plenty of exercise is given, the trouble will pass off. Exercise is one of the best remedies for this complaint, and applies to old dogs as well as to young ones.

AGE IN DOGS

A dog is considered decidedly old if it reaches fifteen or sixteen years. I have had several that reached this age, and they can live even longer, under certain circumstances. There is no need either that the declining years need be unhealthful, or unintelligent. The improvement in the outlook towards old age nowadays, affects both human beings and canines alike. It is now recognised that old age need not by any means be a condition of decrepitude and inaction of physical or mental powers. Suitable dieting, according to the passing of years, is one of the points emphasised by those who decline to forego the usual vigour of mind and body, during the later years of life. The food should be light and nourishing, but not so plentiful as in youth when the perpetual motion and greater energy of everyday life induced a much quicker process of wastage. Exercise should be continued as usual, but without undue fatigue. Above all the mind must be kept usefully occupied, and some sort of steady work is certainly to be advocated.

All these remarks apply equally to dogs increasing in years. I have noticed that dogs, which have some sort of steady occupation, live much longer and more healthily, than those whose only outlook on life is composed in eating and drowsing, with an occasional stroll. Some dogs make duties for themselves, with very good results on their health. It is quite a common idea for the family dog to take it into its head that certain portions of the property can only be intruded upon by strangers who have been viséd by itself.

I have had a small dog which made a little post of observation for itself in one of the hedges near the main gate. For hours it would sit there inspecting each passer-by and issuing forth into the road in a more or less indignant condition, as anything passed to which it took exception. No actual interference would be evinced by the little sentinel, but protest would be made if necessary. All strange dogs were held up as a matter of course, and their credentials required. Where these were refused, by those of independent character, "words" would pass, and Dandie would return in an explosive and gurgling condition to his point of vantage.

Another dog, a collie, had the same sense of responsibility with regard to all visitors to the house. A plot of lawn, on a slight eminence in front of the house, gave him a position from which he could see the entire length of the avenue, and the gate. Here he would voluntarily take his stand each morning, and with eagle eye, espy all visitors. He took his duties extremely seriously, and was extraordinarily discriminating, having varying degrees of welcome, as the case required. Sometimes, when taken for a walk outside the place, his heart would misgive him and he would leave us and hasten back, and would be found perched at his self-appointed task on his eminence, scanning the horizon for intruders. To friends of the family he gave a very gracious and dignified reception, running half down the drive to meet them, and escorting them to the doorstep.

Another dog, in all weathers, escorted his master to the station in the morning and met him in the evening on the platform. This was his "job," and he lived for it, and having it gave him a definite interest in his daily life. I refer to this question of some sort of life interest being necessary to a dog's well-being, in the chapter on training, but here I am mentioning it to emphasise the fact, that some sort of definite motive in life is a great preservative, not only of health but also length of days.

If dogs become fat and unwieldy, with offensive breath, as they grow older, it is because their feeding is not being properly managed. The principle of a mixed diet should always be held to, and the hours of feeding must be very regular: no food left about in between meals. They must also be properly exercised.

CHAPTER XII

Kennelling

" Be thou diligent to know the state of thy flocks, and look well to thy herds."—PROVERBS.

I HAVE already given hints as to the management of the house dog, including its sleeping accommodation, and have recommended a box with sides high enough to protect the animal from floor draughts. Another way is to set aside a comfortable armchair for the dog's own use. A rug thrown over this, which can be shaken every day and which can also be sent to the cleaners every now and then, will ensure a really comfortable rest and protection from draughts. If it is given a nice chair for itself the family friend will not be so liable to covet those of the family.

For out of door dogs, I recommend a wooden kennel placed in a shed or stables. If this is not feasible (in the event of there not being any out-buildings), a wooden kennel with wooden run attached is a good pattern. The latter can be obtained from most dog-kennel makers, or a local joiner could make one easily. The whole construction is in one piece with a door to open and shut from the sleeping compartment into the run. The front of the run has iron bars, but the lower half and the end are boarded to protect from cold wind, and the whole is roofed. There is a door into the run from the outside and also one in the front of the sleeping compartment, in the top section of this door there should be a window. The whole thing stands on its own wooden feet, and should be about a foot from the ground.

I can very highly recommend this form of kennel. It is cheap and extremely sanitary.

Built kennels, while giving a handsome appearance to a place, can never be so sanitary as these wooden ones, nor are they nearly so warm. Concrete or bricked runs are cold for the dogs to lie on, and it is never very easy to keep the ground round about the kennel really sanitary. Now the wooden kennel I have described is movable, and can be lifted about whenever the ground underneath, or round about becomes soiled, and this is a most important point affecting the health of the dog. It can also be moved round according to the way of the sun or wind, and if it is desired to leave the animal inside during the day-time,this considera-tion saves it a great deal of discomfort.

In hot summer weather such a kennel can be lifted into the shade of a tree, or can at all events be turned away from the fierce sun rays. In winter it can be turned south to catch the sun, and yet the dog is well sheltered.

Cleanliness is so extremely important that a form of kennelling cheap enough to afford a relief kennel is a good thing. Each day the one the dog is inhabiting should be cleaned out thoroughly. The bedding in the sleeping compartment should be changed frequently, and well shaken each day, but this is not sufficient. Every now and then after a thorough scrubbing inside and out, a coat of creosote should be given. This is a fine preservative and dis-infector, and will destroy all insects. The creosote must be applied especially lavishly to all the joins and cracks in the wood. The whole kennel can then be left to air for a few days or even longer, and the dog can live in No. 2 kennel, while this process is being carried out. This interchange of kennels ensures absolute cleanliness, and freedom from infectious diseases.

In cold weather a covering of tarred felting all over the sleeping compartment ensures greater warmth. This can be removed in summer, when a good creosoting underneath will furbish it up and destroy any insects which might have found lodgment underneath.

It is no use going on from year to year with the same kennels. This old-fashioned idea is not sanitary, and for this reason also these cheap wooden kennels are advocated above all the most expensively built canine palaces imagin-able, as they can be renewed as often as it is thought advisable, and at no great expense. They are also excellent as breeding houses, or for puppies.

Another useful idea to which they can be adapted is for the purpose of night stations for guard dogs at vulnerable points, when it is not considered advisable that the animals should be loose. These kennels can be mounted on wheels, like a shepherd's hut, and they can then be moved about as desired.

Where a large number of dogs is kept, it will be found very useful to have a number of such kennels which can be placed in a meadow or other convenient place. The ground can be changed as often as is desired. A certain number of kennels above that of the dogs kept should always be available, so as to ensure a frequent spring-cleaning and airing. Lime-wash inside is also a quick and inexpensive cleanser.

Where people already have kennels of other patterns, and do not wish to discard them, perhaps the above hints on cleanliness, and mitigation of the discomforts of heat and cold will assist them in arriving at conclusions as to how their present kennels can be kept as near the right standard of sanitation and comfort as possible.

One thing to remember is, that for nightfall in winter, a wooden kennel out of doors with no door is too cold. The kennel should be lifted into a shed or stable, and, if it is still desired to keep the dog in a kennel during the day-time, another one should be obtained, and the dog transferred to it each morning. Failing this, and if no other night accommodation is available, a door to the kennel should be provided, which can be shut on very cold nights.

The old idea that the same old kennel, in the same old place, with the same biting wind blowing, and the same sun blazing down on to the unfortunate inmate, is absolutely ruled out nowadays. It was *always* cruel, and only the most hardened animals could stand it. Nowadays, dogs are of much higher value. They have been carefully cultivated, and while they can be, and are, perfectly hardy, the improved conditions under which they are bred and trained, make them more sensitive to dirt and unhealthy surroundings. This is no fault in the animals, but is merely a reproach to dog keepers who are ready to tolerate insanitary conditions, if they think they can save themselves trouble.

The feeding and drinking dishes should be scoured each day with hot water and soap. Cold water should be supplied for drinking purposes each morning, and, in hot weather, the water should be renewed during the day. Nothing whatever should be put in the water, such as sulphur, etc.

Straw and hay make useful bedding, always provided they are changed frequently.

In no case should a dog be put to sleep in a shed or stable, *without* a kennel or box to creep into. Such a place except in hot summer weather is not warm enough, and the creature requires a nice sheltered spot in the shed or stable, inside which it can lie, to give it a sense of rest, and also as a protection from cold and draughts.

For official kennels, such as police or military establishments, the wooden kennel as described is the best, and is economically feasible. Drains can be avoided by their use, and this is always an excellent thing, as they are very difficult to keep absolutely sanitary. Drained kennels are also extremely expensive nowadays.

Where there are a number of dogs, the great secret of keeping them in good health is to kennel them separately. It is the greatest mistake to allow a litter, after it is well weaned, to sleep together while the pups are growing up. If they are individually sold, they will in the ordinary course be separated, but if it is desired to keep them all, they should each be given a different kennel. Unless this is done, they will infect each other with every canine ailment which comes along, and the trouble itself will probably be accentuated.

Grown dogs, in the same way, should each be given a separate kennel, and where there are two or three kept in the house, each one should have his own sleeping box not too near his neighbour.

On the first signs of any indisposition, the sufferer should instantly be isolated from his brothers and carefully watched. He should be exercised separately as well, until all traces of cold, eruption, or whatever the symptoms may be, have vanished.

CHAPTER XIII

Man-Tracking as a Protection

> " 'Twas pleasure as we looked behind
> To see how the chase could wind ;
> Cheer the dark bloodhound on his way."
>
> —SIR WALTER SCOTT.

> " His snuffing nose, his active tail,
> Attest his joy ; then with deep opening mouth,
> That makes the welkin tremble, he proclaims
> The audacious felon ; foot by foot he marks
> His winding way, while all the listening crowd
> Applaud his reasonings. O'er the watery ford,
> Dry sandy heaths, and stony barren hills,
> O'er beaten paths, with men and beasts distained,
> Unerring he pursues ; till at the cot
> Arrived. . . . The caitiff vile redeems the captive prey :
> So exquisitely delicate his sense."
>
> —SOMERVILLE.

FOR a number of years before the war I kept a number of bloodhounds, which were kept up to an efficient state of training. Some of the Chief Constables of counties within reach of my residence obtained the right of call for the services of these hounds, in the event of tracking work being required. They were useful in several cases as showing the direction the criminal had taken when he escaped, and a clue was obtained as to certain probabilities, which on being followed up, led to the arrest of the culprit.

One murder call, which took place in Scotland, I could only reach after thirty-six hours had elapsed. The fact that the murderer had left the scene of the crime with blood-stained boots, enabled the bloodhound I took with me to get a good lead, even after such a lapse of time. The criminal had evidently run along a high road, but had branched off into the undergrowth on each side every now and then, to escape observation, as he proceeded. The working of the hound was most interesting. Having scented the blood on the trail at the outset, it was extremely keen, and although the work was difficult and the tracks were constantly being lost on the high road, it persisted in the tracking, co-operating with great willingness in the constant recasting backwards and ahead, in order to locate the temporarily lost trail. The hound steadily kept on for about three miles along the main road, which led to the nearest town. When nearing this place, the road branched, and at this spot the trail became very obliterated and was difficult to pick up. Along one of the branches, after much casting, no trail could be found at all, but along the other branch after going down it some little distance the hound gave tongue joyfully, and started off again. This road led direct to the railway station, but the tracks became quite obliterated when near that place. It was, however, quite clear that the murderer had escaped by train, and the police were encouraged by this clue to persist with greater vigour along that line of research. The man was caught down in England a few days after.

Tracking-dogs are exceedingly useful for the detection of poultry stealers, rick burners, or poachers. A pair of bloodhounds I had tracked a poultry thief to the door of his cottage three miles across country. The theft was committed in the early hours of the morning, and I did not get the hounds on the trail till 11 a.m., but the footmarks and traces of the hens' plumage were clearly visible near the roosts. The hounds got going at once, and led to a barn in a field about a mile off. On entering this we found the thief had evidently stopped to investigate his haul, and a quantity of hens' feathers were in one corner. After recasting the hounds they went straight away over the fields, and, coming to a hamlet about two miles off, made for a cottage and vehemently pawed at the door which was shut. The owner of the poultry had accompanied me, but, as in this case I had merely been running the trail for my own instruction and experience, we had not asked a constable to accompany us, so we had no warrant to enable us to enter the cottage, but we reported the matter to the local police station, and

MAN-TRACKING BLOODHOUNDS AT ALDERSHOT.

p. 160.

they informed us that the man who lived there was a well-known poacher, and was responsible for most of the hen roost robberies in the neighbourhood.

Another bloodhound which went from my kennels to an owner of large property tracked a gang of poachers across country for nine miles. It was in the charge of the keeper who was able to get it on the trail early, before the sun and wind had arisen to obliterate the scent.

All local tracking work, such as would be required for poultry thieves and poachers, could to a great extent be carried out by other breeds than bloodhounds. The latter have always been scarce. They have never been bred in sufficient numbers to make them anything except an expensive hobby.

Man-tracking is a most interesting sport, and both the tracked and the tracker can have a fine morning's run across a good line of country. The quarry makes every effort to mislead the hound by twisting, and if possible breaking his trail, and the handler may have to use a great deal of judgment and persistence in assisting the animal, and recasting it again and again.

TRACKING-DOGS FOR ESTATES

It is always a reason for astonishment to me that landowners do not keep bloodhounds, or tracking-dogs of some sort on their estates, where game preserving is carried on. In these days such preservation is only carried on under difficulties far greater than were experienced before the war. A gamekeeper, who desires to carry out his work faithfully and defend the game, has no easy or safe post, and he probably will not have the support of a number of underkeepers as he had before the war. No one desires violence, least of all the employer. What is wanted is prevention, or, as an alternative, detection without violence. The conditions for tracking under such circumstances are ideal. The evening hours or dawn would be the usual time for working the dogs, and this is the best period during the twenty-four hours, as scent lies well then. The trail would be across woodland or mostly open country. One hound I had under such circumstances tracked the poacher nine miles across country. At this time of day there is little traffic, and the trail in some cases remains practically uncrossed. The smell of the game carried away also helps. Altogether, there is a chance that, very frequently, with one or two good tracking-dogs, the culprit could very easily be run to earth. *The fact of this possibility acts as a very great deterrent*, and is one of the factors to be taken into account in weighing the pros and cons of the matter. It is very much better to have it known that such dogs exist on an estate, ready for immediate use, and thereby hold the intended raid in abeyance in consequence. Even if the raid takes place successfully, from the poacher's point of view, the knowledge is not a pleasant feeling for him, that any moment soon after he has reached home, he may hear the bay of a hound outside his cottage.

At the same time the owner finds he has direct evidence, and all without any violence to his men. The dogs are, of course, only concerned with the tracking, they are not savage at all, and have no evil intent towards their quarry, so that nothing could be brought against them on that score.

I have already stated that the man-tracking dog, par excellence, is the bloodhound. Where a private owner need not consider expense, and where prevention as well as cure is very much desired, he cannot do better than invest in a brace of these dogs. A dog and a bitch would be good from the point of view that it would be possible to breed from them and increase the stock. The only drawback to this is, that at certain times, the dog would be considerably off his work: when the bitch had to be shut up. This, however, would only be temporarily, of course. The name bloodhound is invested with a certain degree of dread and superstition, which in itself is a powerful deterrent. The implication of the name is not clearly understood. A gory victim is a common idea, and under any circumstances, a bloody trail, matching the deep red haws of the hounds' eyes, fill the imagination of the ignorant with apprehensive awe. As a matter of fact, the original meaning of the name is not really known. Some think it refers to the pureness of the breed, as in the term "blood horse." This may be so, but I think it more likely that, in previous centuries, before the use of the rifle for deer stalking, and also when many a wounded raider was flying for his life, the blood trail in both cases would be there, and the hounds would be worked on that.

The deep and somewhat bloodcurdling bay of the hound on the trail would seem to those unacquainted with the breed to threaten severe treatment when the quarry was run to earth. When this sound is heard, however, which is such music in the handler's ear, it implies only deep pleasure and joyful discovery of a sure scent, and no vindictive treatment is in view. I have only owned two or three bloodhounds which were dangerous, and which would have downed their quarry. I think in their case each hound must have thrown back to some savage ancestor, or perhaps to a Cuban bloodhound. The last mentioned hounds were used for tracking runaway slaves on the plantations in Cuba and Southern America. They were cross bred animals of bloodhound origin, but the crosses used had been purposely of very savage strains, such as the native mastiffs. The fear inspired by these Cuban bloodhounds was the means, and was intended to be so in those brutal times, of preventing runaways, and also for punishing them when caught.

Descendants of these hounds are still in use in America, but they are now used only for tracking escaped prisoners from the penitentiaries. They are also now no longer fierce, and do not harm their quarry.

I imported one of these hounds several years ago. It was a much lighter hound than one of our British breed, and was nearly all black, with only a little dark red tan about the muzzle and legs.

It came to me with a very fine reputation, and had done some splendid work at the penitentiaries, on one occasion having run down an escaped murderer after a two days' chase in the mountains. I found it certainly a splendid tracker, and it was a great help for encouraging the young hounds under training.

The average bloodhound, as bred in this country, is not at all savage, and its use is, therefore, quite humane. Apart from superstition, there is no doubt that the uncanny feeling that the escape unseen from the scene of a crime to the refuge of his own house is really no safeguard from detection, and the knowledge that a dog can trace him, even to his fireside, acts as a very powerful deterrent to a man with crime in his heart.

An argument which is frequently brought in here by those whose actual experience under such conditions is nil, is that the dogs would run the risk of being poisoned. It is true such risk may exist and always must do for any animals appointed to do protective work. But in actual practice this result does not follow, except quite unusually. This argument was one of the procuring causes for a very regrettable delay in inaugurating the official guard dogs during the war. One or two officials in Whitehall suggested this possibility, and the matter was shelved. Quite a time elapsed, and much life and property was lost and endangered, before I was able to convince the authorities, that, while such a risk could not be entirely eliminated, it was nothing which need cause any serious stoppage of the proposed Guard Dog Scheme.

As a matter of fact, several hundreds of dogs were trained for this purpose and were distributed all over the British Isles with extremely satisfactory results. The hundreds of reports sent in by officers commanding the various stations where the dogs were sent, testified in a wonderful way to the practical value of this auxiliary aid to the sentries, in guarding every sort of vulnerable point. I do not remember a case of poisoning being mentioned, except once.

It has to be remembered, that, in order to be certain of poisoning the dogs, the stuff has to be administered by giving it, or throwing it, to the dog at its kennel, and that the animal gives warning of the poisoner's approach long before he can get within throwing distance. Even laying poison down is not safe work for him, as where there are one or two tracking-dogs about, even if one of them picks it up, another may track the offender from the very spot where he laid the poison.

It will, of course, be understood that such dogs as these are not held in light estimation by a keeper who knows how much depends on them, and he is not likely to let them stray about, except under his personal supervision.

Bloodhounds have been more particularly associated with tracking than any other breed. Certainly a good hound with strong inherent tendencies, and having been well trained, is not easily diverted from the trail. Even if this is lost, it will continue with extraordinary pertinacity to try to regain it, where another kind of dog might not persist with such insistency. A good bloodhound has the greater part of its brain power concentrated in its nose, and the moment it is taken out, it instinctively walks with its muzzle to the ground. The origin of their use for man-tracking was one of grim necessity, and dates back to two or three centuries ago. Tracking-dogs were used in Ireland and also against the Clansmen in Scotland, and they were used on the border after raiders.

These raiders assumed a very serious aspect in the life of the inhabitants of the border country between England and Scotland, and, indeed, of the whole of the southern part of Scotland. These wild outlaws organised themselves into more or less drilled bands, and descended on the unfortunate dwellers of the fertile districts, seizing anything of value they could lay their hands on, and driving flocks and herds before them as they returned to their fastnesses. These strongholds were usually situated in the midst of the bogs and moss-land, of which the border country was greatly composed.

All the secret paths and ways of escape across the bogs were known to these desperate ruffians, who were called Moss Troopers on account of their place of residence, and also because they wore clothes the dull brown colour of the moss-land. This made them very invisible, and escape easy at all times, especially at night. In this adoption of nature-colouring for clothes, we see the first hint of khaki, and, indeed, the Moss Troopers' conduct in no way differs from that of the modern Bolsheviki. This state of affairs became so serious in the sixteenth and seventeenth centuries that vigorous measures had to be taken by the Crown to protect the peaceful country people. There was a system of beacon fires arranged, whereby, on any warning of a raid, these fires were ignited, and the country people were drawn together to unite against the common foe. It was ordered that tracking-dogs were to be kept in the various districts to assist the Crown forces in locating the marauders across the treacherous swamps.

Leslie, Bishop of Ross, in a volume printed in 1578, states :

"There is also another kind of scenting dogs (I am not speaking of the common sort which pursues hares and roe-bucks), far different from the other ; it is for the most part red, marked with black spots, or vice versa. These are endowed with so great sagacity and fierceness, that they pursue thieves in a direct course without any deviation : and this with such ferocity of nature that they tear them to pieces even by chance lying down in company with many others : for from the first scent the dog perceives (with his master following), although other men meet, come behind, or cross him, he is not at all confused, is not in the least diverted, but constantly sticks to the footsteps of his departing prey. Only in passing rivers they are at a loss, because there they lose the scent : which the thieves and cattle-stealers knowing, they, with many circles and mazes, pressing now this, now the opposite bank, drive off their plunder, and, pretending to make their exit both ways beyond the banks, rejoin at the same spot. In the meantime, the dog, filling the heavens with his clamour, does not desist till he has overtaken the steps of the fugitives."

In Nicolson and Burns' "History of the Antiquities of Westmoreland and Cumberland," published in 1777, there is a statement as to these dogs :

"Slough-dogs were for pursuing offenders through the sloughs, mosses, and bogs, that were not passable but by those who were acquainted with the various and intricate by-paths and turnings. These offenders were peculiarly styled moss-troopers : and the dogs were commonly called blood-hounds ; which were kept in use till within the memory of many of our fathers.

"And all along, the pursuit of hot trod (flagranti delicto), with red hand (as the Scots term it) was by hound, and horn, and voice. And the following warrant ascertains by whom and where those dogs were to be kept :

"September 29, 1616, Sir Wilfride Lawson and Sir William Hutton, Knights, two of his Majesty's Commissioners for the government of the middle shires of Great Britain, to

John Musgrave, the Provost-Marshall, and the rest of His Majesty's garrison (of Carlisle) send salutations. Whereas upon due consideration of the increase of stealths daily growing both in deed and report among you on the borders, we formally concluded and agreed, that for reformation therefore watches should be set, and slough-dogs provided and kept, according to the contents of His Majesty's directions to us in that behalf prescribed."

The method of distributing the dogs and the tax for their keep imposed on the inhabitants is here described:

" Imprimis, beyond Eske by the inhabitants there, to be kept above the foot of Sarke	1 Dogge
Item, by the inhabitants the inside of Eske to Richmont's Clugh, to be kept at the moat	1 Dogge
Item, by the inhabitants of the parish of Arthered, above Richmont's Clugh, with the Bayliffe and Black quarter; to be kept at the Bayliehead	1 Dogge
Item, Newcastle parish, besides the Baylie and Black quarters; to be kept at Tinkerhill	1 Dogge
Item, the parish of Stapylton	1 Dogge
Item, the parish of Irdington	1 Dogge
Item, the parishes of Lanercost and Walton	1 Dogge
Item, Kirklington, Skaleby, Houghton, and Richarby..	1 Dogge
Item, Westlinton, Roucliff, Etterby, Stainton, Stanwix, and Cargo; to be kept at Roucliff	1 Dogge

" The sheriff, officers, bailiffs, and constables, within every circuit, and compass wherein the slough-dogs are appointed to be kept, are to take care for taxing the inhabitants towards the charge thereof, and collect the same, and for providing the slough-dogs; and to inform the commissioners if any refuse to pay their contribution, so as thereby such as refuse may be committed to the gaol till they pay the same."

In his book on the dog, Jesse gives a curious correspondence from James V. of Scotland to the Archdeacon of the East Riding, on the subject of his desire to procure bloodhounds trained to ride on a saddle on a horse behind a man. His mother, Queen Margaret, seemed equally interested in the quest for such dogs, and also writes to the Archdeacon from Edinburgh. It seems uncertain as to what was in their minds, in desiring the dogs to ride in this position, but Jesse suggests that: " These were perhaps to be taken up when the tracks of the marauders pursued were plainly visible in soft ground. Swift pursuit was then made, till hard ground was come to, when the slow hound was dropped again to pick up the trail."

If this was the idea, it was a strange one, as the hounds could easily have kept up with the horsemen by galloping alongside; and it would be next to impossible to get any sort of saddle capable of holding the dog, or, for that matter, a hound willing to sit on such a contrivance, even though some such device could be invented.

The correspondence is extremely quaint, and the polite Archdeacon, in expressing his willingness to gratify the desire of his royal correspondents, conveys many fulsome compliments, and while he does not in any way suggest that the request cannot be complied with, seeks to pacify them in the first place by a gift of ordinary hounds for hunting purposes, procured from his patron, the Duke of Richmond and Somerset, who sent his own huntsman with them for the space of a month, and, furthermore, promises that inquiries will be made as to the possibility of procuring such horseback hounds. I greatly fear he was not successful in his search.

Seeing that tracking was of such great importance at this period of history, when the whole country was in a more or less roadless condition, and the inhabitants in the wilder regions were thus enabled to live securely by lawless means of supply, the soldiery, and, indeed, all the respectable members of society, regarded these tracking-hounds as part of the machinery for clearing the land of desperados, and every method of following a trail was carefully studied. Those who were pursued also took all the " tricks of the trade," so to speak, into account, and, from their point of view, sought out every sort of means to counteract the successful working of the hounds, and made use of every obstacle which it was known would divert them from the trail.

It is a common belief that, if the fugitive crosses water, the trail can no longer be followed, and this is so very often, unless those who are working the hounds have some sort of understanding of the method of assisting them to overcome this obstacle. The only way to proceed is to take the hounds across the river, either by boat or to swim them, and cast them again and again on the opposite bank, until they pick up the trail again. This has sometimes to be done for a considerable distance down the river, as the fugitive may have allowed himself to drift down-stream with the current, in order to confuse the hounds still further. In the case of a lake, or still water of any sort, the fresh cast will have to be made both up and down the opposite bank.

Well-trained, eager hounds will quite understand the desire of their keepers to assist them, and will energetically seek the scent again on the other side. I have even known unusually eager hounds, where the scent has been hot, plunge into the water on their own account, and swim to the other side and commence their fresh search for the broken trail. This is, however, exceptional, as the marauders of old well knew, and hounds usually require assistance in such a dilemma, and during the delay occasioned by crossing and taking up the trail again, the scent is all the time becoming fainter.

Another, and much more serious trick for stopping the pursuit, was for the fugitive to spill blood on the trail. The strong smell of this would completely destroy the fine scenting qualities of the hounds. In some of the punitive expeditions of the northerners, a captive was sacrificed to this end.

It will be seen that the authorities placed considerable value on the services of these tracking-dogs. In the wild, untrodden country of that period and neighbourhood, the hounds would have every chance to follow the trail successfully, and the moist nature of the ground would also be of great assistance in retaining the scent for a considerable time after the fleeing bands had passed, especially if they were driving herds of animals.

At this early period the war dog and the police dog were one and the same, but later on, as the country became more settled, and the bands of marauders were broken up, owing to new roads being made, and the country opened up generally, the criminal began to be much more an isolated individual, which made pursuit more difficult, as naturally one man was more difficult to pursue than a band, and also the fact of so many high roads, with steadily growing traffic along them, presented bad surfaces for scent, so different from the soft, moist mosses of the wilder and uncultivated period. Nevertheless, bloodhounds continued their work with the various bodies on whom devolved the duties of preserving order in the country, until fairly modern times, when they fell to a great extent into disuse. A few people, however, still kept them up and in training, as will be seen as follows.

I give an account from the Press of a case in which a conviction was obtained by the use of bloodhounds at the present day, in this country. I may add that the work was carried out under very great difficulties, but was, nevertheless, successful.

"FIRST CONVICTION FROM BLOODHOUND EVIDENCE

"At the Northamptonshire Assizes, the evidence of Major Richardson's bloodhounds was accepted as conclusive. Shaw, one of Lord Lilford's gamekeepers, who will be well remembered by visitors to the trials of the English Setter Club each spring, was shot at by poachers early in the morning of December 22. Bloodhounds were telegraphed for, and at half-past nine o'clock the same evening, twenty hours after the affray, they were laid on the trail with definite result.

"At the trial, Mr. Simpson, who prosecuted for the Crown, said: 'With reference to the service of the hounds, this was valuable for the reason that on the next morning, as soon as it was daylight, a search was made along the line of retreat (which had been run by the hounds during the night), and the barrel of a gun was picked up, opposite a stile in a field, over which the bloodhounds had gone.' The barrel of the gun was identified, and through it the poachers were arrested, and each got twelve years' penal servitude. This is interesting, as showing that the bloodhounds ran the true line in the dark with a very cold scent, and it is the first conviction obtained from bloodhound evidence."

Mr. Charles Gordon, Superintendent of Police, Saharanpur, United Provinces, India, procured a tracking bloodhound from me some years ago, and took it out to India. He later sent me the following report on the work of the dog:

" My bloodhound was of great service in a dacoit gang robbery, which was committed at a village in the Bulanshar Districts in the autumn of 1920. The dacoits had crossed a line of rails on their way to the village, and had picked up a quantity of stone ballast to use as missiles. The villagers were reinforced, and the dacoits finally bolted, carrying off with them twelve hundred rupees in loot. When bolting, the dacoits threw away the balance of the ballast which they had not thrown, and this gave their line of retreat. The bloodhound was put on the trail next morning, and was instrumental in tracking down three men. As a result of this, twelve more dacoits were arrested, and in the course of the enquiry another dacoity was brought home to this gang, both cases resulting in conviction.

" Autumn of 1911 a dacoity was committed at midnight in Saharanpur District. A bullock-cart in which was some police was attacked by dacoits. The dacoits were Sanasias (an aboriginal tribe of criminal propensities). One dacoit was wounded, and the night being dark, the others succeeded in getting away. My dog was put on the trail ten hours subsequent to the crime. Some indistinct footprints were found on the scene and leading to some fields to the south of the road. One of the dacoits was recognised at the time of the occurrence as being by name Mara (Sansia). He, however, managed to escape. The bloodhound was put on the trail of their footprints, which, however, ceased after twenty yards. The hound ran the trail across country until he came to a canal, which he skirted until he came to a bridge, over which he crossed. Then he continued the trail along the bank of a feeder canal; then, leaving this, he struck across four rice-fields, which had been irrigated from the canal. The water was about four inches deep, and growing rice about five inches above the water. (This was a particularly good piece of work).

" On arriving on the other side of the rice-field, he journeyed across country until he came to a village, through which he passed, and ended up at a house in a Sansia settlement to the far side of the village. Not a single Sansia man was present in the settlement, only women and children. On making enquiry, I ascertained that the house in question was that of Mara. Mara was arrested the following night.

"An amusing episode occurred when Mara and the other dacoits were on trial before the judge. Mara denied that he was present at the dacoity and said he knew nothing about it. 'How comes it that the dog tracked you for four and a half miles from the scene of the dacoity up to your house?' Mara replied that he did not know, but then volunteered the following statement, quite on his own account :

"'Agar Kutta aisa patta pagata Koon shars chouri Karskta?' A translation of this being: 'When the dog tracks in this manner, what chance has a fellow of committing thefts?'"

Some breeds have the sense of scent more highly developed than others. Hounds have most of their intelligence concentrated in this instinct, and are therefore better for the particular purpose of tracking. Different breeds of hounds have been for generations trained to hunt quarry of some sort. Bloodhounds hunt man, foxhounds hunt the fox, otter hounds hunt otter, and so on. Each of these breeds has inherited this particular instinct for certain quarry from generations of ancestry, which have been used for this same purpose, but, while it is always better if serious work is on foot, to use that breed most identified with that branch of tracking one is associated with at the moment, it does not necessarily mean that individuals of other breeds are not capable of being used as trackers, or do not take to the work. On the contrary, many collies and terriers and other sorts of dogs have excellent noses, and only need training to develop very satisfactorily.

One of the best man-trackers I ever had was a cross-bred Collie, and many Airedales are also excellent. During the Middle Ages, and up till quite recent times, dogs were used on the deer forests for tracking wounded deer, and deerhounds, collies and bloodhounds have all been used for this purpose.

HOW TO TEACH A DOG TO TRACK

In teaching the young of any species to track, it is always a help to have one of the older generation running with it to train the budding idea.

Many people are under the impression that all bloodhounds can track, and that this gift is quite instinctive and can be used without any particular training. These ideas are both erroneous. While it is true, that nearly every bloodhound will have a fairly clear understanding of what is required of it, the ability to work out a difficult trail is not acquired by all hounds, nor do they all have the persistency for this. Furthermore, the training of the young hound has to be regularly carried on in the first place, and the old tracker, which has learnt its work, must be kept in practice. The first-class tracking bloodhound will have been selected from several candidates for training, and while his brothers and sisters may have followed his lead, it is this particular one which will have supplied the initiative, and which in difficult situations will carry him through where the others, when by themselves and without his leading, will fail. It would be very much better if the breed was more numerous, as the process of selection would thereby be easier and quicker, and a great deal of labour in connection with hounds of mediocre tendencies would be eliminated.

The same process of selection and training is necessary for other breeds as well, and here, the far greater numbers from which to draw recruits, is a better basis on which to start. Many dogs are possessed of excellent noses, and only need some systematic training in order to turn them into excellent man-trackers. But in no breed, except the bloodhound, is this man-tracking hereditary, and therefore one can pass in review many specimens of other breeds, because they will be quite unaware of the manner in which their scenting qualities can be systematically adapted. This quality will have to be first developed and then the dog gradually taught the use of it. There is, however, this much in their favour. Although they may not have the basis of hereditary training to rely upon, still the natural intelligence of many other breeds is far greater than is that of the bloodhound. There is a far greater desire to understand an order, and also greater concentration in the endeavour to carry it out. The intelligent partnership and co-operation between master and dog is upon a higher basis.

As already stated, I have found collies and Airedales to answer exceedingly well to this training. Many of them have very excellent scenting powers and they take an intelligent interest in the work. Lurchers, also, are often very good and are extraordinarily intelligent. The only thing with them, however, is that they must not have already been trained for sporting purposes, as so many lurchers are. It is better to start the tracking instruction on a mind without a previous bias in any given direction. For this reason sporting dogs whose strong retrieving instincts are connected entirely with game are not advisable, as it is difficult to eradicate this tendency and divert it into that of man-tracking.

Collies and Airedales, on the other hand, are accustomed to turn to the master and to co-operate with him in many personal ways, and they understand that their great duty in life is to reach out to anything that he desires of them. Their constant endeavour is to interpret his wishes, and the pricked ear and questioning eye are indications of this earnest desire. This is a very good point of view from which to start training.

The first thing is to test the natural scenting instinct in the dog. Where there are a number of trained dogs, say a small pack of bloodhounds, the young dog can be allowed in the first place to run with the others. It will learn from them a great deal of the requirements, but it will also need special training on its own account. The best age to commence is from nine months to a year old. By testing the young animal by itself as early as possible, much time may be saved by the discovery as to whether it has any natural aptitude for man-tracking or not.

Many candidates for the work will have to be discarded, as there is not the slightest use putting effort into the tuition of a dog which does not at the outset give evidence of a very good nose indeed.

For this specialised testing and training, which under any circumstances must attend the tracker's education, two people are required. The underlying principle is that of reward. The person who is to lay the trail shows the animal, which is held in leash by the master or handler, a piece of biscuit or meat, and then walks away, calling. For the first few times he should remain within sight, and each time the dog is released he must give it the reward. After this preliminary lesson is learnt, he can make trails which lead out of sight, and as the pupil advances in understanding all sorts of variations and obstructions can be introduced into the trail. Thus it can be doubled backwards, or can lead across, or along a roadway for a time. Crossing a stream, and teaching the animal to look for, and pick up, the trail at the other side, is also an excellent training in intelligence as well as in scenting.

After the actual tracking has been well taught under all aspects, the period between the time the trail is first started and the animal is laid on can be increased. Where, at first, the hound is laid on immediately after the trail has been made, it can be held in leash for some considerable time and then released. It is as well that the person making the trail should go away in full view of the dog, until the latter has become quite expert in tracking after a lapse of time. The reward should also always be shown, and *always* given at the finish of each trail.

It is also important to use the same words in starting, and that the dog should understand thoroughly what these imply. The necessity for this is obvious when the final lessons are given, at which the dog is brought on to the trail with no runner in sight, and still more so, when the length of time is increased, and the trail is consequently weak and needs searching for. If the dog has been trained regularly hitherto on certain words, such as "Get after him," it will know that, whenever it hears them, finding the commencement of the trail is the duty asked of it, and it will immediately begin casting in every direction, until it finds what is sought.

The lessons should not be too difficult in the first place, and no fresh step should be taken until the previous one is learnt. The training should be regular, but not too rigorous, otherwise there is risk of the animal becoming bewildered and losing heart. The dog should be put on the commencement of the trail, and for this reason it is necessary to know exactly where the runner has started from. As the lessons advance, however, the dog can be brought on the *approximate* place of commencement, and with the words, "Get after him," it will learn to search about for the trail.

With regard to the presentation of a piece of the clothing of the person who is being pursued for the animal to smell, there is a considerable difference of opinion as to the utility of this. Personally, I am not prepared to make any definite statement on the subject, but on the whole I do not think there is much in it, except in the case of very exceptional dogs. There is no means of knowing very exactly how far it connects the scent of the clothing with that on the ground, and in practice I have never noticed that the animal pays much attention to the presentation of the article of dress.

Another debatable point is how far the body-scent, as apart from the boot-scent, enters into the successful tracking of the trail. I think that body-scent enters very largely into the matter, and although the dog keeps its nose to the ground all the time it is tracking, this is because the scent given off by the body falls to the ground along the trail. In a still, moist atmosphere this takes place more noticeably, as there is no wind, and the air is heavy, so that the scent is not blown away, but falls with a distinct concentration. I may remark here that I do not, under any circumstances, believe in trailing the dog on anything but the "clean boot"—that is to say, with no assistance to the scent, such as aniseed. Some trainers think that an aniseed trail in the first lessons is a help in attracting the young dog's attention; but this mitigation of difficulty has to be paid for later on as the lessons proceed, and the aniseed has to be debarred. It is much better to start fair, and work upwards from the start.

With regard to the runners used for making the trail, the question of scent enters very largely into their selection. Before the war it used to be fairly easy to pick up odd people of the tramp class, who for a shilling or two, were only too glad to make a trail across country. This type of "unwashed" quarry was excellent, as the body-scent, and the thoroughly impregnated clothes and boots, all left a powerful bouquet for the dog to follow. This was a great aid in the tracking, and a very distinct difference was observable when, as often happened, the trail would be made by a friend or a member of the family.

Matutinal tubs, and decent clothing, greatly decrease the possibilities of successful work, quite apart from any climatic obstruction. The necessity for obtaining outside aid is obvious, as it would not be making any great demand on the animal's powers if it was always trailed after its kennel-men, or anyone whose scent was especially known to it, although, in the first place, it is a help to start the young dog on someone it knows. In fact, the first lesson should be the trail of the kennel-man or some such person. After this has been picked up, and well run, under all sorts of varying conditions, the quarry should be changed as much as possible.

Since the war it is not so easy to find odd labour, and the price asked for using anyone's time at all, even for such a very labourless act as running across country, is often too high to make this sort of training possible in an ordinary way. Schoolchildren make useful little quarry, and are not so grasping in their demands as to payment, but enter into it much for the fun of the thing. Change of scent is what is required, so as to cultivate the dog's ingenuity and intelligence under every sort of difficulty.

Another point, which must be remembered, is that the person working the dog, or the handler, as he is called, must himself have a good deal of practice if he is to make much use of his animal's gift. He must study the peculiarities of scent—what sort of atmospheric conditions affect it, adversely, or the reverse.

Then he must know how to work his animals so that they are always under control, and yet have plenty of liberty to cast about.

It is generally best to leave the dog loose until it has the lesson fairly learnt, merely holding it in the leash while the runner goes away. When, however, the dog really begins to understand and is likely to run clean away on the trail, it is necessary to have it on a fairly long leash, and to keep up with the running animal. The leash is also useful for controlling purposes, when the trail is temporarily lost, as the dog will have to be forcibly drawn back to where it previously was running true, or it may be thought necessary, if this plan fails, to recast again further ahead, so as to strike the trail afresh.

It will be seen that a good deal of judgment is necessary

in all this, and the success of an animal's tracking powers can be greatly helped or marred by the handler.

In giving the above instructions it should be understood that they apply equally to any breed as well as to bloodhounds.

I would again emphasise that Airedales and collies are excellent substitutes for the extremely expensive and scarce bloodhound. They are extraordinarily intelligent, and have (many of them), excellent noses, and only need training to adapt themselves well. There are also large numbers from which to select those which are inherently good at the work, apart from training.

SCENT

The best scenting day is one on which evaporation is taking place slowly. A nice moist atmosphere, with no wind, and a fairly damp soil contribute to conditions whereby successful tracking can take place.

Where there is high wind, or hot sun, the trail very quickly becomes obliterated, and when the ground is very hard and dry it does not lie well.

The state of the atmosphere, just above the ground, is very important, as the body-scent hangs there indefinitely, unless blown or scorched away.

Midsummer is, therefore, not usually a good time for tracking, and springtime is inclined to be windy, but late autumn is very often excellent. Hard frost or very heavy rain are not good. The latter washes the trail away and the other freezes it. I have found, however, that if the trail has been made during the night hours, and before the frost at dawn, it is possible to pick it up again after the frost has melted. Only the dog must be put on immediately after the thaw.

Grass fields and undergrowth in woodlands hold scent well, and for this reason poachers, chicken thieves, and evil-doers of every sort are perfectly trackable, owing to the fact that they seek refuge from observation by cutting across country and avoiding the roads.

Scent will not lie long on hard high roads, but I have

traced many trails with dogs owing to the fact, as explained elsewhere, that the runner had branched off into the fields or woods at the side, where the scent had found longer lodgement. A good deal of practice and judgment is required from the handler in working a trail such as this, as the animal will have to be recast backwards and forwards, and every sign of footmark will have to be looked for as a guide as well. But the puzzling out of such a trail is very interesting.

When there is anything to accentuate the scent, such as blood, or dead game, this helps very much, and it will remain for a long time afterwards. This is another reason why a murderer can be more easily traced, than would be thought, as the blood-scent is very frequently there. There is no necessity that the blood should be on his boots, as the fact of it being on his hands or clothes will leave a trail behind him, and if he has crossed country, as such a man might be quite likely to do, and the tracking-dogs are put on to the trail in time, there is a good chance of success.

Although tracking conditions are frequently not good during the daytime in summer, the night hours and early dawn are quite satisfactory usually, as the atmosphere is cool and still, and the dew moistens everything. Too heavy a dew will, however, wash out a scent.

I have trained many dogs on downland, and have also, at various times, during the last thirty years, been permitted to train in military areas, such as Aldershot and elsewhere. All this sort of ground is very good practice for the animals because it is very difficult. The sandy or chalky nature of the soil does not retain moisture, and the exposed shadelessness, not to speak of unobstructed wind, gives the scent of the trail very little chance of lying long, or in any strength. The dogs have to be very smart at their work, in order to trace their quarry in such ground, and therefore this class of tracking brings them up to a high standard quicker than if they are run always through woods and moist grass fields.

CHAPTER XIV

Dogs in the Great War

" With eye upraised, his master's looks to scan,
The joy, the solace, and the aid of man ;
The rich man's guardian, and the poor man's friend,
The only being faithful to the end."

—Crabbe.

In including this chapter on the work the dogs of Britain did for the British army in the field, I have the twofold object of a desire to show how judicious training can secure to man the co-operation of his best friend, even at the time of most dire peril, and also to show forth and commemorate the fidelity, sagacity, and endurance of the British war dogs during the Great War.

The dogs used were all of native breeds. I mention this particularly, as, since the war, there have been statements made by unauthorised persons that foreign stock was used. This was not the case. I have found from many years of experimenting, both at home and abroad, that no dogs are a patch on our own breeds, in sagacity, courage, or reliability.

When the war opened in 1914 there were practically no military dogs of any sort attached to the British army. The only ones, which had been officially used, were some Airedales I had sent out to India for the Abor campaign, to act as scouts and sentries in the jungles and gullies. There were one or two also with the Durhams, for sentry work, and there was an Airedale which I trained as a sentry, and which went to manœuvres with the 2nd Battalion Norfolk Regiment, and on the outbreak of war accompanied it to France, where it was eventually killed by a shell on the Aisne. For many years previously I had been studying this subject, and as the result of my convictions had accumulated a large kennel of dogs, with which I made constant experiments. The study was also applied to the use of dogs with the police, and my conviction of the great value of trained dogs to the army and police became of the most emphatic character. I brought the matter from time to time to the notice of authorities, and although the police supported the idea to a certain extent, especially the forces in provincial towns, who used a number of dogs for patrolling suburban areas, I could get no generally concerted action taken. I did not give up hope, however, and continued my private experiments. Many people came to me for advice in obtaining safety for themselves or their property. There are very few parts of the world from which I did not receive either visitors or letters, in connection with this subject. Owners of tea and coffee estates, sugar plantations, poultry farms, and animal farms in all parts of the world, penitentiaries in North and South America, rubber estates, large rambling mansions, factories, docks, etc. In fact, all suffering from the same trouble, namely, the difficulty and unreliability of the human being, unaided, to provide the necessary guarantee of security. Each case was treated separately, according to the circumstances, climate, personnel and environment.

As it was necessary to specialise in certain breeds, it was found that, for these particular needs, the Airedale, as an all-round, courageous, reliable and hardy individual, could not be beaten, and the extraordinary way in which he is able to adapt himself to both northern and tropical climates is exceedingly remarkable and useful. I paid many visits to the Continent, to those countries which specialised in trained police or military dogs. In France, tentative experiments with army dogs were carried on, and police dogs were used in suburban areas of large towns. Russia had a definite establishment of military dogs, in which the Tsar took a great interest, and which were attached to many regiments. I may here incidentally remark that I was in Russia three weeks before the war broke out, acting as judge at the army trials of these military dogs. The other two judges were Germans.

Holland, Sweden, and Italy all had canine military establishments, in a more or less experimental stage, and in the case of Italy, the experience gained was put to good use in the Tripoli campaign. I visited Tripoli personally during the war, and gained many valuable hints, and I was allowed to visit the battlefields in Morocco at the invitation of King Alfonso, in the Riff campaign, taking one of my own dogs with me. These experiences, in actual warfare, were added to by a visit to the Balkans, when war broke out there in 1911. The Albanians used many of their shaggy sheep-dogs of ferocious disposition, which rendered excellent service in the mountains as guards to their sentries. The Bulgarians also used sentry dogs. I was able to send out a pair of dogs from my own kennels to the 8th Gurkhas, for the Abor campaign in India in 1911. These were used by sentries and patrols, and rendered considerable service in the dense scrub, by preventing the sentries from being surprised and the battalions rushed. One was an Airedale, and the other a cross-bred sheep-dog.

The official report on the work of these dogs is as follows:

"Before the encounter of November 7th, one of the dogs accompanying the advanced guard gave timely warning of the presence of the Abors. The dogs are also employed at night time, being used by the Gurkha sentries, who keep them on a chain, to supplement their own vigilance."

It was in Germany that I found a fairly organised service of both military and police dogs. Between the years 1900 and 1914 I paid several visits to their training establishments, and admired many of their methods, but I quickly saw that we had the advantage in this country, by the possession of a better choice of dogs for the work; and also I questioned whether the immensely detailed system of training the keepers of the dogs, and also the dogs themselves, was to any useful purpose. It seemed to me that, as in other forms of German organisation, not enough attention was directed to the psychology of the subject, and too much to the letter of mechanical instruction. I knew that in the event of dogs being employed at all in war, large supplies and quickly trained would be needed, and that, therefore, a quicker system of instruction was required, at all events for our country, where no preparations were being made in peace time, in this branch.

When the thunderbolt of war fell in this country, the

In the Trenches, Morocco.
Riff War, 1911.

School of Instruction.
Training military dogs.

p. 182.

first shock seemed to bring to the surface, among other things, the fact that we had been harbouring quantities of bitterly hostile, treacherous aliens, about whom only one thing was certain, which was, that we could not trust them in any direction whatever. Our whole nation began to be immensely on the alert within a few days, and I saw at once that a properly organised system of sentinels and guard dogs, all over the country, would be of enormous service in guarding bridge-heads, magazines, factories, and valuable property of all kinds. I judged, from my experience of years in the same sort of work for civilians, how immensely valuable an adaptation of the same idea would be for the army. I very urgently represented this, and offered to present my whole kennel of trained dogs to the army, that experiment might immediately be made. My ideas were, however, not in any way understood at the time, and I could make no headway.

When my offer of sentry dogs was rejected in the first days of the war, I turned to another branch of work in which I had frequently experimented in previous years—that of tracing the wounded on the battlefield. These dogs were, of course, used with ambulance sections. At this period, a war of movement was the only method conceived, and also we, in this country, were convinced of the inviolability of the sacred symbol of the Red Cross, whether on man or beast, hospital or ship. Had these conditions obtained in this war, ambulance dogs would have been of great assistance.

It was found, however, that with a retreating Army, they could not be used. Furthermore, when the fighting settled down to entrenched warfare, any attempt to use the dogs, even though provided with Red Cross saddles, was frustrated by the enemy firing on the animals and their keepers. Their use was therefore forbidden in both the English and French armies.

I had offered my services to the British Red Cross Society with some trained ambulance dogs, and was sent by them to Belgium early in August, 1914. I made my way as far as Brussels, only to find the enemy entering the city from the east, and the Belgians falling back, while our own army had not come up. I succeeded in getting out of Brussels with the dogs and reached Ostend, but the conditions on the Western Front soon became, as I have said, impossible for the successful use of ambulance dogs.

After some months I received a number of requests from officers, privately, for dogs for sentry and patrol work. I did my best to supply these, and found Airedales answered the purpose well. I also sent some to the Belgian army. During this time, I understand many officers were writing to the War Office, asking that dogs should be supplied officially, for several purposes. In the summer of 1916, I received a letter from an officer in the Royal Artillery, in which he expressed a great desire for trained dogs, to keep up communications between his outpost and the battery during heavy bombardment, when telephones were rendered useless, and the risk to runners was enormous. He asked if I would train some dogs to carry messages, and I promised to do so. I made many experiments with a large number of dogs, and at last I got two dogs to carry messages homewards, regularly, without a hitch, for two miles. They were both Airedales, and their names were Wolf and Prince.

They left for France at the end of 1916, and went direct to Thiepval, under escort of a gunner. The dogs were very intelligently managed in France, for although they had been trained without any of the adjuncts of war, they settled down successfully, and began to carry messages regularly. Colonel Winter, R.A., to whom they went, was very kind in assisting me with suggestions, and I found the hints he gave me very useful later on. The first report on these two dogs was as follows :

" From O.C. 56th Brigade, Royal Field Artillery.

" To R.A. Headquarters, 11th Division.

" In continuation of my letter No. 549 dated on the 7th inst., during the operations against Wytschaete Ridge, two messenger dogs attached to this Brigade were sent forward at 1 a.m. One was attached to the forward liaison officer, and one with the group forward observation officer.

" After being led up through communication trenches during darkness, they went forward as soon as the attack was launched, passing through the smoke barrage. . . . One was dispatched at 10.45 a.m. and the other at 12.45 p.m.

" Both dogs reached brigade headquarters, travelling

a distance as the crow flies of 4,000 yards, over ground they had never seen before, and over an exceptionally difficult terrain. The dog dispatched at 12.45 p.m. reached his destination under the hour, bringing in an important message, and this was the first message which was received, all visual communication having failed.

(*Signed*) " O.C. 56th Brigade, R.F.A."

Two other reports on these dogs are as follows :

" When the Germans withdrew their line in the spring of 1917, the dogs were taken up the night before to a wood east of Bucquoy. They were then sent up to a forward observation post, 4,000 yards to the east of the wood, and were released with important messages. They found their way back, through masses of troops on the march, to the wood, although they had only arrived there the night previously, and the ground was quite unknown to them."

" On the attack on the Vimy Ridge the dogs were employed with an artillery observation post. All the telephones were broken, and visual signalling was impossible. The dogs were the first to bring through news."

The definite results obtained through these two dogs, and through Colonel Winter's initiative, led the authorities to enquire into the question of establishing some means whereby supplies of these messenger dogs could be provided for the army. I was ordered to the War Office to discuss the matter. Suffice it to say, I was glad to propose a definite plan for starting an official school of instruction for military dogs, and that my ideas were agreed to. It was decided that the school should be formed at Shoeburyness, for the reason that the constant firing of the big guns would be excellent training for the dogs.

A certain number of men were to be sent to the school each month for instruction in handling the dogs, and these men, at the end of the course, which lasted about five weeks, took the dogs overseas. A depot was formed in France as a base, and the dogs and men were all assembled here and drafted to sectional kennels, behind the front line. Each sectional kennel was in charge of a sergeant, and had about forty-eight dogs and sixteen men allotted to it. From these sectional kennels the dogs were sent with their keepers, to the proportion of three dogs to one man, to the active sectors. His dogs were then taken away from him by certain men detailed from the infantry battalions in the Brigade, and were led up to the front line. The keeper remained at Brigade headquarters, watching for the dogs' return, and ready to deliver the messages they brought to the officer commanding. Very careful regulations for the correct management of the messenger dogs, and their keepers, were drawn up and issued. This method of concentration and supervision soon began to give excellent results.

In the meantime the training work proceeded steadily at the War Dog School at Shoeburyness, and class after class of trained men and dogs were sent overseas, where they were concentrated, in the first place, at the central kennels, before being distributed to the sectional kennels. A new branch of activity had also commenced at Shoeburyness. As the demand for fighting men became increasingly insistent, large numbers who had been doing guard duty all over Britain were withdrawn, and the security of munition factories, magazines, and vulnerable points of all kinds was an anxious problem for the Government. I was sent for and questioned as to whether the dogs could be of service at this juncture, to act as guards, and replace man power. I said most emphatically they could. From my experience, however, in pre-war years, as applied to civilian needs, I knew, that, in order to be successful, careful management of these guard dogs would be necessary, and therefore I drew up a list of regulations which was issued to each centre where these dogs were employed. Once this branch was fairly started, applications began to pour in from all parts of the country.

At this time, also, a request for sentry dogs for use with the troops at Salonika in the mountains, was referred to me. The desire was particularly for Airedales, and they were to be used in the listening-posts in the front line, to give warning of enemy approach. There were thus, at this time, three separate branches of training, proceeding at the school. With these increasing demands it was found that the supply of suitable dogs, so far obtained, was becoming inadequate. At first the only supply was from the Home for Lost Dogs at Battersea. Then the Birmingham, Liverpool, Bristol and Manchester Dogs' Homes were invited to help by sending any suitable dogs to the school. Many a homeless, deserted " stray " was saved from the lethal chamber, and transformed into a useful member of His Majesty's Forces. Later, the Home Office ordered the police all over the country to send all stray dogs, of certain breeds, to the school. Finally, when even these sources were not sufficient, the War Office decided to appeal to the public for gifts. The response was exceedingly generous. The country was, at this time, passing through especially serious times, and many people were only too glad to help by sending their dogs. The food shortage also was much accentuated, and it was felt that the family friend would be certain to receive good food and care in the army.

A splendid collection of dogs was daily assembled. Many of them were fine show specimens, while others of humble ancestry nevertheless came with wise faces and willing hearts. They were one and all welcome, and were made to feel so. The attitude of mind was, in most cases, that of a schoolboy plunged into a large public school—bewilderment and sometimes home-sickness for a short time—but, as it was found that reassuring, kindly human voices were all round, and that excellent dinners were going, they soon became quite at home. Added to this, life offered most interesting companionship with other dogs, and also a completely new experience, in what seemed to the dog, the learning of a new sort of game.

Each recruit was carefully tested for three different duties—messenger, sentry, or guard work. Sometimes they failed in one, but succeeded in another, and all had a good chance to show some sort of initiative. In the event of a dog showing no desire for work of any sort, it was returned to the source from whence it came. The more one has to do with the canine race, the clearer it is seen that, as regards psychology, there is little difference between it and the human race, and I much regret to say that it was my experience to find occasionally, the canine "conscientious objector" among the recruits. There was, however, a convenient method of dealing with the offenders, which, unfortunately, is not available for human beings—an excellent lethal chamber at Battersea!

We had many distinguished visitors. Earl French inspected the school, accompanied by General Lowther. This was before the results of the work that was being done had been fully demonstrated, and the genuine interest Earl French showed in the dogs, and the few words of helpful encouragement he gave me, at a time when very great difficulties were being overcome, will always be remembered with gratitude. A large number of officers belonging to the Allied and neutral countries also visited the school, besides various travelling parties of Allied and Colonial editors. During the summer of 1917, so numerous were the requests, from various officials, to visit the school, that a special day had to be set aside once a week for this purpose, so that the training should not be hampered.

The demand for more, and yet more dogs, both as messengers and guards, became insistent. The former proved themselves speedy and life-saving, in maintaining communication in the field, and the latter as a means of substituting man-power, and protecting Government property of every kind. In June, 1918, I made an inspection of the entire messenger dog service in France. I visited also the French front, and was greatly interested in the work done in the French army, with dogs. I had a conversation with the famous General Gouraud, whose wonderful defence near Rheims in July, 1918, will always be remembered. The general is a great believer in dogs, and in speaking of messenger dogs he said: "If only two out of six dogs come back, with their messages, I am satisfied."

Previous to this I had already paid two visits to the dogs on the French front. In April, 1915, I visited the French 6th army at Villers Cotterets, and also in December the same year I visited the 7th French army in the Vosges, where I was hospitably received by Monsieur Paul Megnin, who has done so much to forward this work in the French army.

On my return to England a large extension of the work, and a proportionate increase to the establishment of the War Dog School, was ordered by the War Office. By this time it was found that the available training-ground at

Shoeburyness was becoming too congested. A new site was therefore chosen on Matley Ridge, above Lyndhurst. There was a splendid stretch of country here, and the training went on satisfactorily until May, 1919. During that month, the school was again moved to Bulford, on Salisbury Plain.

In November, 1918, the Armistice came, but just before that event the latest instructions for divisonal attack were issued. In these it was ordered that all infantry battalions in the attack were to be provided with messenger dogs. This seemed to set a seal on the work. The long uphill struggle, the open sneers, the active obstruction, the grudging assistance, all was forgotten, in the knowledge that countless men's lives had been saved, and that this fact had now been realised, and acknowledged.

Field-Marshal Earl Haig, in his final dispatch on the war, pays a tribute to the work the messenger dogs did in the field.

THE TRAINING OF THE MESSENGER DOG

The training of the messenger dog differs from that of any other dog. In the first place, the dog has to work entirely on its own initiative, and it may be miles away from its keeper. It has to know what it has to do, and to think out how this can be done. The only training that approaches it is that of the shepherd's dog, where a man may send his dog up the hill-side with directions to gather in the sheep. But the distance is not so great, nor are the difficulties to be compared. It is easy to understand, therefore, that the messenger dog has to be trained in such a way that it takes the keenest delight and pride in its work. The highest qualities of mind—love and duty—have to be appealed to, and cultivated. Coercion is of no avail, for of what use would this be, when the dog is two or three miles away from its keeper? In fact, it may be said that the whole training is based on appeal. To this end, the dog is gently taught to associate everything pleasant with its working hours. Under no circumstances, whatever, must it be roughly handled. If it makes a mistake, or is slack in its work when being trained, it is never chastised, but merely shown how to do it over again. If any of the men under instruction are observed to display roughness, or lack of sympathy with the dogs, they should be instantly dismissed, as a promising young dog could easily be thrown back in his training, or even spoiled altogether by sharp handling.

In the early days of the dog's training, it is not asked to travel very long distances, but before it is considered ready for the field it must have been in the regular habit of carrying messages over different sorts of country, for three and a half, to four miles. The ground over which the dogs are trained must be varied as much as possible. They must be taught to travel along high roads, amongst lorry and other traffic, through villages, and past every sort of camp and cook-house temptation. They must be taught not to be afraid of water, or of any inequalities in the ground. To aid the dogs in overcoming these difficulties, all sorts of artificial obstacles are introduced into the route of the dog's journey, over and above those he would meet in the ordinary way. Barbed wire entanglements, palings, fences, water dykes, smoke clouds, made by harmless means, etc., should intercept its homeward journey, and it must be induced at all costs, one way or another, to surmount these difficulties by going over, through, or under. It is left to the dog to choose, but come he must. Competition with each other is a very strong educator here, and one of the great aids to training. When a dog begins to be keen on its work, it takes great pride in everything connected with its training, and is greatly displeased to see another passing it.

It was my custom at the school to divide the messenger dogs into classes, according to their progress. There was a first, second and third class. Sometimes one class would be left in, while the others were taken out for work. If the first class, which was the most highly trained, happened to be left in, it was most amusing to watch the indignation and contempt with which the incoming effort of the lesser-trained dogs were greeted by its members. They generally elected to watch the proceedings, perched on top of their kennels, and loud choruses of derision were hurled at the raw recruits. When the turn came, afterwards, for members of the first class to exhibit their prowess, great was the assumption of superiority, and determination to show how much better they could do.

In order to accustom them to gunfire, the best method is to encourage the young recruit with a daily practice under rifle fire, with blank ammunition. One or two rifles are sufficient at the start,and the number may be increased, as the dogs get accustomed to them. Afterwards thunder-flash bombs can be used, at varying distances. At Shoeburyness, the dogs were taken daily to the batteries, first of all to the 18-pounders, and afterwards to the heavies. Much gentleness and careful treatment is needed here, so that the dogs may not be unduly scared at first. The whole process must be gradual.

It is a good plan to feed the dog with tit-bits during the firing. It is remarkable how soon most dogs get accustomed to the heaviest firing. I am frequently asked how long it takes to train a messenger dog, and to this no very definite answer can be given, as so much depends on the individual dog's intelligence, and stamina. For, it must be understood, that not only has the mind to be instructed, but the health, and muscular activity have to be brought up to a high standard. The great proportion of the dogs sent to the school had been previously living indoors, sometimes in hot kitchens. The change to an outdoor life was quite an experience, and it took a little time for them to become hardened to weather conditions.

Then again, very few dogs have been accustomed to gallop several miles every day over every sort of surface, and their feet were rarely in good working condition. Another point is, that the usual manner of feeding a single house-dog on any odd scraps that may be left over from the household meal is not a good preparation for the steady working diet provided for them when under training. It was quite difficult for them to believe that dog biscuits, cooked with horseflesh would really very soon seem to them the most delightful fare that could be provided. It may be stated that no dog should leave the war dog school under five weeks, and only a few should do so then, the majority requiring six weeks to two months, to become thoroughly trained and hardened.

It was found that the best method of kennelling the dogs, when at the school, was for each dog to be chained to a separate kennel. These were of the box pattern, with a sloping roof, which opens upwards, and with a sliding door. Each kennel had in front of it a movable shelter, with a wooden roof and floor. These shelters were a great comfort to the dog, as they gave protection both from rain and the sun. Such kennels proved exceedingly satisfactory, and the health of the dogs was very good indeed. They were also easily shifted about, so that the ground did not get foul. This system of kennelling was also adopted at the Central Kennels, in France. The kennels should be periodically, and frequently white-washed inside.

A man should be set aside to attend to the grooming of the dogs. In the case of the old English sheep-dogs, it was well to clip the legs, as all that long fur was uncomfortable for the dog when in hard training, and when it got wet. In fact, all working dogs, with extremely shaggy coats, should be trimmed, especially about the legs, leaving only a good thick saddle of fur along the back. One good, reliable man was put on duty as head nurse. He had to be kind, gentle, and practical, and not fond of dosing, as sick dogs are far better without any drugs. Rest, warmth, and dieting in an intelligent manner is the quickest and surest way to bring dogs into health again. I may also add that prevention is better than cure, and if the dogs are kept in the manner directed, well fed, well groomed, and exercised, they will be happy, and when dogs are happy they are generally healthy. In the case of wounds or bites from other dogs, I am very much against putting on any ointment or medical dressing of any sort, beyond sometimes a mere bandage soaked in water. I find that the healing takes place much quicker if the wound is kept clean, and left alone.

The hour of training was eagerly anticipated by the dogs, and they were in a high state of excitement, when let out on to the parade ground by the keepers. It was better, if possible, that each man should concern himself with two dogs only at this time, but, in the case of the more advanced classes, it was sometimes necessary, if the number of dogs under training was very large, that each keeper should have three, or even four, which were taken from their kennels on leads. A certain amount of "swank" was evident among those members of the classes, who considered their work was approaching that quality known as "haute ecole." This was for the benefit of the less accomplished, and especially for the last comers, who were drawn up in a line on the opposite side, and were attached by their leads to posts. These raw recruits waited until all the dogs who were capable of returning from some distance had departed. This morning parade was an excellent time for the officer in charge to conduct a thorough inspection of all the dogs on duty. Signs of sickness were noted, and condition of health in every particular, including coat, skin, and so on.

All dogs were classified according to their work, and those at the same stage of training went out together, with their keepers, in groups. As I have said, they were at this time in such a high state of complacency that their behaviour was apt to get on each other's nerves, and the natural desire "to take each other down a peg or two" sometimes resulted in squabbles of an undignified nature. These were, however, soon ended, and the next moment the combatants were trotting off quite happily, as though nothing had occurred. It may be added that this is the only occasion when a scolding was administered.

I might remark here that the best weapon for stopping a dog fight is a heavy stable broom with good stiff bristles. By bringing it down, bristle end, on the dogs' noses, it will be found they will quickly realise the game is up. The broom need not be used heavily, as they dislike the bristles very much, and usually let go without further trouble.

The first training each day was the firing drill. The entire parade of dogs, excluding the new arrivals, were led up to a large shed, where a certain number of keepers were drawn up with rifles loaded with blank cartridges. Several rounds were fired, and many of the haughty spirits, that had been making such a display on the parade ground, were now inclined to put up a sorry show. Much gentleness was, however, extended at this lesson, and any dog that showed timidity was taken further away until it got accustomed to the firing. This they very soon did, and the old hands proudly stood right under the firing keepers.

After this there was a system of bomb-firing, which was a further call upon nerve force, and had often to be carried on for some time. The dogs were also trained to run among the keepers, who were firing their rifles from a recumbent position across the road, by which the dogs have to come. They were also taken to the batteries and accustomed gradually at varying distances to the sound of 18-pounders up to the 12in. guns. Another lesson was the water training, and in this case the dog had to cross a stream, either by jumping, swimming, or wading, and there was also the obstacle crossing, which might be barricades of barbed wire, fencing, or thorn-hedging. The smoke barrage had also to be met and conquered. This was made by setting alight bundles of straw or hay, or by harmless smoke bombs, and the dogs had to run through it.

In all these tests the dog had to do the work voluntarily. It is not coerced, or compelled. It must want to do it. For this reason it will be understood how much patience was required, and that no definite time could be laid down for each dog's training. Those that refused were gently asked to try again, and would be perhaps given a much easier test, and so were led up to the point, which was at first rather beyond their intelligence. The classes were now ready for the running work, and were taken out shorter, or longer distances, according to their capabilities, and were slipped back to the training post.

In the meantime the new dogs were dealt with. Each dog was taken singly, by a keeper, and slipped back, and this system was carried on over and over again, and at increasing distances. The officer in charge of the training found a high platform very convenient, from which he surveyed the surrounding land, to inspect the running of the dogs, and note each one's behaviour. The eye soon became practised where the training ground was in open country, to distinguish the running dogs from a long distance, and note would be taken as to whether the dog came steadily, or if it stopped and why. This training was carried on twice a day for all the dogs, except those of the highest class, which would probably have been taken out four miles or so in the morning, and slipped backwards, thus bringing their run up to about eight miles. In their case, that was sufficient for one day. When the evening hour came, they were all very ready to seek the quiet rest of their individual kennels, and to feel, with proud consciousness, that they were daily learning a little more of a very honourable task.

The following nominal roll of men and dogs attached to a sectional kennel, gives a good idea of the class of dog found most suitable. It brings out the fact that the gift of intelligence necessary for message carrying cannot be said to be confined, in particular, to any one breed. It should be noted that many of these dogs had slight crosses in them, and this is especially so in the case of the retrievers, many of which had a strain of collie in them.

MESSENGER DOG SERVICE

NOMINAL ROLL OF DOGS AND KEEPERS, NO. 3 SECTION. N.C.O. i/c SERGT. W. BONNEY

No.	Description.	Sex.	Name.	Keeper's Name.
101	Airedale	Dog	Buller ..	3133 Cpl. J. Coull
102	Collie	Dog	Trick ..	do.
103	Setter	Bitch	Nell ..	do.
104	Collie lurcher ..	Dog	Yellow ..	491793 Pnr. H. Bevington
105	Airedale	Dog	Rocket ..	do.
106	Airedale	Dog	Jame ..	do.
107	Airedale	Dog	Tags ..	361465 Pnr. H. Monagham
108	Old English sheep ..	Dog	Tweed ..	do.
109	Retriever	Bitch	Lill ..	do.
110	Irish terrier	Dog	Paddy ..	449951 Pnr. G. L. L. Griffiths
111	Irish terrier	Dog	Mick ..	do.
112	Irish (missing) ..	Dog	Cocoa ..	do.
113	Airedale	Dog	Dale.. ..	432401 Pte. P. M. O. Oldroyd
114	Airedale lurcher ..	Dog	Badger ..	do.
115	Bloodhound (missing) ..	Dog	Duke ..	do.
116	Retriever sheep ..	Bitch	Curly ..	234830 Pte. W. T. Rea
117	Airedale, Irish ..	Dog	Gyp ..	do.
118	Irish..	Dog	Dick ..	do.
119	Lurcher	Dog	Sharp ..	360178 Pnr. J. Ferriby
120	Irish water spaniel ..	Dog	Coffee ..	do.
121	Yellow lurcher ..	Dog	Vulcan ..	do.
122	Lurcher	Dog	Dan ..	360700 Pnr. R. Young
123	Retriever	Dog	Black Petal ..	do.
124	Collie	Dog	Flight ..	do.
125	Terrier	Dog	Georgie ..	369186 Pnr. C. Welham
126	Spaniel	Dog	Spotty ..	do.
127	Retriever	Dog	Hanky ..	do.
128	Brown setter ..	Dog	Ginger ..	360167 Pnr. J. Cousall
129	Collie	Dog	Ben ..	do.
130	Airedale	Dog	Moses ..	do.
131	Lurcher	Dog	Frolic ..	443982 Pnr. W. Taylor
132	Collie	Dog	Willard ..	do.
133	Spaniel	Dog	Drummer ..	do.
134	Collie	Dog	Jim ..	525929 Pnr. H. Cotton
135	Old sheep	Dog	Jock ..	do.
136	Bedlington	Dog	Dick ..	do.
137	Irish Bedlington ..	Dog	Paddy ..	360174 Pnr. T. W. Woof
138	Brown lurcher ..	Bitch	Lady ..	do.
139	Lurcher	Dog	Roger ..	do.
140	Small retriever ..	Dog	Darkie ..	210148 Pnr. G. W. Allcock
141	Retriever spaniel ..	Dog	Prince ..	do.
142	Collie	Dog	Flier ..	do.
143	Whippet	Dog	Skim ..	360173 Pnr. R. Windle
144	Irish..	Dog	Links ..	do.
145	Whippet	Dog	Forest ..	do.
146	Lurcher	Dog	Slick ..	360188 Pnr. J. Dunn
147	Collie lurcher ..	Dog	Rapid ..	do.
148	Lurcher	Dog	Sailor ..	do.

Several hundreds of such dogs crossed the channel, fully trained for their humane work, with our soldiers.

The following list represents about one month's output, and still further shows forth the breeds used:

Breed of Dogs	No.
Collies	74
Lurchers	70
Airedales	66
Sheep dogs	36
Retrievers	33
Irish terriers	18
Spaniels	11
Deerhounds	6
Setters	4
Welsh terriers	5
Bull terriers	5
Greyhounds	2
Eskimos	2
Dalmatians	2
Bedlingtons	2
Pointers	2
Bull dogs	1
Whippets	1
Total	340

It will here be seen that the collies and lurchers take the highest place as regards numbers, and Airedales the next. Some of the other breeds were good at the work, but were of a scarcer breed, and therefore more difficult to obtain. Of these I would particularly mention Welsh terriers. Some deerhounds also showed a great aptitude, but they are, of course, rather scarce.

It will be observed, however, that the first four breeds are all such as have been associated, some of them from prehistoric times, with man, in connection with his work, and therefore have instinctively a sense of calling inherent in their minds. The collie or sheep-dog is quite one of the most ancient breeds, and has always been the companion of man, for guarding his person and his flocks. The lurcher is a mixture of working dogs, the greyhound part of him being adapted, on account of the fleetness to be derived from this breed, to the intelligence of the other part of him, which may be a collie or an Airedale, the two portions combining into a very clever, reasoning, working dog. The Airedale has, for many generations now, been adopted as a very personal dog, mostly for the guarding of person and property, and he also takes life as quite a serious business. This natural instinct for work is, of course, a great point on which to base the training.

In estimating the value of the work of the messenger dogs in the field, it is necessary to remember certain essential facts when comparing this means of communication with others more commonly in vogue. Runners and telephones may certainly be sure and rapid in peace time, but the imperfections of these are only too well known to those who had to depend on them under war conditions. If, under peace conditions, it may seem that these forms of communication should take precedence, it will be found that in the upheaval that takes place in war time the more mechanical methods become displaced, and the dog is then more than equal to any of them.

In support of this I may mention an instance of a brigade signal officer issuing instructions that, as far as possible, all important dispatches were to be sent by dogs. On numerous occasions the dogs were the first to bring back information of important operations, and many urgent messages. On dark and stormy nights they were invaluable, and the time in which they did their work was approximately the same as in the daytime. The average speed of the dog was one-half to one-third of the time taken by runners in the daytime, and at night still less. Runners have come in cut and bleeding from barbed wire and other obstacles, after having been lost for several hours in the darkness, while the dogs have come through safely, and without delay.

I here give some statements of the work of the messenger dogs in the field, which were sent to me by the keepers, when the dogs first went overseas. I have already stated that the importance of their work was not properly understood at first by either officers or men of the regiments to which they were attached, nor in the army as a whole. Later, when the real service they could render came to be understood, and when the regulations governing the dogs began to be enforced, all ranks were much more ready to assist the dogs. One of the most important rules for the troops to observe was to refrain from enticing or checking a dog on its journey.

Keeper Goodway, who was one of the earliest men to be trained, and to go to France, mentions the difficulty for the dog by this regulation not being properly understood.

"The two are doing well, the black lurcher bitch especially. She is splendid, takes no notice of the guns or anything; they have both been running regularly day and night this last fortnight from advanced H.Q. to the rear. They used to do it in about seven or eight minutes, where it takes a man over half an hour. The officers think they are splendid, and I know they have sent in a good report. One thing I was rather afraid of was the runs at night, when there is generally more shelling, but it makes no difference; they run quite as well in the dark as the daylight. The only fault about the big collie 'Scott' is, that he is rather a good-looking dog, and everybody will make a fuss of him if they get a chance, therefore if any soldier calls him he will stop to be made a fuss of; the bitch being a bit savage-looking doesn't get spoken to, and she is absolutely the best."

Keeper Rea, who also went to France in the early days of the movement, makes the same complaint. These men both testify to the fact, which was amply proved later, that the night time made no difference to the dog when at work.

"Old 'Tray' is still as steady and faithful as ever, and is as sure as day and night, and he can jump as good as any of them. 'Joseph' is a good one and fast, only not as good as old 'Tray.' In rough ground 'Swallow' is doing grand. I am keeping him in practice all the time. Pte. Reid, of the 13th R.H. of Canada, is at the same place as myself and we work the dogs between us. I take his, and he mine. It is a hard job to keep the lads from making a fuss of them; it seems as though man and dog were made to go together. We are down on our old front again.

The dogs are running from three to six kilos per day, so keep in good condition. We have snow on the ground, and it has been very cold ; to-day it is thawing a little ; the ground is covered with snow still. Some very heavy strafing going on—steady here now. We got a bunch of Germans last night, all dressed in white overalls and white smocks. I was thinking they would be a good rig for the Salonica dogs at night practice. I have good places for dogs, and lots of good food."

Keeper David in his statement refers also to the question of night work.

" ' Joe ' and ' Lizzard ' have done some very good work out here, both day and night. The dog is as good in the night as he is in the day ; he is worth his weight in gold, and the bitch is very good. I have had them come three miles at night in twenty minutes, and they are just the same on any front that we go to. The dog can always be relied upon."

These statements from the keepers in the field were a great help to us in the training work at the School. For instance, we were not certain as to the effect of gas on the dogs. Keeper Brooks mentions this matter in a report on his dog ' Tom.' As a matter of fact, they were not so sensitive to this, on the whole, as one would perhaps have imagined.

" The dogs I brought out from England were taken away from me to be distributed amongst the other men, for we have to have three dogs each. I had three of the first lot sent out, and the names are as follows : ' Tom ' (black and white spaniel), ' Moses ' (black, with a little white in neck, sheep-dog), and ' Fritz ' (the large German sheep-dog). I am very pleased with them, and they are doing some very good work. They are running from the front line to Batt. Hdqs. which is a good mile and a half, and their average run is from five to eight minutes, which the officer thinks is very good. ' Tom ' has been gassed and got a bit of shrapnel, but is quite well again. I am going back on the 25th for fourteen days' rest, which I think we earned."

A later report of 'Tom' is as follows:

"No. 10 Cross Spaniel has been on the Ypres Sector for the last twelve months, having done some good work bringing back some urgent messages from the Ninth Division and the Highland Light Infantry, being gassed and wounded in the shoulder, and getting some very close shaves from shrapnel going through the barrage. Was in the advance until it finished."

Keeper Nicolson seems to have brought his dogs through a gas attack well.

"I have tried my three dogs in the trenches and found them all very satisfactory. The first time I sent them forward, 'Jim,' the dog without a number, did record time; the journey he did used to take a man one hour and ten minutes to walk, and 'Jim' did it in twenty-two minutes, through barbed-wire entanglements, and a large number of batteries. I noticed when he got near home some of the gunners tried to draw his attention, but he took no notice, and came straight to the pill-box where I was billeted. It was very difficult ground he had to travel, and the other two dogs were a bit slow. We are in again for the second time, and I tried all three. 'Jim' was sent up to the Test Station yesterday afternoon, and did his journey in seventeen minutes, which would have taken a man three-quarters of an hour to walk, and the little Irish terrier was sent up this morning before daybreak and he did the same distance in fourteen minutes.

"The night before last we had a very nasty attack of gas, and my dogs' helmets were not available, so they had to stand bare-faced, and took no harm. I think they will stand it much better than man. I had a bit of trouble with 'Jim.' He got wounded in the head, so I dressed the hair off, and got a syringe and some dressing from a Red Cross man, so he is doing very well."

Keeper Osbourne gives an interesting instance of his dog 'Jim' notifying the approach of gas. This was a small cross-bred retriever spaniel and was a most intelligent little animal, and is a different dog from the 'Jim' mentioned in the foregoing statement.

MESSENGER DOG.
Message being inserted in collar for return to headquarters.

MESSAGE RECEIVED.
A distance of three miles has been covered by these dogs.

p. 200.

Keeper Osbourne's Statement :

" You will be highly gratified to learn that little ' Jim,' by his excellent services and consistency, has justly earned our C.O.'s commendation, who thinks he is easily the finest dog we have in France.

" One or two of his services to wit. While in the recent offensive in Belgium, he carried important dispatches in wonderful quick time, and it is certain no one else could have delivered such dispatches under such terrific and heavy shell-fire without meeting with bodily harm.

" At present we are on a much more quiet part of the front, where long distances of trenches have to be traversed, and invariably little ' Jim ' covers the distance of approximately four kilos. in the very good time of fifteen minutes. And I feel sure you will agree with me that with his consistency this wonderful little dog is invaluable.

" On another occasion while in the first-line trenches, little ' Jim ' was instrumental in first giving the warning of gas, due no doubt to his highly-sensitive nose ; thereupon he was immediately released with the warning to Headquarters, arriving there a little more than three-quarters of an hour earlier than the warning given by wire. His worth is beyond value, and his services beyond praise, and I feel honoured to take care of such a very serviceable animal.

" At such times when gas is about I have to see to the putting of ' Jimmy's ' head in a man's P.H. smoke helmet, and I should be greatly pleased if you could inform me where to secure a mask for his proper protection, as, of course, a P.H. helmet is made solely for the requirements of a man, and does not adequately safeguard a dog.

Official Report of Above Dog " Jim " :

" Dog 36.—Black. Cross between retriever and spaniel, about three years old. Brought from England by Pte. Osbourne and worked with 1/6th R. War. R. since August, 1917. The most reliable dog ; has often done distances up to 4½ miles.

" The speed in covering this distance was proved to be three or four times the speed of a runner."

Keeper MacLeod gives an account of the way the dogs under his control picked up, after being gassed, and of the plucky behaviour of little " Paddy " in reporting himself at Headquarters, although wounded and left for dead. In it will be seen one of the many instances of courage and determination displayed by these dogs. " Paddy " was an Irish terrier.

" I left for France with three dogs in Nov. 1917, and went back to my old Division—the 34th. The G.O.C. Divison appeared to be greatly interested in the dogs—that alone gave me some encouragement to do my best for the dogs.

" I went into the line at the back of Monchy, and kept my dogs beside me for a day. They were taken up on the second night. They were sent back in the morning with a trial message, and all three of them did well. They were kept there for a fortnight, always running home in the morning. They never made any mistakes at all. We were sent into the line on December 27, until the end of January——five weeks, during which time the dogs ran once every 24 hours, covering the distance—a little over five kilos—in something like 20 minutes, over very rough country, which always took the runner over one hour. The dogs always brought messages, and usually saved a midday runner.

" We left on April 14, 1918, and went up to Hazebrouck with the dogs ' Whitefoot,' ' Prince,' ' Paddy,' ' Mop,' ' Shag,' ' Swift,' ' Lloyd,' ' Jack,' ' Jock,' ' Wolf,' ' Tim,' and ' Champion.'

" When the 29th Division came in, and relieved the 31st, there was a small advance made then—the dogs did great work then—that was in Nieppe Forest Sector. The G.O.C. 88th Brigade wrote out, and had a note typed of which I got a copy, giving great praise to dogs 83, 94 and 65. The first two were ' Jock ' and ' Bruno,' and the other ' Champion.' That was the first official praise we had from anyone. Then came another small advance, which proved the mettle of three more dogs, ' Whitefoot,' ' Paddy,' and ' Mop.' The first two were badly gassed, but carried on. They were three weeks in hospital after they came out of the line, but during the gas bombardment they never failed to give the greatest satisfaction. Once again there was a slight advance made, in which two dogs, ' Bruce ' and ' Blue Boy,' were to the fore. Bruce came four different times from the front line to Brigade Headquarters, with messages which were of great importance.

" ' Blue Boy ' was killed in the first attempt to cross over from an outpost to the Headquarters. Two runners had been badly knocked out trying to get through.

" About this time there was another slight advance in the Nieppe Forest Sector, but nothing out of the ordinary took place. At that time, ' Paddy ' was badly gassed in the front line, and came right back to the Section Kennel—a distance of 17 kilos. When he came in he was totally blind, but went direct to his own kennel and lay there till I went to his assistance. In three hours he had his eyes open again and was as lively as ever. We were then transferred to the 19th Corps Signals in and around Kemmel Hill, and between that and Ypres. The first time that any dogs were in that part they did not do anything worth mentioning.

" However, there was going to be a big stunt on that front, and all the men and dogs were taken into the line together and placed by the Brigade Signals Officers who were in charge. The first message to come through was brought back by the dog ' Roman.' He brought through a request for reinforcements in men and ammunition, thereby saving a nasty situation. At the same time ' Paddy ' was again in the wars. He was led nearly up to the top of Passchendaele Ridge with the Infantry ; he was along with an officer and a runner at a farm-house which contained Germans. A German came out and took a revolver and shot the dog, which was left on the field for dead. He had laid there a long time before he came to himself. He reported at Brigade Headquarters, and word was sent to me to go and fetch him as he was badly hit."

The dog " Roman " mentioned at the end of Keeper MaCleod's statement, was a pure-bred tri-colour collie, of the show type, carrying a splendid coat, and with a long narrow head. He was a curious character, rather self-centred, and fond of taking his time on the journey, but imbued with a strong understanding always of the absolute necessity of making his way homewards. In this connection

I may here remark, that it is instructive and interesting to watch the growing of conscience—the sense of right and wrong in the dog while under training. As the idea of duty becomes implanted in its mind, the uneasiness at stopping at any point en route becomes gradually more marked. A promising dog that is beginning to understand the high responsibility that is placed upon it, even if it is tempted to linger, will generally make good, by increasing its pace when starting again.

It is amusing to come across two or three dogs, at a point some distance from home, and watch them unobserved. They are going back with their messages, and are keeping up a steady lop, generally led by the best dog. Suddenly something will attract one of them, and they may even all stop for a minute. The dog that knows its work best, however, will not long tolerate delay, and it soon trots off, and now sets the pace at a fast gallop, which the others are bound to follow.

While it is, of course, better that each dog should make its journey alone, it is impossible, while under training, and when sometimes fifty or sixty dogs are out in various directions, to keep them entirely separate, when they are released to bring their messages home. But in the long run it is a point of not much importance, as even if a promising dog may be momentarily detracted from the path of complete obedience, by one less trained or less conscientious, he himself will sooner or later come to see that it is much better to go straight, and will assist in impressing this on his more faulty comrade.

The dogs " Paddy " and " Roman " are both mentioned in the following official report.

Official Report:

" Dogs.—These were most useful. In the right Brigade the first intimation received that the final objective was reached was brought back by a dog in 40 minutes. Dog 54 was shot and wounded by a German officer, who in turn was shot dead by an officer of the 6th Wiltshire Regiment. This dog was reported killed in error by the Brigade, as it subsequently turned up. In the left Brigade a message by a dog was received in 50 minutes, saying that the Bluff had been captured—distance covered 6,000 yards. Another important message came back by dog which was of importance to the Division on our left.

" Some of the dogs had never been in the line before, and, considering this, their work was good throughout."

Unfortunately poor " Blue Boy," after faithful service, laid down his life at Nieppe Forest. Keeper Matheson speaks of him when working under his charge.

Statement of Keeper Matheson :

" I had two very good dogs and they did very good work. No. 67, a Bedlington, 'Blue Boy' by name, was a very reliable dog ; he did very good work when the enemy tried to take Mount Kemmel last year. He was shot at Nieppe Forest, bringing a very important message, as the 31st Division was held up. The poor dog was liberated under a barrage of machine-gun fire, and was killed on me.

" Poor old 'Mop,' No. 60, did very good, and would run a message, say four miles in 12 minutes. She was very reliable."

To revert once more to the subject of pure-bred dogs, I may mention a collie called " Nell," which was one of the first to go to France. This was a sable and white, perfectly pure-bred dog, sensitive and highly strung, and to look at her one would have thought there was no room in her narrow skull for brains. Nevertheless, she developed very wonderful intelligence, and worked steadily to the end of the war. It can safely be said that this dog alone saved hundreds of lives. She is now living in honourable seclusion, in the home of her keeper to whom she was devoted.

Keeper Dowdeswell tells of the wonderful sense of duty displayed by his dog " Smiler," which was a lurcher cross. The dog brought his message in safely, although severely wounded.

" I am sorry to have to tell you that I have lost poor old

'Smiler.' The Staff Captain had taken him up the line and sent him back with a message, which he brought back in 20 minutes—a distance of three kilos. The poor old fellow's jaw was hanging down, being fractured by a bullet. I knew there was not much hope for him, but I took him to the A.V.C. after binding him up, and they immediately shot him. He had been going up the line with the General each morning and bringing his messages back in good time always. The General was very fond of him, and told me yesterday he was sorry I had lost him."

After the first few months of experimenting, I was able to bring the training of the dogs to gunfire up to a much more effective standard, and shell-shock became much the exception. Keeper Swankie, who went out early with two dogs, "Creamy" and "Ginger," mentions an unpleasant experience whereby "Ginger" suffered from shell-shock.

"I left here in September for Poperinghe, was there for five days, then went to Canal Bank with the 18th Divisional Headquarters, from there to Varna Farm, where I was attached to the 54th and 55th Brigades. It was there both my dogs were blown up by a shell. I found one that night, but lost the other one for three days. My first night there, which was by no means comfortable for me or my dogs, I had to stand all night with my dog by my side. Next morning 'Creamy' was taken out by the Brigade Major to the front line trenches, leaving at 7.30 a.m. Released at 1 p.m. arriving back 1.25 p.m. with a few messages and a map of the new position taken that morning, Poel Capelle Brewery. Approx. distance six kilos., time taken 25 minutes. The third day 'Ginger,' my other dog, was brought back to me, and I found he had shell-shock. I tried my best to cure him, but without success."

"Ginger," however, greatly recovered later on, and was constantly in use in the field. Keeper Swankie's report continues:

"On one occasion the Division General came to see the dogs' work. Their duty that day was to carry two messages sent out by message rocket back to Brigade Headquarters, a distance of 1,000 yards—time taken, three and a half minutes.

"After we had got the kennels fixed up, orders came for eight men and 24 dogs to go up the line. I was amongst them and next morning went to Gentilles Wood, where I was attached to the 47th London Division. The dogs did splendid work there, and were working day and night. I lost one dog there, an old collie—he had carried five messages that day, and was on his way back with his sixth one when he was killed by shrapnel. By this time the French had taken over that part of the line, and we had to go to a place called Vignecourt where we were attached to the Australian Corps. My first trip up the line from there was to a place called Villers Bretonneux, where I was for seven days, and during that time my dogs were working day and night. From there I went back to the compound for seven days' rest, then back to Villers Bretonneux for another seven. This time it was pretty rough in this part and the dogs had plenty of work and did it well."

The dog "Creamy" was a cream-coloured cross-bred lurcher with a semi-rough coat—a most affectionate and intelligent messenger. It did most of its work under Keeper Swankie, to whom it was greatly attached. A further statement as to its work is as follows:

"The last time this Division (18th) was in action, I was sent to Brigade Headquarters. After being there for one night, my dog 'Creamy' was taken out during an attack and carried a map of —— also a message from the front line trenches back to Brigade Headquarters. Time taken was 25 minutes, whereas a man took from two and a half to three hours. Under the conditions and heavy shell fire, it was very good, and my officers were highly pleased with it, for the map and message were very important, and all other means of communication at the time failed."

Further testimony as to "Creamy's" sagacity is sent Keeper Reid:

"I may say that Swankie's bitch 'Creamy' helped the 3rd Londoners from being cut off on the right of Villers Bretonneux. She and 'Tweed' kept the Battalion in touch with Brigade Headquarters. There was no way of getting a message through, only by a runner or a dog, and the dog kept the way open."

Keeper Reid makes the following statement regarding his own dogs:

"I am writing this to let you know how my dogs are doing. I may say I have tried them all ways and they come home. To-day I had 'Tweed' and 'Jock' acting Battalion runners from Battalion Headquarters to transport lines, and they have done splendid. I had 'Tweed' up the line and brought back a very important message through heavy shell fire. I am highly satisfied with my dogs.

"On May 2, 1918, I was sent to the 18th Division. There were no dogs that had been up before. On May 2, at 10 p.m., the Hun came over on the Q.V.R.—my dog was up at their Battalion Headquarters. They were cut off from the London Regiment; they released 'Tweed' with the message: 'Send up reinforcements and small round ammunition.' He came through a Boche barrage—three kilos. in 10 minutes. The French were sent up, and filled the gaps, and straightened out the line, otherwise Amiens would be in the hands of the Germans. On May 8 I was with the Australians, 48th Battalion. They had moved forward, no runner could cross the open in the daytime—pigeons could not fly at night; they were in a bad place, so they sent for 'Tweed.' He made three runs at night, and one of the runs he was out on patrol; they sent him back with a message, 'The Germans are preparing for a raid,' and spoiled the Huns' plans."

The dog "Tweed" mentioned in the above statement performed some wonderful services. He was a Highland sheep-dog, and took rather longer to train than usual, owing to his highly-sensitive nature; in fact, he was nearly rejected altogether, and it was only through the urgent representation of Mrs. Richardson, who discerned "Tweed's" fine character through his shyness, that he was retained and his training persevered with. Patience and great gentleness in handling eventually overcame his reluctance and timidity, and the clever management of "Tweed" in the field by his keeper brought this dog up to a very high standard.

A further account by Keeper Reid shows that the messages brought by the dogs, besides being frequently of the most vital importance, were at times of comparatively minor value, such as this one with the request for socks, but which, nevertheless, would make the greatest difference to the comfort of the troops:

"For six months the three dogs were in constant work from the line. This same dog was with my Battalion, 13th R.H.C., at Passchendaele on November 8, 1917. The Battalion had to go in and support the 3rd Canadian Division. The O.C. wished dry socks for his men. There was no way to get a message back in daytime; he released 'Tweed' with message 'Moving forward to-night. Send socks for men and some S.O.S. lights."

"Tweed's" fine behaviour at Amiens, mentioned by Keeper Reid, deserves special commendation, and there are other occasions that stand out particularly when other dogs did specially brilliant service. The attack at Kemel Hill brought many of them into prominence. Amongst others, two dogs called "Flash" and "Boxer" deserve mention. The former was a brindle lurcher, the latter was a large, powerful Airedale. They were devoted to their keeper, Dixon. He reported on these two dogs as follows, soon after he arrived in France with them:

"The two dogs I took out are doing well, I should say exceptionally well. I have not the least hesitation in saying there is not a brace of better dogs in this or any other country as messenger dogs. 'Boxer,' the Airedale, is running like an engine. The lurcher bitch 'Flash' beats him on this week's running by 20 minutes, which is not a lot considering the breeds. The General of the——Division said that the Airedale was the best dog he had seen. 'Boxer' was a bit long on Thursday; he had been at some carcase and tried to steal past into his bed, but I saw him—he knew he had done wrong. The conditions are very bad for running dogs—such a lot of rubbish and dead carcasses and abandoned cook-houses, etc."

In this report will be seen the temptations which confront the messenger dog in the field, and to which poor 'Boxer' at first succumbed. The distinguishing sense of right and wrong is very highly developed in many dogs, especially in those which are trained, and "Boxer's" sense of duty evidently rose above the temptations of the flesh, as Keeper Dixon later reports on him:

"A staunch, reliable dog, ran steadily, and never let me down. Best time 3 miles in 10 minutes. On one occasion he went over the top with the Kents. Released at 5 a.m. with important message. He jumped at me at 5.25. A tip-top performance—about 4 miles. A great dog!"

"Flash" was a very fast, clever dog, and Dixon reports:

"She ran every alternate week except two, and was never once behind time."

These two dogs were both at Kemmel Hill. Dixon states in this connection:

"About the best week's running I did, in my opinion, was at Kemmel Hill in October, with the 34th Division, when all my dogs did well. The times seem slow, but they were really good, as the dogs were running belly deep in mud. It took a man two hours to go to the line. The conditions were horrible."

Keeper Hedley testified to the good work of his dogs at this time, and also during the last offensive of the war:

"I can faithfully say my dogs did excellent work, especially on two occasions. The first offensive which the Germans made on Kemmel Hill between the dates of April 16 and April 25, 1918, and the second was when we made the large offensive commencing September 28, 1919, at Ypres. They came back in splendid time."

TYPICAL GROUP OF MESSENGER DOGS.

ONE OF LIEUT.-COL. RICHARDSON'S AIREDALES
Trained to lay signal wire on a supposedly dangerous zone and thus to save human life and time.

(*See page* 259.)

Keeper Young had in his charge a very good cross-bred dog called "Dane." He was a powerful dog and did his work faithfully and well:

"'Dane,' No. 29, he did good work all the time, but I did not know what the messages contained, but during the German offensive on Kemmel in April, 1918, he fetched the situation reports every morning for 10 days, sometimes when all other communications were broken and very heavy shelling going on."

Keeper Brown had two good dogs, but unfortunately there is a tragedy in his report following the dog's good work at Kemmel Hill:

"My dogs have done very good work in the field. I was on the Hazebrouck Sector part of last summer and my dogs, 'Trusty,' No. 79, and 'Peter,' No. 78, were doing good work there taking messages, and then I went to Kemmel Hill, where they were taking in messages day and night. The Officer i/c Signals there was highly pleased with the work the dogs had done, taking in messages day and night, and I went from Kemmel Hill to the Ypres Sector, where my two dogs were killed with one shell, also the runner that was taking them to the front line—that was on September 28. I was very sorry to have them killed as they were very good dogs."

The official report on the work of the dogs at Kemmel is as follows:

"On April 17, during the German attacks on Kemmel Hill, three more messenger dog groups were sent up by road to 22nd Corps, and re-allotted straight away by them to the 9th Division. These dogs were sent to Scherpenberg, which was the advanced 9th Divisional Headquarters. When they arrived, however, the Division was already retiring, and the groups were left for the use of the Brigade. It is of interest to note, that these dogs did sterling work between Kemmel and Scherpenberg, during the whole of the German attack on Kemmel Hill.

The report continues :

" The messenger dog groups, which had been allotted to the 15th Corps had been re-allotted by them, two groups to 1st Australian Division, and two groups to 1st Guards' Brigade. The Australian Division re-allotted one group for use with their Brigade at Flêtre, and one group was used with the 2nd Brigade at Borre. The 1st Life Guards used their two groups in the Forest of Nieppe. These two groups were used by the 1st Guards' Brigade during the heavy mustard gas attacks on April 22, which caused so many casualties. Two out of the twelve dogs were badly wounded, and all the dogs suffered from the gas, although they ultimately recovered.

" Exceptionally good work was done by these dogs through the forest of Nieppe, and interest in the messenger dogs, as a means of communication in heavily shelled areas was aroused."

I may say here, that during a tour of inspection which I made during the war, I myself saw the dogs working through the Nieppe Forest, and was greatly pleased with the manner in which they negotiated this difficult sector.

After the Armistice, I again made an entire and close inspection of the entire battlefields, with the object of studying the various sorts of surfaces the messenger dogs had to traverse. The Ypres sector is, of course, one of the worst, and in this shell-torn ground the dogs must have had all their energies called out. In wet weather, when every step brought a risk of drowning in the terrific shell-holes to the human runner—and this apart from the ceaseless firing—a message would have a far greater chance of being brought through safely by a dog. If the dog fell into a hole, it could easily swim and scramble out, and it would certainly be able to negotiate these obstacles much more quickly, creeping lightly along the lip of the craters.

At Passchendaele also, the terrible slope presented unending dangers to anyone forced to move rapidly, and here, too, excellent work was done by the dogs, which would have been appallingly difficult, if not impossible to runners.

Other parts of the line presented different features, but

in every sector I came to the conclusion that message carrying could be carried out with far greater dispatch and certainty, as long as the rules for working were enforced, and the troops given a good understanding of the work the dogs were doing.

As showing the tremendous amount of ground covered by the messenger dogs during their work in the war, I may quote from the official report on this point, which even then only deals with the time after the formation of the dogs into concentrated service, and does not take into account the period previous to that, when they were allotted to battalions.

" During the nine months the Messenger Dog Service was working as a complete service, the three section kennels were moved thirteen times, and shifted practically from one end of the line to the other.

" During this period section kennels were placed at Kruistraatt, Kemmel, Noordpeene, Wallon Capell, Morbeque, Hinges, Villers au Bois, Viller Bocage, Vaux, Dury, Menin, Blandain, Lille.

" Both at Lens and Villers Bretonneux, dogs had to run through towns, which the enemy daily saturated with mustard gas. At Lens especially, the dogs were called upon to use their intelligence."

Another portion of the official report reads :

" Proceeded to Battalion Headquarters of 1/14 Rifle Brigade. The C.O. who had been using messenger dogs from the front line trenches back to the ramparts at Ypres, told me that all the dogs he had used had done extremely well and proved very reliable.

" Visited A.D. Signals 19th Corps, who showed me some reports which had just arrived in from different divisions on messenger dogs. The divisions continue using their dogs, and taking them up with them as the troops advance. Excellent use is being made of the dogs, and in two cases, the first news that their objectives had been taken, was brought in by messenger dogs."

Keeper Errington in the following report gives an account of his three dogs "Jack," "Whitefoot" and "Lloyd." "Jack" was an Airedale, and the other two were Welsh terriers of a large size.

"I started running these dogs in difficult circumstances at Strazeele on April 14, 1918. The roads were busy with traffic, and stray dogs in abundance. Cattle, sheep, and poultry were being killed by the heavy shelling. We had 10 dogs running, in which the dogs were thoroughly tested. I found the greatest difficulty at first was the relay post. The dogs were sent to this post, a distance of two kilos., and had to wait there until another runner came to take them to the front line, one and a half kilos. The waiting here was from 30 minutes to two hours, therefore the dogs usually stopped at this point on the first few runs, but with practice it was soon all right.

"I started at Nieppe Forest (Hazebrouck Front) in May. The dogs did some excellent running—the distance was five kilos. at first, the average time 45 minutes ; the front got quieter and the distance was reduced to three and a half kilos. 'Whitefoot' acted as runner for Brig.-Gen. Taylor, who personally took the dog to visit his battalions in the line. After receiving the Intelligence Report, he released the dog, which ran to the Brigade Headquarters. Seven runs in succession. This dog's time was 23 and 25 minutes. The greatest difficulty here was gas which affected the pads of the feet, especially during damp or wet weather. 'Jack' was killed and 'Whitefoot' and 'Lloyd' were footsore, but soon were running again.

"During damp weather and when it was muddy and heavy running for dogs, I used to clip the hair between the toes (pads) that prevented any gas in the mud from adhering to the feet and causing inflammation.

"At the taking of Villers Bretonneux in August 'Lloyd' arrived in 10 minutes, after being released, and was slightly wounded in fore leg, the message stating that 'their objective had been taken.' 'Whitefoot' ran the distance in 12 minutes, with a message asking for stretcher bearers or R.A.M.C. men.

"During October the enemy was falling back, and we

were moving every other day although we still kept running the dogs. On October 14 the dogs were taken to the firing line and had to cross the Canal by boat. They were liberated on the 16th by the Scottish Rifles. No. 59 message was 'they were still advancing.' Time 65 minutes—distance unknown. 'Lloyd' was killed by shell and was found several days later. During this running, I found that dogs ran faster and keener if they were on strange ground, but should, as far as possible, have at least 10 hours in their new home to give good results, but in cases we have run them after only two hours and with good results. 'Whitefoot' never failed once, and was very reliable and fast. 'Lloyd' was also a good dog, but not so fast.

"In one division on certain days there was no communication by telephone, as they suspected the enemy of tapping the wire with some instrument, and the dogs did the running, which was usually a list of requirements to be taken up at dark, as no one was allowed to travel during daylight.

"The dogs kept in good health, and the food was all right, and the veterinary surgeons were always ready to give any help."

Keeper Errington's remark on the length of time which the dogs should be given in a station should be commented upon. What he says is, I think, perfectly sound, namely, that the dogs should be given, if possible, a day in a new point. He, however, has found, he says, that they have worked with good results after only two hours in a new place. This rapidity of adapting themselves to a new environment has been confirmed by other keepers. On many occasions the dogs have arrived at night and within an hour or two have been taken up through the darkness to the front line, to be released in the early morning. This sense of direction and remembrance of where they last left their keepers is certainly marvellous. It points to a sense of location, which, in the human being, is much less developed.

The rate of speed with which the dogs accomplish their journeys was, of course, an important point, and the following statements from different keepers touch on this. While a rapid dog was of greater value than a slow one, still the question of reliability is the most important point of all, and a dog which might not make such a brilliant show on the time sheet, might nevertheless be worth its weight in gold on account of the absolute certainty of its steady if somewhat slower return. On this point Keeper Macgregor says:

"I wish to let you know that my dogs are doing well over here. I have them running from one company to another. The retriever did eight kilos. in a little over half an hour, and the other in 20 minutes."

Keeper Ferriby sends the picture of his dogs with their running prize, the result of a competition:

"I am writing to let you know that my mate, Woof and I won the silver cup with my three dogs 'Coffee,' 'Vulcan,' and 'Sharp.' The latter is the dog which I brought out with me. He has done 1 mile in 1 minute, 50 seconds.

Keeper Bevington, in the following report, speaks with pride of the rapidity with which his dogs returned to him, and the trouble to which he went to verify the timing. The fact may also be observed that the dogs had to start their work after being only two hours in their new quarters:

"I was sent up to No. 3 Section at Amiens, and all three dogs were sent up with the troops. In that big attack on July 4—you will remember that, as the Americans were in it for the first time—two of the dogs were taken over the top in the attack with the Australians, and No. 106 did a good run also. 104 he did a very good run for the Artillery Officer. The forward observation post he ran from, and 105 was lost for a time, but in my opinion he was stolen, as I found him with some artillerymen on a different part of the front.

"The next important front where they were working was on the Vimy Ridge Sector, and they did some very good runs there. In one small attack there my dogs were sent up in the attack, and it was running on duck boards that time, not on open country, and they brought back all these messages in very good time as anyone can see by looking at their records, that should be at the 8th Army Corps.

" They also ran some very good runs at Maroc, from Hart's Crater and Harrison's Crater. Then we began to advance, and our kennels were in Hythe Tunnel. This will show that my dogs were very fair dogs—they were sent out of the tunnel to the forward post Battalion Headquarters, a distance of three thousand yards, and came back in four minutes, with what I believe was an important message ; it was a map of the German lines. That four minutes' run was done by two dogs, 104 and 106, and you can imagine how they must have run to have done it in that time. It was a night run and was very dark. Anyway, I will convince you that what I have said is true.

" The two dogs came in to the tunnel. I got the messages out of the carrier and was half-way to the signal officer, when I was met by the R. E. corporal who said that my two dogs had been released. Of course, I told him that they had reached me—well ! he said, he would not believe it that a dog could beat a telephone message. Evidently when the dogs were released the telephone man had telephoned through to say the dogs had been let go. I was not satisfied ; I wanted the thing correct, so I went to the signal office and asked the man at the forward post what time he released the dogs, and he replied that they had been released exactly six minutes, so as it was a minute's walk from the kennels to the signal office, and with the time it took to get the messages out of the dogs' collars, I saw they did their run in four minutes, and there was not a dog beat that time.

" The last important place they ran, was from a wood that the Germans held part of, in front of St. Amand, near to Valenciennes. There was an attack there one night and my three dogs were sent in that. I may add that they had only been with me two hours at this place before they were sent up to the front line company, and they came back in fairly good time. The officer spoke well of them."

Keeper Waters had two black-and-white collies, " Pierrot " and " Domino." They were both handsome dogs, " Domino " especially. Unfortunately he had to be sent back from the line on account of shell-shock.

" I went to the 15th Corps on the 26/7/18, and went into

the line to the 9th Division near Meteren, and was sent to the 26th Brigade. My dogs were running through Meteren to Flêtre, about 6,000 yards. I had a black-and-white collie ' Pierrot.' He was a good dog, and did some very good work. The black-and-white collie, ' Domino,' was not of much use. He had been with No. 3 Section and had shell-shock, and would not run when there was any shelling going on. I then went to the 30th Division, 93rd Brigade, on the left of Flêtre. I went up the line with two dogs, ' Pierrot ' and ' Domino.' As there was heavy artillery fire on that front ' Domino ' was useless, but ' Pierrot ' made some good runs."

Keeper Fergusson, in his statement, confesses to his predilection for Airedales for the work, and while it is true that they are remarkably hardy dogs, and not inclined to be nervous under fire, I have convincing recommendations as to other breeds from keepers in the field.

" I consider the most useful dogs for the work are Airedales, pure or cross-bred. They have not great speed, but they are sure, and soon find their way on strange ground.

" The most outstanding instance of usefulness which I have on record was with my Airedale dog, ' Jock,' No. 73. He, on several occasions in the month of June, 1918, was taken forward with the attacking forces, and was sent back with messages stating that the positions had been captured, giving the estimate of casualties, and giving map references of the new line taken up. This dog, also ' Bruno,' dog No. 72, did many other good runs. I have omitted to state that the distance which ' Jock ' carried previous-mentioned messages was five kilos.—times ranging from 23 to 28 minutes (five kilos. = $3\frac{1}{2}$ miles) over rough ground swept by machine gun and shell fire."

Keeper Shayler, who gives the following report, was one of the earliest men to be trained. The whole Messenger Dog Service owes a debt of gratitude to those loyal keepers who gave their whole mind and energy to overcoming great obstacles in the first few months, when the work of the dogs was hardly understood at all by those in the field. It will be observed, from his statement, how much easier it was for both dogs and keeper to work where they were received with sympathy and interest.

"After one month's training of messenger dogs at Shoeburyness, I proceeded to France on July 13, 1917, with two dogs, one an old English sheep-dog, 'Betsy,' and an Airedale, 'Jim.' Landing at Le Havre, we entrained for Poperinghe, Belgium. I reported to the 14th Corps Headquarters. After four days there I went forward to Brigade Headquarters at a village named Elverdingh. This place was heavily shelled, but the dogs ran very satisfactorily for the first time under shell fire. I stayed there for about seven weeks. I then reported to the 19th Corps Headquarters, and then went forward to Ypres. I stayed there for two months. My dog 'Jim' was killed by a shell. He had been a good reliable dog. At this time of the Dog Service it was uphill work for both men and dogs, as the work was not properly understood in France. From Ypres I came out for a rest.

"The next move was to Flesquieres, near Bourlon Wood, but only staying there for a few days. The continual movements made it nearly impossible to use the dogs on this sector very much. In February I received orders for Central Kennels, Etaples. At this place men and dogs of the Service were made into sections of sixteen men and forty-eight dogs, with one sergeant. I was placed in No. 1 Section. On April 15, four men, including myself and dogs, proceeded to Nieppe Forest, Hazebrouck Section. These were the first to leave Etaples, and were for trial before the full sections were settled. I stayed in this sector for 10 days; the dogs proved satisfactory. They were sent forward a few hours after arriving at Brigade Headquarters, to the 2nd Corps Headquarters, at which place we made a Section Compound, other men and dogs being sent up to form this section.

"We only stayed there for three weeks, and then went to the 22nd Corps Headquarters at Houtkerk, which was the position of No. 1 Compound for some time. I went forward from Section Compound to Kemmel Hill Sector, 18th Brigade, 5th Division. At this position my dog 'Betsy' ran well and in good and regular time. I was relieved after seven days' work here, and returned to the compound, where the dogs were kept in training. My next week's work was at Ypres, where the dogs had a very difficult place to work, as they had only two ways of returning, either by going round to a bridge or through a tunnel under the canal bank. At this place my dogs worked for the York and Lancashire Battalions, for whom they carried good messages.

" My next place after a week at the compound was at Battalion Headquarters between Ypres and Kemmel Hill. This place was well under the observation of the enemy and heavily shelled, causing communication by wire to be frequently cut off, and making it impossible for runners to be used in the daylight, and so the dogs were very much called for. I was working here for the A. and S. Highlanders, 33rd Division. These men were good with the dogs, and my dogs carried good messages for this battalion. At this time I was doing 14 days in the line and 14 out. During these 14 days, my dogs worked for the Cameronians and Scottish Rifles, two good battalions for dogs. My next 14 days was the same position with the 1st Middlesex Battalion and 1st Queen's. At this time I had a new dog called 'Tiger,' who was a good reliable dog. I never knew him to fail. He carried good messages in very regular time. The route he ran over was very heavily shelled.

" At the end of 14 days, I returned to the compound, which was still at Houtkerk. I went forward again to the same place, reporting to the A. and S. Battalion Headquarters, and the 1st Battalion 118th Regiment, U.S.A., where 'Betsy' did some very fine work, always doing 12-15 hours' forward duty and returning in good and regular time. Usual time 10-15 minutes, often wet and covered in mud. The U.S.A. troops were good with the dogs. My dogs carried Dealed Code, maps and other messages from raiding troops. After being buried in this sector by a shell, I returned to Etaples, not going up again as the Armistice was signed."

Keeper Dempsey gives a graphic description of his work in the field. Conditions were, by now, getting much easier for the keepers, as the work of the dogs was understood by the officers under whom they had to work. At the same time it is extraordinary the amount of prejudice there has been to overcome. I have come across officers with a pile of official reports on successful dog work in front of them, and who have never themselves tested them, who blandly remarked that they did not believe in dogs. It is this unreceptive attitude to new ideas that has been at the bottom of so many mistakes in the war.

"My first turn in action was on the Kemmel front, where the dogs did very well, although the ground was very rough, in fact the conditions were very bad indeed. I stayed there for seven days, and was then relieved, and went back to Corps Headquarters for seven days. Then from there I went to Ypres Ramparts. During my seven days there my dogs carried very important messages day and night. On one occasion, when with the York and Lancashire Regiments, 'Paddy,' one of my dogs, carried a message, when all other means of communication failed. This message was about the artillery.

"Another of my dogs, 'Prince,' also carried sealed messages. I do not know what they were about, for the signal officer was awaiting the dog's coming in, and took the messages out. The time taken by 'Prince' was 15 to 17 minutes, while 'Paddy' did it in 10 to 11 minutes. The distance was 3½ to 4 kilos. The ground was very rough for dogs. 'Paddy' was gassed here, and still he carried on with his work day and night without fail. After my seven days there, I went back to Ypres again, and stayed in for 14 days with the 49th Division, my dogs carrying messages all the time. Sometimes the dogs were taken away in the morning, and released at night, then they would change, and would take them at night and release them in the morning. My dogs 'Prince and 'Paddy' always brought important messages. Most of them were sealed.

"The signal officer was always eager for the dogs to come in. In fact the officers, N.C.O.'s and men of the division were all interested in the dogs, and would trust them with all sorts of important messages. It took the runners one hour and five minutes to go from my dug-out, whereas it only took 'Paddy' 11 and 'Prince' 15 minutes.

The dogs can get over very rough ground far quicker than can a man. Later I got a very good dog called 'Rags.'

"I then went back to Ypres and got attached to the 29th Division. I used my three dogs there, each of the three bringing important messages, and coming in first-class time. I worked there for the Royal Dublin Fusiliers, Leinster Regiment, and K.O.S.B.'s, and they were all very well pleased with the dogs, as there was always a heavy bombardment on, and it would not be safe for a man to bring the messages. I then got relieved for seven days. I went back to the same division on the same front. They were preparing for a big push. It began on September 28. The Royal Fusiliers took two dogs, 'Prince' and 'Paddy.' They were away for two and a half days, as all the lines of communication kept good, but they got cut with shell fire, and both dogs were released with messages and returned all right. I do not know what the distance was to be exact. The officer told me he thought it was about nine kilos.

"It was raining very hard during that time, and that made the ground very difficult to get over with the heavy shell fire and troops advancing. I then got relieved and came back to Houtkerk. I stayed there 10 days, training and exercising the dogs. I then got orders to go up the line, and got attached to the 36th Division. I joined the 107th Brigade, 36th Division, two miles from Dadeszeele, and stayed for one night and marched into Dadeszeele, next morning at 3.30 with Brigade Headquarters. My dogs were taken away at 4 p.m. and the division advanced about ten kilos., October 14. On the 16th two of my dogs, 'Prince' and 'Rags,' arrived with messages. While I was with the 107th Brigade, Keeper Buckingham was with the 108th Brigade.

"On the morning of the 14th this division advanced, and the enemy put up a terrific barrage. All the lines of communication were cut and a battalion released a dog, which returned to Buckingham, and thus gave news of the plight of this battalion. The dog was thus the means of getting reinforcements sent up to the relief of the Inniskillings, and that gallant body were saved from being wiped out. The Brigadier-General was delighted with the dogs' performance, and congratulated Buckingham on his management of them."

The "Paddy" mentioned by Keeper Dempsey is a different one from that in Keeper Macleod's possession, and which has been mentioned earlier. There were several Irish terriers in the Service, and I am afraid the tendency to call them all "Paddies" was too strong to overcome, although there were also a number of "Mikes" and "Mickies." Keeper Hammond had a "Paddy" upon which he reports favourably:

"I left Shoeburyness the first week in October, 1917, taking with me two dogs, 'Paddy' and 'Nansen.' I first ran them at Passchendaele, and was on that sector until the beginning of March, 1918. 'Nansen' was killed on the first run, but 'Paddy' was a splendid dog, and never made a mistake during the six months I had him. I consider his best record was carrying a message from Battalion Headquarters on Passchendaele down nearly to Ypres, a distance of five miles, over about three miles of duck-boards. You can imagine the time saved when 'Paddy' did it in 27-30 minutes, and the Battalion runners were doing it in nearly two hours. After being transferred to the Messenger Dog Service, I did not go up the line again, as I had suffered severely from shell-shock, and my health gave way. Ramsey took 'Paddy,' and I have no doubt at all that he is one of the best dogs that ever went to France."

Keeper Alcock gives an account of a very nice collie he had:

"*Re* No. 140. This dog went over the top with three or four brigades of Australians on several occasions. One occasion, in particular, was when an attack was made on Villers Bretonneux on the Somme. He came back with a dispatch 'Urgent,' which contained the details of the attack—a distance of 4½ kilos. in 18 minutes. There was very heavy shell fire at the time. While in front of Douai this dog advanced roughly seven miles, and brought the only message received when Douai was captured, as all the wires were broken. He completed his journey in 55 minutes. The other dogs I had were taken out in attacks and did good work also. I am sure they must have saved a large amount of life."

Another of the men was Keeper Corporal Coull. He took a very intelligent and conscientious interest in his work, helping to educate public opinion, as well as working the dogs. He states :

" Directly under my personal care were ' Buller ' (Airedale), ' Trick ' (collie), and ' Nell ' (setter bitch). At the outset ' Buller ' was somewhat inconsistent, but in a very short time he blossomed out into a very fine working dog, and did some very fine running. He carried messages, such as requisitions for ammunition, material, food, and the most common, but not the least important—the situation reports.

" When the Australian troops were making repeated attacks on the fronts between Villers-Bretonneux about April and May, the service of ' Trick ' was repeatedly and specially in demand, and on various occasions on that front he brought back the first messages of the progress of the attacks, and also requests for further materials necessary for the successful carrying out of operations. On one occasion special mention was made in divisional orders of the good work done by ' Trick ' and another dog, called ' Willard,' on the front of the left of Corbie. On that occasion ' Trick ' and ' Willard ' brought back the first message of an important and successful operation by the Australian troops. By his good work ' Trick ' was always sought out by any signalling officer when any message of importance and urgency was to be sent, and never once did he prove untrustworthy.

" A black retriever dog called ' Dick ' had a wonderful record, worthy of the V.C. While carrying a message in the Villers-Bretonneux Sector he was wounded very severely in the back and shoulder. The dog completed his run in good spirit, and was ultimately sent to the section kennel for treatment from the veterinary officer. As no foreign bodies could be located in the wounds, they were stitched up, and he was soon healed up and at work again. He did his runs in the line as well as before, and seemed all right when we moved to the 8th Corps. A day or two after moving the dog was seen to be suffering, and the attention of the vet. was called to his state. After a few days' observation, the veterinary officer concluded there was some foreign body in the wound, and so, as poor Dick was on the point of death, he was ordered to be destroyed.

" At the post-mortem examination it was discovered that a rifle bullet was resting between the shoulder and body, while near the small of the back a piece of shrapnel was found lodged close to the spine. Through all his suffering the dog carried out his duties cheerfully and most faithfully, until he was overtaken by death."

The keepers found considerable difficulty at first in working the dogs with the Australian troops, as the latter were somewhat indifferent in observing the regulations with regard to the dogs in the field. When, however, a commanding officer possessed the gift of discernment and recognised the real benefit of using the dogs, and seeing that they received proper treatment, the result appears to have been satisfactory.

Lieut-Colonel Owen H. Read, Canterbury Regiment, sends the following report :

War Dogs. " During the winter of 1917-18, while the Division was in the Ypres Sector, I had two of these attached to my battalion.

" Owing to the broken nature of the ground we were holding, and the bad weather which was experienced, communication between the Company and Battalion Headquarters was exceptionally difficult, and the dogs on several occasions proved of great value in conveying messages, when other means of communication failed, being far more rapid than runners, who in some cases were unable, owing to heavy shell fire to deliver their messages.

" Although the conditions in this sector were very trying, the dogs always carried out their work in a thoroughly satisfactory manner and were, on many occasions, of great assistance.

(*Signed*) " Owen H. Head, Lieut-Colonel,
" Canterbury Regiment,
" N. Z. E. F."

Another Australian officer told me that one of the sights that impressed him most was his first sight of a messenger dog. He saw it first coming from the direction of the front-line trenches—a little Welsh terrier. The ground it was going over was in a terrible condition, and was absolutely waterlogged. The little creature was running along hopping, jumping, plunging, with the most obvious concentration of purpose. He could not imagine what it was doing, until it came near, and he saw the message carried on its neck. As the dog sped past him he noticed the earnest expression on its face.

Keeper Sergeant Brown was a very intelligent handler of the dogs, and he not only worked then in a scientific manner, but he also did excellently in educating the men in the understanding of the benefit to be obtained by adhering to the regulations governing the dogs. He says:

"When the men understood the use of the dogs, I had no trouble, but before that they did not know they were being used as messengers. I got permission to go to the battalions in my division and give the men a lecture about them, and after that all went well. We then moved to another front. I looked over the ground and found it very rough, with holes and wire, and a great distance from the line—about 6 miles. The officer wanted me to work the dogs over this, which I did, for a few times, till my dogs were getting very bruised and cut, so I stopped them.

"The officer found the great use they were, as the men were taking about three times as long. I then worked my dogs in a very dangerous part, from the battalion to the post, as it was not safe for a man even at night, and the dogs worked at night. When the brigadier heard the work the dogs were doing, he wanted a great many more. I was then called back to the base, and they were anxious for me to leave the dogs behind, as they knew they had been the means of saving scores of lives. The runners were more than sorry, as they were always asking for more dogs. The old idea was that a dog's life was nothing, but after the experience I have had with them in the field, it has taught me to love and respect them as never before.

"I was moved to another sector, and after I had

explained the use of the dogs to the men, all went well, and one and all were surprised at their good work, as they had to run about three miles, through a forest, with streams and ditches. They were in the open and on the move all the time, and it was quite impossible for a man to get through the gas sometimes. The dogs worked there for three days, and then they required rest, as they were done up and some were wounded. One little bitch, 'Sulky,' nearly had her leg cut off, but it did not prevent her from coming in, and as it happened, she was carrying a very important message. On one occasion I sent a dog with an officer and his runner, who was going out on patrol, and when out on No Man's Land the officer was killed. The dog brought back the message and the position, so that another officer could be sent out. I also remember a dog being taken on a bombing raid, which was undertaken with the object of finding out just who was in front of us. The dog 'Vulcan' came back with some papers and a shoulder strap off a German's coat with the regimental number on it.

"On another occasion, in the advance on the Ypres Sector (1918), the same dog was taken over by the colonel of a battalion, but he was out of touch with the corps I was with, till the dog came in. I did not know what the message contained, but it was an important one, as this particular battalion wanted to keep up the advance, and they wanted the Belgians to advance as well, in order to make it a success, as they found little opposition in front of them and were well through.

"I understand also that the first news of the capture of Hill 60 was brought in by one of the dogs. On one occasion we had attacked a German sap, and were trying to hold it. We had run out of bombs, and the doggie was sent back with the casualty report, and for more bombs to be sent up."

The Americans had no dogs of their own, and viewed the messenger dogs with envy. Keeper Sergeant Brown says on this point:

"I had great trouble to prevent the Americans from appropriating the dogs, as they had no dogs of their own, and they all spoke of the great success of them everywhere."

Corporal Taylor sends the following report, in which will be seen the difference it made to the men when they came under an officer who took genuine interest in the work of the dogs, and also the difficulties experienced in working them, when the troops were not sufficiently instructed as to the importance of refraining from petting and feeding the dogs. This was constituted a disciplinary offence in the German army, and was severely punished.

"I landed in France with my two dogs, 'Major' and 'Maggie,' and was sent to my old brigade. Their headquarters were in an old slag heap, just to the rear of Hermies village. I did not get much help, nor did I find anyone very interested in the dogs at first, but on coming out of the line for a rest, I was taken over by the Brigade Signal Officer, Lieut. Parkes. He was very interested in the dogs, and did a lot for me. The consequence was, that next time we were in the line, the dogs were used night and day, with good results. We were in the line from January 25 till February 21, and the dogs were running from the front line to advanced Brigade Headquarters.

"At different times, our officer had silent days, when no wires were used, only runners and dogs. Of course, the dogs beat the runners every time, and never made one mistake. It was a very unhealthy spot—a lot of shelling. Poor 'Maggie' was shell-shocked. I buried her in a little hut I used to keep her in. It would have been a great thing if all officers had taken the same interest in their dogs as did Lieut. Parkes.

"I returned to Etaples when the Dog Service was reorganised, and my next venture was at Kemmel Hill, April 16, 1918, and went up with Keepers Young, Headly, Ferriby, Radford, and Ferris, with eighteen dogs. The men had nearly all the same dogs they brought from England. We went to the 9th Division, and ran the dogs for the 26th and 27th Brigade. Their Headquarters were just to the right of La Clythe. Here I found I was wanted to run dogs from Spoil Bank, close to the Canal, through Voormazeele, a distance of 14 kilos., so made a relay post at Ridge Wood, leaving Keepers Young and Ferris at Headquarters. It was here men and dogs had a rough time, as the enemy was doing a lot of heavy shelling, ready for his attack and capture of Kemmel Hill, 10 days later.

"My own dogs were 'Major,' 'Rab,' and an unregistered dog. The work was difficult for the dogs, as Brigade Headquarters moved about so much. After the dogs had done about six journeys, Headquarters moved, so that the dogs had to turn to the right on the Dickebusch Road, instead of to the left, where they had been running before, but four out of the six dogs did it all right. My bitch, 'Rab' was hit by a piece of shell on her second journey. She managed to stagger in with her message, but I could see there was not much hope for her. I bound her up, and carried her down to Brigade Headquarters, but she died the next day.

"I was watching for the dogs the next day to come in, and 'Major' and that fast bitch of Ferriby's—I forget her name—racing back over the ridge. As they were passing a battery of artillery, the enemy opened out with eight-inch stuff.

Ferriby's bitch was killed, but 'Major' got through. I could see that 'Major' was actually dodging the shells. He took a wide sweep from where the first shell fell, and kept working out further. The time for that run was a record—about six minutes. It took me an hour to walk and run the distance. Radford's dogs were doing the night duty, also Ferriby's, and never made a mistake. Hedley's dogs also did all that was asked of them. They were on day duty.

"I might mention here, that I found one or two of the dogs were losing time, so I went forward to find out the cause, and found them in a trench, on their chains, and a lot of pieces of bully beef put in a tin in front of them. Very kind, of course, but spoiling the dogs. I at once informed the signal officers of both brigades, and it was stopped. That was one of our greatest troubles—troops feeding and fussing about the dogs.

"On April 25, I was wounded in the attack by the enemy on Kemmel Hill, and was in hospital some time. I returned to No. 1 Section early in October. I only had one turn in the line, however, with my three dogs, as 'Jerry' threw up the sponge. I might say, that 'Major' was given to Keeper Hunt, when I was in hospital, and he did hundreds of runs for him. One run he did for Hunt is worth telling.

Taken forward in an attack, an advance was made of 17 kilos. without much opposition. 'Major' was then released by the Brig-General's orders with a message asking for help at once. 'Major' did the 17 kilos. in one hour. He isn't much to look at—a cross lurcher and deerhound—but a heart of gold."

The following report given me is of interest:

"In July, 1918, when the main force of the German attack had subsided, and our policy appeared to be to cut off small portions of German salients preparatory to the great general advance, small battalion offensives were in vogue, with a view to taking and consolidating strong points, from which larger offensives were eventually pressed forward. In these small offensives (which were more than raids, inasmuch that the ground taken was consolidated and held), the messenger dogs proved of invaluable service. Telephone wires were almost impossible from the front lines of newly-acquired territory, and, as these offensives were carried out invariably by night, pigeons were useless. The result of a raid, or minor offensive, giving the line captured and consolidated, had to be returned to Higher Command by runners, or dogs.

"In one instance in an attack on a small factory, half a mile west of Vieux Brequin, the attack had to cross very flat, swampy ground, with two small streams, the advance originating from the western edge of the Foret de Nieppe. The report that the attack had been successful, and a plan showing the line consolidated, reached Corps Headquarters by messenger dog in 50 minutes, the total distance being 13½ miles. (I regret I do not know how far from the Corps Headquarters were the kennels, and how much of the distance was done by the telephone, but I should say very little). The next report, which was a duplicate, sent off at the same hour by runner to Brigade Headquarters, and thence by telephone, arrived at Corps Headquarters one hour and thirty-five minutes after the messenger dog report arrived. This statement was published in Corps intelligence and in the 29th Divisional Orders of that month.

(*Signed*) "K. E. Milford,
"(Major R. F. A.)"

The record of the dog's work was kept by the keepers when on duty at the front, on time sheets.

The actual wording of the army instructions is as follows :

" It will be impossible, at any rate during the early stages of the advance, to depend upon telephonic or telegraphic communication in the forward fighting zone, the transmission of information will, therefore, depend principally upon wireless, visual signalling, liaison officers, messenger dogs, and pigeons."

Another part of the instructions read :

" Messenger dogs. A group of messenger dogs (two keepers and six dogs) should be assigned if possible to each battalion Headquarters. Their employment as message-carriers may save the use of runners. Dogs should be allotted to definite companies, and should always be released separately."

It was after the printing and issuing to the army of the above, that the reports from the front regarding the results of the use of messenger dogs were so satisfactory, and the demand for more was so insistent, that I received orders to immediately double the capacity of training and issue at the War Dog School. This was now the third time of enlargement. The Armistice, however, came at this moment, and the need of course ceased.

It may be pointed out here that the advantage which dogs have over pigeons is that the latter can only work from a fixed base, whereas the dogs can move their base almost continuously. Wherever they *last* left their keeper is their base. Also pigeons cannot fly at night or in mist, whereas these conditions present no obstructions to dogs.

In the event of another great war, it would be impossible to say just what form it would assume. No doubt the air fighting would take premier part, but it is safe to say that wherever infantry are used, dogs will always be of use as messengers, sentries, and carriers.

GUARD DOGS

The above reports among many received give a slight idea of the work of the dispatch-carrying dogs, but this was not the only service they were able to give.

Guard dogs were also trained and issued to stations all over the country.

The selection and training of these guard dogs was one of the chief duties of the War Dog School. As each dog arrived, it was first tested for dispatch-carrying, and if, after a time, it showed no aptitude for this it was then tested for guard duty, and put on a special part of the ground set aside for this branch of the training. The dogs rested during the day, and were trained at night, and the men, who were especially selected for the training of these guard dogs, rested during the day like the dogs, and came on for duty on night shifts.

The dogs were attached by a running chain to long wires, each fifty to one hundred yards long, fastened to stakes in the ground. Each dog had a kennel to retire to in case of inclement weather at night. The duty of the trainers was to advance at various distances and angles, and observe the growing acumen of the dogs, as their sense of sight, hearing, scent, and general alertness became trained.

I have already said that the demand for these dogs came at a time when the man-power question was becoming very serious. It was increasingly difficult for the stores, magazines, and filling factories to be adequately guarded. The advent of the dogs seems to have saved the situation, whereever they were employed.

It was further arranged that an N.C.O. from each protection company was to visit the War Dog School for two or three days' instruction in the proper placing of the dogs, in relation to the needs of his particular station, and also to be taught the correct method of management. It may be mentioned here, that on the correct placing and management of the dogs, depends the whole success of the idea. A list of regulations was carefully drawn up, based on a study of the dogs' needs when on duty. A well-trained dog will give valuable results if these regulations are carried out, and not one of them can be relaxed if the highest efficiency is desired from the dog. For instance, the rule that the dog must be removed during the day to a quiet spot to rest, is an extremely important one to observe.

Many people imagine that dogs can be on guard during the whole of the twenty-four hours, but this is not so. They need sleep as much as human beings, and it is better that they should have it during the day, when the property can be supervised by the sentries without assistance. Then the necessity of a short walk is also important, as is also correct feeding at the right time, which is on coming off duty in the morning. The result of these rules, properly carried out, is that the dog goes on duty very fresh, and quite comfortable in every way. Now the placing of the wires for the dogs round the areas to be guarded requires the exercise of intelligence and common sense. On one occasion I found the dogs placed close to a building inside of which there was a constant roar of machinery, whereby their sense of hearing was getting quite blunted.

In another case the dogs had their wires placed in such a way that the only footsteps they could hear were those of the sentries. These positions being adjusted, the dogs were able to carry out their duties properly.

The sense of guardianship, which is inherent in some dogs, and by judicious training can be intensified, is wonderfully shown forth in the following reports, chosen out of several hundreds of similar burden, which were sent in by the officials in charge of the dogs, at the various centres where the dogs were stationed. The great point to notice is the general consensus of opinion, as to the efficient manner in which the dogs did their work, also that in nearly every case, the presence of the dogs enabled the number of the sentries to be reduced, and giving to those remaining a greater sense of security.

In the first report, the dog is considered of greater value than a sentry:

Verwood Magazine

"I have the honour to furnish the following respecting the magazine guard dog under my charge at this station

I have not the slightest hesitation in stating that this dog was by far a greater protection than a sentry, and the part patrolled by him was undoubtedly absolutely secure; he was so generally feared by the people here, that they would not approach the precincts of the magazine, and have approached the county police with a view to getting the dog removed, a matter that met with no favour from me; the chief reason of this complaint was that the R.E. fencing was no boundary for him, as happened on two or three occasions.

"The dog's work consisted of night patrol, resting through the day, approximately 120 yards' run, and by the state of the track he did it well, as it was beaten to a hard path; the dog was secured to a lead, and this ran on a line extending the 120 yards, as it was not fixed near the fence, and a rather long lead; the dog did practically one half of the sentry work of the enclosure.

(*Signed*) "C. Monk,
O.C. Det., Verwood Magazine."

The next report confirms this opinion:

Thorne

"I beg to report that the dogs I had under my charge at Thorne rendered very valuable assistance to the sentries on duty, especially during the night.

"They were attached to wires, which enabled them to traverse the full length of the stacking ground, and it was practically impossible for anyone to approach the stacks without the dogs warning the sentry; in fact, in my opinion, they did their work quite as well as a flying sentry. At the least sign of any person approaching they were always on the alert.

"I have the honour to be, sir,
"Your obedient servant,
(*Signed*) "H. Denton, Cpl."

In the following report, the scenting power of the dogs has been noted:

Group of Army Guard Dogs.

p. 234.

North Walsham

" I have pleasure in informing you that the three guard dogs which have been used at Stalham, Martham, and North Walsham, have, in each instance, carried out their duties in a very satisfactory manner.

" By their use it was possible to mount only a single guard at night, instead of the double guard, as is usual in the case of guards for ammunition dumps.

" It has been found that these dogs will scent a stranger approaching at night a very considerable time before their presence was known by the soldier on his post, and, in my opinion, these dogs have quite justified their employment in ammunition dumps as watch dogs.

(*Signed*) " B. T. WARD, Major, R.F.A.
O.C. 1206th Battery, R.F.A.

" North Walsham, Norfolk."

I used generally to ask the officers to report to me any case of attempted aggression, but the fact of dogs being employed seems to have been sufficient in nearly every case in preventing anything of this sort. The next report illustrates this :

West Beckham

" The following report on the watch-dog doing duty with this unit is forwarded for your information :

" The dog was posted outside the entrance to the main ammunition dump of the 223rd Mixed Brigade. The possession of this dog enabled the military authorities to reduce the guard from fifteen men down to a patrol of seven men. The dog had wonderful intelligence—he knew the footsteps of the patrol, and when hearing strange footsteps he created a tremendous disturbance, thereby warning the occupants of the hut a few yards away from the dog's post.

" There was no instance of prevented aggression—it had become well-known that the dog was on the spot, and I think that this fact prevented would-be intruders from attempting to gain admission to the dump. I had one man told off to care for the dog—the animal got used to him—but no other man dared go near him.

"In my opinion, watch dogs are a great asset in the service, and I would like to see them fully utilised in the peace-time army.

(*Signed*) "B. S. BALL, Capt., R.F.A.
416th Amm. Column.

"West Beckham, Holt, Norfolk."

These reports all testify the saving of man-power:

Banbury

"With reference to a report on the work of the dogs, I can only say that experience has proved that the factory has been adequately guarded, and I am satisfied that the dogs have been an important factor in the guarding of our stores. Of the four dogs, three were placed on duty at dusk, and taken off at daybreak, each dog having one day off in four. Long runs were provided at each of the three stores, which contained large quantities of explosives.

"With the aid of the dogs, we were able to guard the whole of the stores area with six constables (two on each of five shifts of eight hours), whereas had it been necessary to place constables at each store, a matter I should have considered had we not had the dogs, this would have necessitated employing at least a further six constables. I am pleased to say that no instances of aggression have occurred at this factory.

"Yours truly,
(*Signed*) "H. F. SNOWBALL,
"General Manager.

"Banbury, Oxon."

Hayle

"In reply to yours, 25,000, dated February 12, 1919, one of the two dogs was kept at Pinhoe, and the other at Monks Road, Exeter, to assist in guarding stores of cordite at those places. On arrival of the dogs, the guard of each place was reduced from two N.C.O.'s and twelve men to one N.C.O. and seven men. There was a barbed wire entanglement round each store (formerly brick works), and the dog was kept inside the entanglement. There is no recorded instance of aggression having been prevented. The dogs were very intelligent and well trained, and quite well suited for their work.

(*Signed*) " WILLIAM THOMAS, Capt.,
" O.C. No. 251 Protection Company, R.D.C.

" Hayle."

Georgetown, Paisley

" I am pleased to inform you that the work of the war dogs on this station has been entirely satisfactory. To begin with, we had twenty-four dogs, three of which died, so that all through we have had twenty-one dogs, which were employed by night only on the loneliest and most dangerous posts to accompany the sentries, and relieve them of as much strain as possible. Each dog was attached to a long wire, which ran the length of the sentry's post.

" Had there been no dogs, it would have been necessary on many of the posts to have employed double sentries, so that the saving in man-power has come to about twenty men per night. There has been no occasion on which aggression was prevented by the dogs, although on many occasions their own aggression was a source of great inconvenience to visiting rounds.

(*Signed*) " P. FORREST, 2nd Lieut.,
" for O.C. No. 202 Protection Company, R.D.C.

" Georgetown, Paisley."

Colchester

" The unit under my command find the guards at three ammunition dumps, and I have had a war dog at each.

" The dogs have been on a running chain, and have enabled one post at least, at each of the dumps, to be dispensed with. They have only been employed at night. The dogs have released for other duties at least nine men.

"I have no knowledge of any instances of aggression at any dump.

(*Signed*) "I. H. CROSS, Major,

"Commanding 69th Protection Company, R.D.C.

"Colchester."

Dorchester

"I beg to report that there have been two dogs attached to guards under my command: one a chow, with the detachment guarding the Hamworthy Magazine; the other, a mastiff, with the detachment guarding the Verwood Magazine.

"The officer i/c of these guards reports that both these dogs have done excellent work; by their use I have been able to release six men on each guard.

(*Signed*) "J. WORTH, Major,

"Commanding Prison Guard, R.D.C.

"Dorchester."

Bourne, Lincs.

"Four of the dogs were utilised as sentries at the Holwell Magazine and proved most useful, particularly during the darkness of the winter months, and it was only necessary to have one post, employing three men by night and by day, the dogs doing the rest, thereby saving at least nine others.

"At Dudley, where only one dog was utilised, the same thing applies, the saving of three men from sentry go.

"Yours obediently,

"(*Signed*) Capt. ——

"O.C. 165th Protection Company, R.D.C.

"Manor House, Bourne, Lincs."

Newport, Mon.

"The number of men employed as sentries, on the police patrol system, was four for one post.

"To effectively guard the magazine, without the aid of

the dogs, would have necessitated twelve men for three posts, so that it may be taken that eight men were in this way released for other duties.

" The dogs were employed to give warning to the sentry on duty of the approach after nightfall of any person to the vicinity of the barbed wire fence surrounding the magazine enclosure. They were placed one dog on each of the four sides of the enclosure, inside the fence, and attached to a wire run of about twenty-five yards, parallel to, and about three yards from, the fence.

" No instance of actual aggression has been reported to me, but I have no doubt that the dogs acted as an effective deterrent, and may be considered as effective for the class of work on which they were employed.

(*Signed*) " M. BRUCE, Lieut.,
" O.C. Det., 331st Protection Company, R.D.C.

" Athletic Grounds, Newport, Mon."

Glenfield

" Five dogs were used here to guard the ammunition dump. They always gave warning of the approach of any strangers. The guard used to consist of eighteen men before the arrival of the dogs, and only nine after their arrival.

(*Signed*) " Pte. ——
" For O.C. Det. 136th Protection Company, R.D.C.

" Heather Brickworks, Glenfield."

St. Thomas

" I have to report that the dogs at this depot were used for guarding the premises, which at that time consisted of several scattered buildings and a large yard. Without these dogs it would have been necessary to have a standing guard of six men and one N.C.O. ; with these dogs it was only necessary to keep one man on night duty. This, I consider, was of great service, and proved a great saving to the public.

(*Signed*) " S. Bird, Lieut., R.A.S.C.
" Officer i/c Supplies, Exeter Sub-District.

" R.A.S.C. Haven Road, St. Thomas, Exeter."

At certain centres the dogs were used by the sentries on patrol duty, when they were usually taken out on the leash. The following reports illustrate this method of working:

Salterforth

" In reference to your order *re* dogs, the duty which the above were doing was magazine watch-dogs; each dog did about one mile patrol, on a lead, with a man. They proved satisfactory in every way, also whenever a civilian came near they would bark. The dogs were not on a loose wire, but always on a lead.

(*Signed*) " T. A. Aaston, Sergt.
" For O. C. 153rd Protection Company, R.D.C.

" Salterforth."

Newcastle-on-Tyne

"Two dogs which are being returned to 200th Company on the 12th inst., have been at Stockton Hay Storage, where they performed very useful work by giving assistance to the sentries under a very difficult patrol, on which there was a considerable amount of trespass. The dogs accompanied the sentries on their patrol, being on the leash, and almost invariably gave warning of an approach before the sentries heard it themselves.

" The dogs were used alternately on the Stock Yard, which was a very large one, and on the chopping shed and loading wharves.

" The latter was really a very difficult patrol, as the shed had, as well as the chopping machinery and supplies, forage in it, a lot of disused iron-rolling machinery, and covered a large area.

(*Signed*) " JAMES BRAND, Capt.,
" 151st Protection Company, R.D.C.

" Handysides Buildings, Percy Street, Newcastle-on-Tyne."

Aberdeen

" I have the honour to report that the work of the dogs with outlying detachments of this company has been satisfactory.

" It was estimated that these dogs were equal to one sentry, and a reduction in personnel of ten men was attributable to their presence.

These dogs are doing patrol work along with sentries on night duty, and were also employed inside barbed wire entanglements to prevent approach of unauthorised persons to certain Government property.

" No active aggression has been attempted, but notice was always given by the dogs barking freely at any strangers approaching, and also of people loitering in the vicinity.

" I have the honour to be, sir,
" Your obedient servant,
(*Signed*) " M. TAYLOR, Major.
" Commanding No. 214 Protection Company, R.D.C.

" Fonthill Barracks, Aberdeen."

Binfield

" The watch-dog at Binfield Magazine was worked as follows :

" Acted as sentry from 5 p.m. until 5 a.m. He used to patrol the magazine with sentries at the time of clocking up the tell-tale clocks every hour. No strangers dare come near—he always gave warning. Owing to his work, the guard was reduced from one sergeant and twenty-eight men to one corporal and six men. He did his work most satisfactorily, and we are sorry to lose him.

" For O.C. 6th Batt. City of London Regt."

The report of the dogs used at the Chislehurst Caves shows how useful they can be for searching this enclosed sort of ground:

Report on Two Dogs used at Chislehurst Cave

" These two dogs were used on patrol, and did the work in searching out the dene holes, undergrowth of the woods, and throughout the woods. On the word " Search," the dogs searched the undergrowth to look for suspicious persons, and I consider the work of the dogs was excellent. They were used for guarding ammunition stores in the caves.

" At night, without the dogs, it would have been impossible to patrol the woods. In these holes any persons could easily be concealed.

(*Signed*) " Corp. SPARK,
" For O.C. 103rd Protection Company, R.D.C."

Chislehurst

" I have the honour to report that war dogs which were under my command at Chislehurst were invaluable in the work they were used for.

" They were taken on patrol work, and used to search undergrowth and dene holes where it was impossible for a man to obtain a foothold.

In this case they did not release any men, the guard having been reduced before the dogs arrived.

(*Signed*) " E. H. RINSEY, Lieut.,
" For O.C. No. 103 Protection Company, R.D.C.

" Chislehurst."

It was found that these dogs very quickly distinguish between soldiers and civilians.

Report on Watch Dog at Verwood

" This dog was on duty from dark to daylight, working on a steel wire 140 yards in length; he took the place of one sentry by night. He was a very valuable dog in his services, being very dangerous to civilians and not allowing anyone in or near the magazine.

(*Signed*) " Pte. Gow,

" For O.C. 254th Protection Company, R.D.C.

" Verwood."

Ratby, Leicester

" Three dogs were used for guarding the munition dump; they were on wires during the night, but taken off during the day and fed once in the morning. If any civilians came near, they always gave the alarm, and would have attacked. Two sentries patrolled alongside the dogs at night.

(*Signed*) " Pte. ——

" For O.C. 156th Protection Company, R.D.C.

" Ratby, near Leicester."

Report on Watch Dog at Dartford, Kent.

" This dog has been on an attached post at Fort Halsted; he was used with the sentry on a lead from 10 p.m. to 6 a.m. He distinguished well between civilians and men in khaki, and he even knew the steps of the relieving sentry at night, but did not take any notice, while he always barked at the footsteps of civilians.

(*Signed*) " Rogers, Corpl.,

" For O.C. 118th Protection Company, R.D.C.

" Dartford, Kent."

Dringhouses

" The following four dogs, which were sent to Middleton Colliery, I found to be fierce when approached by a civilian. They were all capable of the duties for which they were intended:

" Black smooth-haired retriever, black curly-haired retriever, black and tan Airedale terrier, black and white cross-bred Pom, and English terrier.

(*Signed*) " A. Humphries, Corpl., N.C.O. i/c Guard,

" For O.C. 200th Protection Company, R.D.C.

" Dringhouses, York."

The moral effect of the presence of the dogs in most neighbourhoods seemed to be strong, as is shown in the following report :

Oldbury

" The establishment of this detachment guarding tanks and tank-testing ground was, previous to June 3, 1918, three N.C.O.'s and twenty-eight men, providing four posts, the men doing ordinary sentry go, two on and four off.

" With the advent of the dogs we were able to release eight of these men, the remaining twenty doing patrol work, four hours on, and twelve off, mounting the dogs with them at dusk, and relieving them soon after daylight.

" There were no particular instances where aggression was actually prevented, but the moral effect was great, as the general impression prevailed in the neighbourhood that it would be preferable to encounter an armed sentry than one of the dogs.

(*Signed*) " O. Stafford Lamber, Lieut.,
" O.C. Det. 261st Protection Company, R.D.C.

" Site ' C,' H. M. Factory, Oldbury."

There is strong evidence to show the greater sense of security which was felt by the sentries as the result of the presence of the dogs :

Loughborough

" I was in charge of six watch dogs at 156th Protection Company, Normanton Hill, Loughborough. I had six dogs on four posts ; they were posted just before dusk. The dogs were on wire runs about twenty yards in length, guarding a T.N.T. compound. They were satisfactory, and gave warning of any approaching strangers. The sentries felt more secure with the dogs than without them.

(*Signed*) " Bring, Corpl.,
" For O.C. 156th Protection Company, R.D.C.

" Loughborough."

Report on War Dogs' Services with 154th Protection Company, R.D.C.

(1) Barnbor	10-runs	6 sentries dispensed with.
(2) Middleton	4 runs	2 sentries dispensed with.
(3) Loisterdyke	5 posts	1 sentry dispensed with.
(4) Coldre Vale	2 runs	1 sentry dispensed with.

Work Done: Garrisoning

(1) Munitions factories.
(2) Explosives magazines.
(3) Forage store.
(4) Picric acid store dump.

How placed.—1, 2, and 4, on wire runs adjoining sentry posts. 3, Fixed posts.

Value placed on dogs' services.—Useful work done, particularly by night, as additional ears and eyes for the sentries.

Ipswich

"I am pleased to report that the dogs have been very serviceable in their duties as watch-dogs over ammunition dumps. In all cases where they have been in use I have been enabled to reduce the guard by half; they have always given due notice of anyone approaching the post, besides being a source of security to the guards and patrols. Posts and wire have been in use in different positions, and the dogs put on different wires at differed times; this has worked well.

(*Signed*) "E. H. Coombe, Major, and O.C.
"Ipswich."

Ringwood

"I beg to report that the dog which is in use at this store as watch-dog is certainly a success, as the animal does not only give confidence to the night watchman in discharging his duties, but I should say also releases three men from such duty. The dog is comfortably housed, but, up to the present, there have been no aggressors.

"For your information, please.

"Yours obediently,

(*Signed*) "HARRY BAILEY, Corpl.

"Storekeeper, Hay Store, Ringwood."

Leighton Buzzard

"I beg to report that the work of the dogs on the Woburn Sands Magazines has been very effective.

"They are very keen on their work, and their continued use reduces the strength of the guard required there to a minimum.

(*Signed*) "J. W. GREGORY, Lieut.,

"O.C. Det. 70th Protection Company, R.D.C.

"To: O.C. 70th Protection Company, R.D.C.

"Leighton Buzzard."

A reduction in the hours of duty of the sentries is here noted:

"With reference to the work of the war dog, attached to a detachment of this battalion, stationed at Binfield, the following is a statement made by men of the guard:

"With the aid of this dog, it was possible for each sentry to do six hours on duty instead of two hours on and four hours off. This probably means the release of three or four men.

"The duty engaged on was guarding a magazine at Binfield.

"The dog was with the sentry while at his post, preventing anyone approaching, and going the rounds with the guard, preventing anyone loitering near the magazine.

"The men state that the dog was extremely useful, and a very valuable sentry.

(*Signed*) "C. CLAY, Capt. and Adjutant,

"For Officer Commanding,

"6th (R) Batt. City of London Rifles.

"Bramley."

Some very fine Airedales were sent also the Base Headquarters in Italy. The officer in whose charge they were wrote to me:

" I am satisfied that the dogs have been a complete success.

" They have taken the place of four N.C.O.'s and twelve men daily."

The following report deals with the last work of the guard dogs before they were demobilised:

" With reference to your visit with the O.C. Troops and your queries as to the usefulness of watch-dogs, I have to report that I find these dogs of the greatest assistance in closed stores.

" When I took over the supply depot two months ago, I was having stores broken into nightly; but since the advent of the dogs, there has been no case of a store being broken open.

" On two occasions stores had been tampered with, and it is evident the persons attempting the entry of the stores had thought better of it, on discovering the canine occupants.

" Lieut-Colonel SYKES,

" O.C. R.A.S.C., Bulford Sub-District.

" Bulford."

All the dogs mentioned so far were trained on the principle of a fixed base, that is to say, they were given a definite spot to guard. There is another branch to this training, however, which is also extremely useful to the soldier and requires a rather different treatment.

SENTRY DOGS

The sentry dog can be of enormous service both in peace and war. In this case it has to be taught that its work is to detect the approach of a stranger and acquaint the soldier sentry of the fact, but it must understand that it has to do this at *any* given spot, and with *any* man with which it may be detailed for duty. The sense of possession and mastership is imbued into the animal in the same way as in the guard dog, but in a more general sense. This requires a more intelligent and acute disposition in the creature, and sentry dogs require very careful selection and training indeed, as they represent the *haute école* of guardianship.

During the first few months of the war, before any official action had been taken in the direction of training military dogs, I had supplied a good many to the armies on the Western Front, and also to the expeditionary forces in Egypt and Mesopotamia.

An Airedale I supplied to an officer of the Berkshire Regiment was taken on patrol one night. It suddenly stopped and began to growl. The party heard and saw nothing suspicious, but the officer ordered the men to lie flat. Immediately afterwards an enemy patrol passed by close to them, without noticing. Our patrols then rose noiselessly, and captured them all.

Some dogs that were sent out to an infantry regiment in Egypt, averted what might have been a serious disaster. It was on the same day as the yeomanry were so severely attacked, and when there was a dense mist. The infantry were also attacked, but the dogs were too quick, and so clearly indicated the approach of the enemy that an order was given to fire into the mist. This had an immediate effect, and the attack was checked. When the mist cleared away, large numbers of enemy dead were found.

I also sent some good Airedale sentries to the flooded areas of the Belgian Front, and they were much appreciated, and there were eighteen Airedales with the South-West African Force. General Botha was very pleased with these, especially on one occasion, when they were the means of warning of a large enemy ambush, whereby a considerable capture of the enemy was effected.

Sentry dogs are particularly suitable where the conditions are those of open warfare. For this reason, there was not so much interest taken in them for the Western Front as the position of our army became more entrenched. On certain parts of the front, however, which were not so consolidated, and especially towards the end, they would have been useful.

I have mentioned already that some sentry dogs were

trained at the War Dog School, and were sent out to Salonica, Airedales had been especially asked for, so they were all of this breed. They formed a very handsome contingent, and went out in charge of some specially trained men. Very good work was done after arrival, and no doubt very large use would have been made of this sort of sentry aid on this front, as it was found that on forward posts in the mountains, the dogs were of great service in detecting enemy movement at night. About this time, however, the fighting began to subside. There is not the slightest doubt that these dogs would always be of inestimable service at all isolated posts open to enemy attack at night.

On the North-West Frontier of India, for instance, there should be an organised permanent sentry dog service. It would be extremely difficult for a sentry to be approached at night, even by the most subtle rifle thief, without the dog giving him sufficient warning to put him on his guard; and the fact that he had such an ally by his side would give him greatly enhanced confidence.

I have elsewhere referred to some sentry dogs I trained, and sent to the Abor Expedition in 1911 and gave the report on them.

On another occasion the dispatch sent was as follows:

"The expedition has now reached Rotung, a gathering place of the Abors, which was found to have been burned. After marching unopposed to the limit of the made road, the striking force began the ascent of the rising ground beyond the Lelek river, through a thick bamboo forest.

"Information had been received to the effect that a stockade might be met with, and the Gurkha scouts, who were accompanied by Major Richardson's war dogs, were accordingly ordered to keep a sharp look out.

"The dogs again proved their efficiency, as they gave warning to the outposts of the presence of the enemy's scouts, before they were seen by the Naga coolies."

Another report also brings out the point of view I am advocating, namely, that sentry dogs should be considered the natural accompaniment of the sentry:

" I beg to forward a report called for, on the value of the dog presented to my company by Major Richardson. The dog, an Airedale terrier, arrived just before brigade training. Major Richardson forwarded full instructions as to its care, feeding, and training. On three occasions I had the opportunity of using the dog on outpost duties at night. Each time I found the presence of the dog to be of the greatest value. He either remained beside the sentry, or went with a patrol. His value consists in the fact that he can, and does, detect the approach of human beings some considerable time before the eye or ear of the average man can distinguish anything. The result is that the sentry or patrol is fully on the alert, and it is impossible for them to be either ambushed or rushed.

" The dog is no expense, as he feeds on the remains of the men's dinner. He is never allowed to run loose in camp or barracks, and no one is allowed to feed him except the man in charge of him. I am of opinion that it would be a very valuable asset to have four of these dogs attached to every infantry battalion for service in the field. I hope at next company training to make more extensive trials of his usefulness. I should add, that his method of indicating the approach of anyone at night is nearly silent. It consists of a low growl, and a stiffening of his body, almost like a pointer.

(*Signed*) " A. C. TEMPERLEY, Captain,
" Commanding No. 4 Company, Norfolk Regiment.
" September 23, 1912."

A good, powerful Airedale, trained in the above manner, would be a valuable safeguard to all officers on duty in India, in frontier stations, and other isolated places, especially if they have their wives and families with them.

The terrible murder of Mrs. Ellis, and the capture of their daughter, in Waziristan this summer (1923), might have been averted if they had had such an animal. It will be remembered that the tragedy took place in the midst of a terrific storm, and that, in the clash and clamour of the elements, the officer friend, who was sleeping in another part of the bungalow, and who had especially come in to act as a protector to the family during the absence of Major Ellis, failed to hear the sound of the attack.

A dog specially prepared for such emergencies, would have heard at once, and would have given instant warning of the approach—in the first place of the assassins—and would also have done excellent attacking work in the event of their entry. It is doubtful, however, if the assault would ever have taken place if such an animal had been on duty. It would almost seem, in fact, that officers in such isolated positions should be provided by the Government with sentry dogs, for the protection of their wives and families.

Among army officers I have found many objectors to the idea of using dogs with sentries, and the arguments they advance are always the same ; I should say, however, that the objections come in every case from those who have not tried the dogs. I have not found any of the objections proven in actual practice. I will admit at the same time, that this work in the army must always be administered by an expert. The dogs must be properly trained at the training school, and the whole service supervised and controlled by an officer, who thoroughly understands the necessities of the work from the dog point of view as well as that of the army.

I will here mention the arguments of the objectors :

(1) That there is danger in the fact that a sentry, having a dog to depend on, will be tempted to be careless in his work.

(2) That the dog's barking would reveal the position, and draw the enemy fire.

My answer to the first objection is, that under those conditions where there is no particular danger to life from enemy attack, and where the sentry might, therefore, not feel the same necessity for alertness, the work is likely to be done better if a dog is posted with him. If the sentry is naturally lazy, or open to bribes, there is no remedy, if he is by himself ; whereas the dog cannot be bribed, and does not sleep, so that, at all events, the situation is rendered more difficult for the intruder, as he can never count on the dog, even if he thinks he might undermine the sentry's alertness or fidelity.

In the case of active warfare, the sentry, in his own

interests, is less likely to sleep, and the danger of a man doing so, owing to undue fatigue, or any other cause, is greatly lessened if he has a dog with him.

The sentry dog does not sleep at night, and will either keep his sentry awake, or wake him up, and in fact, represents the second string to the bow.

The whole matter may be summed up by emphasising the obvious fact, that, where it might be difficult to approach a sentry post with only a man on duty, it would be a hundred times more so, if there is also a trained sentry dog to reckon with.

In dispensing with these dogs it may be said that a very effective means of defence against unwarned attack is neglected.

In the case of the second objection, that the dog would give warning and draw the enemy fire, it may certainly be admitted that there are occasions when absolute silence is essential. At these times it would be safer not to post the dog, although even here, by the use of a strap muzzle, any noise which the dog would make could be controlled; while, by its alert attitude, it would give the sentry warning, long before he himself was aware of enemy movement. Apart from this, there are scores of occasions when no risk whatever is incurred by the dog growling, or even barking.

The Saving of Man Power

Sentry dogs can also be the means of greatly reducing the sentries, and are thus a valuable asset for the reduction of man power.

The Type of Dog

The qualities required in these dogs are: acute hearing and scent, sagacity, fidelity, and a strong sense of duty. Any dog showing these attributes can be developed into a good sentry dog, provided it is the right size, which must be that of a collie, Airedale or large Irish terrier—in fact, middle size.

White dogs should be avoided, and, as a whole, dogs are better than bitches. There are exceptions to every rule, but

I find that dogs are rather more aggressive and less self-centred than bitches, which are of a milder and less alert disposition.

It seems to be supposed that Airedales are essentially the best for this work, but this is not necessarily the case, as many other breeds of this size are equally good. The Airedale standard is certainly a good one, as the hardiness and fondness for the master exhibited by this breed are excellent qualities on which to start work. But many collies and retrievers of the rugged sort, are first rate, as well as crosses of all these breeds. A good weather resisting coat is necessary, even if the dogs are for service in a hot climate. During the hot weather it is easy to clip them, and the hair can be allowed to grow again as the cold weather approaches.

The Training

The training of these dogs must be carried out at the official training school, and must be under expert management. It is useless to imagine that any dogs, picked up here and there, can be utilised by a unit for its sentries. The dogs, to understand the work properly, must be carefully trained, and this must be done at night at the school. The training commences at dusk, when the dogs are led from their kennels by soldier keepers to various posts in isolated spots. Persons representing the enemy are instructed to approach from various directions. Accurate note is taken of the time and the distance at which the dog first takes notice, and how much ahead he is of the sentry in detecting the approach of the enemy. After a course of this training, the dog becomes well aware that he is expected to be on the look-out, and his senses, already naturally acute, are developed in a remarkable way. The training is somewhat slow, as it is not possible to do more than two or three attacks each night, and a good deal of patience and understanding is required of the trainer, and of those in charge. Day training is not necessary, and it is essential that the dog should rest during the day, so that it may be thoroughly alert at night. In any case, in the daylight, the sentry can easily detect the enemy himself from afar, so that he has no need for the dog at this time.

Feeding and Kennelling

Sentry dogs, both when under training, and after they are drafted from the training school to the various units, must be kept during the day in a quiet and isolated spot, and not visited by anyone except the men told off as keepers to attend to them. These men should be selected on account of a previous knowledge of dogs, and when posted to a unit, supervision over both men and dogs should be carried out by a specially detailed officer. The isolation of the dogs is a most important point, as if they become accustomed to see strangers constantly, they lose their alertness and sharpness. A good way is to place their kennels, which should be the ordinary box variety, in a stable or compound, which can be locked up. They should be made very comfortable, with straw in their kennels, so that they rest well.

Their meal should be given on coming off duty in the very early morning, and should be ample. They must, on no account, be fed at night.

Correct Posting and Management

When sentry dogs are first drafted from the training school to any unit, a little consideration must be shown them in the first instance, on arrival. They must be allowed time to settle down, and the first tests must not be too severe. After a few days, the dogs will have developed the possessive sense of their new environment, and the sentries will also understand the method of handling them. It will be understood that these dogs will have already gone through a considerable period of training, and all that is necessary now, is that those who have the handling of them should be themselves sufficiently educated in the methods of communication employed by the dog, to be able to interpret those signs. Therefore, the training of the sentries should also include definite instruction on the rules to observe when sentry dogs are employed. It should be pointed out that the effect of employing dogs and of carefully observing the rules of management, will greatly safeguard the sentry, and enable him to carry out his duty with increased efficiency.

Telephone-laying Dogs

At the present time, I still continue the training of dogs for army work, and I have lately, among other new experiments, found that a very useful asset to the Signalling Corps is a dog trained to carry a reel of signalling wire on its back. As the animal goes forward, the reel pays out the wire.

For crossing a dangerous zone, and thus sparing the lives of signal wire operators, this idea should prove helpful. The dog will go much more safely and quicker.

HOMING INSTINCT

Before closing this chapter a few remarks on homing instinct on which sense the whole training of messenger work is based, might be of interest.

This instinct in the dog teems with interest, not only on account of the wonderful results to be obtained by its exercise, but also because it is one, which man does not possess in anything like the same degree. How is it that the dog, without any of the material aids of direction open to man, can find his way homewards, across totally unknown country? How is it that the messenger dog, which has been taken up to the front line, through the trenches, will choose very often to return by night as well as day, and do so successfully, across the open country, often with every sort of obstacle in its path? What is it that guides it? It cannot be sight, as darkness would be an insuperable hindrance, and they work as well at night as by day. It cannot be hearing, nor is it by the sense of scent, as the dog does not necessarily choose the same route for its return, even in the doubtful and in most cases impossible likelihood of there being any trail.

It must be confessed, that in trying to account for the cause of this wonderful instinct in his four-footed friend, man is hopelessly nonplussed, and can only admit with admiring humility, that in this respect at all events, dog beats man completely.

In connection with the training of dogs for messenger

work, I have found two points in connection with the homing instinct, which rather seem to contradict each other. First of all, it is observable that they take note of objects on the road, to assist them in their return homewards. One finds this by noting that a young dog under training will sometimes take a correct course homewards, and then at cross roads take the wrong turning; showing that it has noticed the fact of the break in the road, but has erred in the choice of the next move. I have seen such a dog, a little further advanced in his training, run down the wrong road some way, then stop, hesitate, turn back, regain the cross roads, and carry on along the right road. In this case the dog's sense of direction had been, first of all, guided, then misled, by the visible appearances of the route.

Now the second point is interesting, because it practically excludes the theory that, noticing the aspect of the country over which it has previously been taken, is the manner in which the dog returns. It is, that dogs work as well at night as in the day, and equally so in mist. In fact, I may say, that observations seem to point to the fact that trained dogs, and even half-trained ones, work better under these conditions than in daylight. And this was also borne out in the field. The keepers have related to me that, on certain nights, when the conditions were so bad, the night so dark and thick, the ground so water-logged and shell-marked, and on certain occasions quite new to the dogs, that they were fearful that these would prove too much even for their faithful followers.

But the curious point was brought out, that the dogs seem to work much better than usual at such times. As one man said: "It seemed as though 'Jock' divined my fears, and put out an extra effort to show they were needless."

I remember one test I made at the school with forty dogs. They were taken in various directions simultaneously, for two miles outwards, and released at a given moment. The night was especially chosen, being moonless, and with a dense fog as well. It was, in fact, pitch-dark, of such darkness as could be felt. The average time for the return was fifteen minutes, though a few did it in ten minutes. A few also took twenty minutes. Only one took over half an hour.

Of course, one reason for the more rapid return at night, is the absence of temptation on the road, such as other dogs, vehicular traffic, and people. But this does not wholly account for the undoubted fact, that, although these temptations are absent, there are other difficulties intensified, and yet excellent results are obtained. It appears to me, therefore, that dogs observe points on their outward journey, of which they make a note in the daytime, perhaps without any conscious intention ; that the newly-trained dog does this especially, in order to help its sense of direction, but that, as the training proceeds, the dog finds this sense developing, and the safest thing to go by in the long run, and discards more and more the signs by the road as guide-marks, so that it soon prefers to take the bee-line rather than trouble with the road, by which it was taken out.

I am further of opinion that this is so, by the demeanour of the dogs on being led away for training. The young dog seems to keep a wary eye on its surroundings as he goes along, as though registering the details in its memory. The old hands, on the contrary, trot off gaily enough, and I have noticed them, when passing through a village on their outward journey, amusing themselves with passing fancies, such as hurried inspections of dogs, cats, and other trivialities which could not possibly help them on their return journey, and, when released, they would as likely as not ignore the route by which they had come, village and all, and take a nearer line across country.

At night-time, when there was no possibility of any help being received from the memory of the aspect of the outward route, the effort has to be concentrated on the sense of direction only, and that, as this is the real and legitimate source of the homing faculty, the results are at once more certain and rapid.

It would seem, therefore, that the causative guiding source of the homing faculty has its origin in the realm of metaphysics, rather than in external phenomena, and if any explanation is sought, it is here that investigation should be made.

First of all, we find an overwhelming desire in the dog's mind to get to a certain place. I, of course, discovered, as I have already explained elsewhere, that the surest foundation from which to arouse this desire, was the love of the dog for its master. Love being an ever-primal, and therefore an eternal quality, the effort involved in carrying out duties under this impulse, is such, that it is strong enough to sweep aside obstructions of every kind, and is the most dependable instinct available.

Starting with this all-guiding impulse, it is of interest to follow out the working of it in relation to the phenomena which come to the dog, in its attempt to reach a certain spot.

It would therefore seem that our animals, under stress of definite necessity, become conscious of certain phenomena of which they make use. That we ourselves do not realise what these are, is no argument that they are not there, nor, in our anxiety to explain the manner in which the animals accomplish the results, need we pin them down to our limited methods of understanding in any particular direction. Rather let us learn from the animals, and see if we cannot regain certain qualities of mind which we no doubt originally had, but have now lost, and which they retain.

I gather, therefore, that the intense desire to reach a given place impels the dog forward; that, as it yields to this impulse, a certain guiding sense, which is, in itself, quite independent of any assistance from external phenomena, comes to its aid, and the sense of direction is in this very sense; that the dog desires to be there, and follows this desire, rather than troubling about the aspect of the surroundings in getting there. The more it becomes accustomed to throw all its efforts into this intuitive prompting, the more it discards any temporary assistance it may be tempted to use; in the first place, such as noting turns in the road and other external aids, and also the more it improves in its way-finding duties. The deduction, in fact, seems to be plain, that the desire itself brings its own lesson, and a world of intelligence is opened up to the dog, and to all animals, under stress of this governing force, of which we human beings are quite unconscious, because we have not yet exercised this particular mental effort along the same lines as the animals.

It will be seen, that those promptings which have their origin in what we call instinct, are due to an intelligence quite apart from, and infinitely above, any guidance from the senses. While man accepts gratefully the many wonderful inventions which have come to him as aids in his present manner of living, there is no doubt that in his increasing dependence on material contrivances, he has sacrificed much wonderful knowledge, which would have come to him, had he trained himself to listen more attentively to the "still, small voice" within. That we will eventually be compelled to depend wholly on this guidance, and wholly discard the material props we rest on to-day is certain, and we can, even now, see evidences of the tendency in this direction in the gradual dematerialising of so many original forces. Thus, telegraphy is no longer confined to wires, light is obtained from certain elements in combination, propulsion from the evaporation of gas. Matter itself is disappearing under analysis, and appears as the "electron" which our chief authorities in the world of chemistry define as "energy," and frankly admit that from this point they hand the whole question over to the metaphysician.

Thus it is apparent, that in some ways, we can still learn much from the animals, and that in their dependence upon the intuitive utterances, derived from voices long unheard by man, they are on the right road towards the solution of many things, which at present remain a mystery to us.

Under this mental propulsion, the senses of sight, hearing, and scenting become greatly intensified, and the great desire in the dog's mind to detect sounds in the far distance, in the performance of its work, is the great impetus whereby the trainer can cultivate hearing and scenting in the sentry and guard dog.

And it would seem that these senses have their origin in Mind.

CHAPTER XV

DOGS FOR THE POLICE

"My hounds are bred out of the Spartan kinde
So flewed, so sanded ; and their heads are hung
With ears that sweep away the morning dew ;
Crook-kneeded, and dewlapp'd like Thessalian Bulls ;
Slow in pursuit, but matched in mouth like bells,
Each under each. A cry more tuneable was
Never halloed to, nor cheered with horne,
In Crete, in Sparta, nor in Thessaly ;
Judge when you heare."

—SHAKESPEARE.

Tracking dogs for the police. Unfortunately, the bloodhound breed, which was small enough in numbers before the war, has decreased still further in this respect since then. The expense of keeping up a kennel of these large dogs, and the difficulty of feeding them during the war years, was greater than most people could manage. Since then they are being bred again, but are still too expensive to be of any practical value to any extent for the police, for that very reason. An adult hound pure-bred and trained, would cost anywhere from £50 to £200. At this price they are not economically feasible. With proper training, however, other breeds, as already stated, can be utilised for man-tracking, and not only would there be plenty of choice from which to select the individual tracker, but the cost of purchase, in the first place, would, of course, be quite moderate.

Apart from bloodhounds, I find collies and Airedales have the best noses and the greatest intelligence for man-tracking. There may be individuals in other breeds which show good scenting powers, but, after having experimented largely in all likely breeds at home and abroad, I find that these two far excel any others in point of numbers, which are found to be capable and reliable. After some training, I have found many of these extraordinarily good, and also very keen and interested in the work. Their general intelligence is far greater than is that of the bloodhound, and in this way they are able to meet the trainers' endeavour by their brain power, in cases where the bloodhound might carry on by his hereditary persistency alone.

For all local tracking work I have no hesitation in saying that, with proper training, such dogs could be used quite as successfully as bloodhounds. Whether they would, as a whole, be able to have followed some of the trails which I have traced in years gone by, and some of which are already described, where great difficulties presented themselves, including delay in reaching the scene, I am not prepared to say. There is this much to be said, however, that had those same episodes occurred since the war, it is uncertain what measure of success would have attended them, even with bloodhounds. The modern tar-sprayed roads present a formidable obstacle to tracking. Plain macadam ones were bad enough, but the scent of tar on the top completely obliterates any other scent which may lie there.

Another feature which makes tracking of crime by dogs increasingly difficult, is the use of motors by which the criminals escape from the scene. Still, there are many occasions when tracking dogs can be of very great service. For one thing, criminals do not always work in gangs with motors to carry them away, but on the contrary, the culprit may be solitary and creep away through the woods and fields seeking to escape observation. In any case it is usually only the high roads which are tarred, and the side roads and lanes, under favourable conditions, can hold scent for a certain time.

It is useless to say that the criminal generally gets caught in the end. This is certainly often the case, so clever and persistent are the means adopted by the police to attain this end, but there is also undoubted evidence that, after the first crime, the escaping culprit has time to commit several other outrages before he is caught.

Now there are many occasions where a good tracking dog, *put on the scene early,* will give great help. Most crimes take place in the dark or in the early morning hours. Scent lies well usually at this time, and were such a dog handy and put on the trail within an hour or two of discovery, which as a rule takes place early and before traffic begins, successful tracking is quite possible, even in quiet streets, and more especially so in the country districts. A common feature of many crimes is that the guilty person does not at first go far from the scene, but hides in surrounding woods, and only makes his way to the towns after the hue and cry has somewhat subsided. From the dog's point of view this is always good. In the hands of the police themselves, and put on early enough, there are many occasions when such dogs would be of very great assistance.

It is no use for those who are opposed to the idea, to point to the wide assistance which telephones, motors and even wireless offer to the police nowadays. All these are made use of and necessarily so, but even with these aids, the percentage of burglaries, assaults with violence, incendiarism, etc., is increasingly high, and furthermore there is risk, as the population grows, that the mere struggle for existence will induce conditions whereby crime will be the outlet for the fierce contentions of the lower grades of the populace to a still greater extent.

It is, however, only under certain definite conditions that tracking dogs for the police can be made really practical adjuncts to the force. They would have to be organised and trained at a centre from which they would be distributed to the various county constabularies. This system would be based on that which worked with great success in connection with the war dogs during the war.

A Police Dog Training School. At the Police Dog Training School the animals would be first of all selected (by no means an easy task), and then carefully trained. Any dogs which deteriorated or turned ill while out with the constabularies, would be returned to the training school to be retrained or doctored. In this way a large number of dogs could be kept perpetually in a high state of training, and individually animals would be distributed to the county constabularies as required. Here they would be actually lodged, so as to be ready and on the spot to accompany the police any time they were required. Many of these dogs would also be excellent for patrol work at night, and would serve two purposes. Constables could be sent to the training school to be instructed in the correct working and management of the dogs. One or two, or even more dogs, could be kept at the local county police stations at which kennels would be provided, and ration allowances for the dogs' keep would be fixed. Visits of inspection would have to be made in the areas by an officer from the training school, to see that correct management was carried out.

In this manner really well trained animals would be at hand for police service, and could be distributed widely enough to be near to an actual crime, so that they could be put early on the trail of the criminal, whereby the latter might be actually run to earth, or at all events a line given as to the direction he had taken, which, in many cases, leads up to a clue resulting in ultimate capture.

Until this system is inaugurated, police dogs of any sort, whether only for patrol purposes or for tracking as well, will never give the measure of aid to the force which they are quite capable of doing.

Patrol Police Dogs. The object, all through this book, has been to show that a dog is capable of safe-guarding person as well as place. This is a fact which will be found especially true, in connection with the policeman on his nightly beat. Many policemen already use dogs, but if the force, as a whole, were supplied with suitably trained animals, the night work would be even more efficiently done.

These dogs would be issued from the training school, and in some cases they would combine both tracking and watching qualities, but in the majority of cases they would be for guarding and detecting only.

A great deal is written about dogs for the police which is not based on true or feasible premise.

At the outset let me emphasise the fact, that the best dogs in the world for this work (either for tracking or patrol) are to be found in the native breeds of the British Isles. The necessity for stating this clearly, is that there is a tendency in certain quarters to thrust forward foreign animals as being superior to our own breeds. Under no circumstances should anyone be taken in by this. It is only an insidious device to decry our good native stock, and is carried on entirely for commercial purposes to sell these foreign dogs.

These dogs are called " Alsatian " for selling purposes,

but they are really German sheep-dogs, and emanate from Germany in the first place.

Furthermore, these fancy and foreign animals are of no use whatever, economically, for the police. They are priced high, and are therefore impossible, apart from other disabilities.

The Police Dog Training School should have every sort of suitable breed pass through it, and cross-breds of every kind of a certain size as well as pure-bred Airedales, collies, retrievers, etc., would be welcome. Many of these would probably be gifts from the public, and others would be cheaply purchased after testing by an expert officer in command. He would be assisted in this work by members of the force, who would be sent to the school as students, and would go back to their local constabularies with a dog or two which they had themselves helped to train.

In this way, a body of constables expert in managing dogs, and also a large number of animals well trained for guarding and tracking, could be dispersed gradually all over the country, and each single constable's value would be greatly increased in consequence by this auxiliary aid.

In this country we should have no difficulty in getting plenty of canine recruits for police work. The characteristics which have made, and which will conserve the British race for what it is, are mirrored in the minds of many of the native breeds of dogs. Some of these are the most wonderful animals in the world, and cannot be approached by the dogs of any other nation.

There is a movement, in certain directions, to decry our British dogs, and to attribute extraordinary virtues to foreign dogs, which have been used abroad especially in Germany for police purposes.

One does not wish to decry any class of animal, but these are being pushed under a constant implication that they are better than our native breeds, and our police must not be imposed upon by such inspired statements, which are untrue.

For police work we have many dogs in our own land which are better suited for our people, and which are much more intelligent for actual work in this country. They are more courageous and better tempered.

In Germany, they do not have the same choice of suitable breeds as we do in England, and they make the most of what they have.

DOGS FOR THE ARMY

If the above suggestion of a Central Official School of Instruction for Police Dogs and of their working were inaugurated, it would also be possible to use the same organisation as a nucleus for dogs for the army. Sentry dogs could be trained there also and distributed to the army as well. While there is no prospect of war at present, it is not necessary to wait for such an event, which one prays may be far distant, in order to make efficient use of watch-dogs in our present-day army.

During the war, guard dogs were used, as I have shown, extensively up and down the country for safe-guarding magazines, powder manufactories, and the hundreds of buildings in which was valuable plant of every description. They were quietly issued from the War Dog School, and the whole movement was kept very secret, as the school was, or the greater part of the time, on the sea coast of Shoeburyness, where there were frequent air raids, and there was a danger of bombs being dropped on the training ground of the dogs.

Another advantage was found also, that, by the use of guard dogs in this manner, sentries could be reduced by more than half all over the country, as the capacity and efficiency of those remaining was so greatly enhanced, that far fewer were needed. When the man-power shortage became acute, this economy was, of course, greatly appreciated by the authorities. From the officers in charge of protection companies I received, as Commandant of the School of Instruction, several hundred reports, and it was most interesting to see how in every case the use of dogs made it possible to immediately reduce personnel.

The official regulations issued to the various stations to which the dogs were sent, commenced :

" The employment of guard dogs enables an enclosure to be adequately guarded with the minimum of sentries or watchmen, and, owing to the dogs' keen sense of hearing and smell, gives greater security than can be obtained by men alone. The presence of dogs becomes a well-known deterrent."

CHAPTER XVI

British v. German Police Dogs

A ROMAN TRIBUTE

"When the bold game turns back upon the spear,
And all the Furies wait upon the war,
First in the fight the whelps of Britain shine,
And snatch, Germanicus, all the palm from thine."
—WHITAKER (FALISCUS).

SINCE the first edition of this book was published a good deal of interest, and also of controversy, has been aroused by some amateur police dog trials which have taken place in this country.

There is a good deal of misunderstanding as to what these trials are supposed to represent, and also as to the capabilities and origin of the dogs which are shown doing the various exercises, and perhaps it may be of interest to go fully into this matter. For this reason a special chapter has been added dealing with the subject.

The breed used has been the German sheep dog, which is at present incorrectly known in this country under the name of the " Alsatian Wolf Dog."

The general public are confused because they find that all the history of this so called " Alsatian " seems to lead to Germany and German methods of training. They cannot understand it, and so the following remarks may give some enlightenment.

The history of this breed is as follows :

For many generations this wolf-like dog had been used by the shepherds of Germany for guarding the sheep. The dogs of South Germany were of a larger size than those in the North, and one or two German breeders thought that by crossing the two types they could get a larger and stronger dog. The shepherd dog had always been crossed every now and then with wolves, to keep them fierce, and now that the large, strong dog was purposely manufactured by expert breeders, it was again thought advisable to bring in a strain of wolf once more, to ensure the character, and several of the first dogs registered in the "Deutchershaferhund Vèrein" (German Sheep Dog Club) were half wolf. This accounts for the curious character of the breed—the mixture of timidity and ferocity which lurks in so many of these dogs.

Herr Meyer and Captain Von Stephenitz originated this amalgamation in the first place, and formed the club in 1899 at Stuttgart, the capital of Würtemberg.

In all wild beasts there is a certain furtiveness which is very difficult to overcome, and this is noticeable at once in the progeny of any domesticated animal which may become crossed in such a way.

The Germans, however, find this fierceness satisfactory, from their point of view, when the dogs are used with their police. There are two reasons for this, one being that the German police prefer a dog capable of serious attack. Their law does not, as with us, pre-suppose the innocence of the prisoner until guilt is proved.

In Germany there is also nothing like our sensitiveness to public opinion with regard to people being bitten.

The German police dog as trained by the German police is a powerful animal, capable of great severity. That such an animal needs a considerable amount of control may well be understood, and, with the usual capacity for dragooning everything with which he comes in contact, the German official has instituted a form of training "according to plan" in which strict discipline is inculcated by various words of command. This discipline is strictly necessary with such a dog, as otherwise it would be very unsafe in public. As it is, one sees persons constantly being attacked in Germany by such dogs in a manner which would never be tolerated over here.

As witness to this wolf cross, I would refer to such breeders as Herr Strebel and Monsieur Sodenkamp, well-known continental breeders, who bear testimony to the fact of the crossing with the wolf. As a matter of fact, I find from personal investigation that the cross is still being made at local Zoos in Germany. This is now not openly divulged in England, although no secret was made of it to me in Germany. I have already explained that the Germans like dogs with a streak of ferocity in their disposition. They like an attacking dog, just as hitherto they have approved of war for war's sake. They are very pleased with the wolf cross and consider it renders the breed virile and determined. Their point of view, in fact, is quite opposed to that of dog lovers over here. There are some English owners of the dog who are now trying to disclaim this wolf cross, but the most trivial inquiries amongst present day German breeders and exporters to this country confirm the fact, and they seem to do so with pride. Herr Strebel mentions the curious behaviour of the Borzoi at a show in Dresden whenever the well-known German sheep-dog (Alsatian) " Eulan I " (which was a wolf cross), passed their benches. The Russian Borzoi is, of course, used to chase wolves, and they showed the same desire to slay this wolf dog as it passed. This " Eulan " figures in the pedigrees of many of the present day so-called " Alsatians."

A letter, dated February 20, 1924, and sent to me by a gentleman living in Holland, says :

" I have been very interested in reading your letter in the *Times* of Monday last about Police Dogs, and for the following reason. . . . I have myself a wire-haired fox terrier which I brought from England a year or two ago. I say ' fox,' but I imagine he is a mixture and with a fair amount of Airedale in him.

" Now this little fellow finds his greatest pleasure in hunting Alsatians of all sizes. He invariably puts them on the run, and even if they show fight he invariably gets the best of it. . . . I myself attribute the marked antipathy my dog showed to this breed as being due to the wolf strain in the ' Alsatian,' which he no doubt instinctively recognizes."

The letter referred to by the above writer was one written to the *Times* by me, in reply to a comment in a leading aritcle on the German Police dog trials held in England this winter.

"POLICE DOGS

"*To the Editor of the Times.*

"SIR

"I have very frequently noted your leading articles which appear now and then on animal psychology. They are clever and illuminating, and I take the liberty of commenting on that one in the *Times* of to-day.

"I gather that the first attribute necessary in the dog which is to be used with the police is self-control. Your article is perfectly correct, and it is for this reason that the German sheep dog (which is at present called Alsatian to popularize them over here) will never be so suitable for police work in this country as dogs of our own native breeds. In my training experiments I have studied the psychology of dogs in all parts of the world during the past 30 years, and one thing I find incontrovertibly proved is that dogs, which are above all other animals so closely in touch with man, partake in time of his very soul, and become in fact the reflection of their masters, for better, for worse. Now these 'Alsatians' (so-called) are essentially the sheep dog of Prussia. They are half wolf, half Prussian, and strongly retain the characteristics of both origins. In Germany then like a dog with a capacity for attack, just as in the same way the nation has always believed in war for its own sake. Our police do not require dogs of this nature, which are more or less innately savage. Police patrol dogs are only of use in country districts, and the average country constable wants a dog he can control easily—a good sensible, discriminating "pal," whose attitude is detection and defence—not attack. Our own native breeds are more suitable, as they are much more easily controlled and are better tempered. Foreign police dogs may suit the Germans, but they would get our police into trouble.

"At the present moment there are in all parts of the country large numbers of perfectly trained, trusty retrievers, Airedales and collies going out nightly with their constable masters—without advertisement or display, and using their sagacious and kindly, yet courageous and discriminating, intelligences in safeguarding the persons and property of sleeping citizens. What more do we want ? Can any breeds touch ours ? I trow not !

" Yours faithfully,

" E. H. RICHARDSON, Lt.-Col.

" Wormley Hill, Broxbourne, Herts, Feb. 9.

" P.S.—I understand Scotland Yard have refused these foreign dogs, and wisely so. Liverpool and other districts use Airedales."

Mr. Horowitz, who is one of the authorities of the breed over here, says, in his book on the ' Alsatian " :

" That certain strains of Alsatians do contain Wolf blood can be taken for granted, if only on the authority of such a great expert of the breed as Monsieur Otto Rahm, of Switzerland, who has told us that the great grand dam of the well-known Hector von Wohlen was the product of a mating between a dog wolf and an Alsatian bitch." Mr. Horowitz also says "It is quite possible we shall see anon that Alsatians were crossed with wolves, but naturally the fanciers concerned in such practices kept them secret."

The ordinary enquirer would naturally ask " Why this secrecy ? "

With regard to the name " Alsatian," by which the breed is nicknamed over here, I have already shown how the present type of dog was formed into a club at Stuttgart in 1899 under the title of " Vereinfür Deutsche Shäferhunge " (German Sheep Dog Society). The headquarters of the club is now at Munich, Bavaria.

A branch of this club was extended to Switzerland under the name of Club Suisse du Chien de Berger Allemande (Swiss Club for the German Sheep Dog). After that, another branch extended to France, where it was called Club Francais du Chien de Berger Allemande (French Club for the German Sheep Dog).

After the war, however, everything German was naturally anathema in France, and, as Herr Schwabacher says in his book on the breed: " In 1915 this name was changed into Chien Berger Alsace. The reason is apparent, as at that period there were no purchasers of German dogs." He continues : " In justice to the breed I must protest against its country of origin being given as Alsace. . . ."

As a matter of fact many of the Alsatians who owned dogs of this breed disclaim this fraudulent camouflage, and have now formed a club for themselves, in which the true name registered is as before, " Chien Berger Allemande. "

With regard to the English Club, it is probable that in the first place a few of our returning soldiers, after the Armistice, brought some dogs back from Alsace under a misapprehension as to the real name and origin of the breed and, in enthusiasm at a new idea, a group of people who were new to the doggy world petitioned the Kennel Club for registration.

That such a request was acceded to was a pity, and already it is giving rise to disputations on the part of many of the owners of the dogs who know the true name and origin of the breed. Many honourable owners of these dogs openly state that they would much prefer to let the dog stand or fall on its own merits, and under its true name, as is the case with Dachhunds. They greatly resent the attitude which they have been compelled to adopt.

Herr de Groote, a specialist judge, who was invited to judge the breed at the Special Show held in July of last year, in his report rebukes the exhibtors for the false name under which the dog is being shown in England, emphasising the fact that it is the " German Sheep Dog," not " Alsatian."

The fact that these alien dogs have been largely purchased by the public under the desire for something new, and with the mistaken impression that they were a native breed of Alsace, has caused a considerable amount of distress to some of our own people. Many of our Tommies on settling down to civilian life again have invested their savings in one or two good bitches of the breeds they know so well—terriers of all sorts—collies, retrievers, bull dogs, etc. They thought to keep the pot boiling, in hard times, with a litter or two of good pups, which they could sell at advantageous prices. Many of these good fellows have found that the people who should ordinarily have bought them are supplied with these foreign dogs. Of course, such a state of things will not last, and especially when the truth becomes known, but it is a pity that it has ever happened.

While dogs of this nature, and such a system of training, may suit German ideas, it is clearly seen that natural initiative is not encouraged. It is the same old Prussian system of dragooning " according to plan," and for patrol police work, such as we require over here, such dogs and such training is not only unwise but totally unnecessary. For this reason, it is not likely that the interest in the trials of these German dogs will be long sustained. The fact that our people are not accustomed to seeing people attacked and bitten by dogs, whether by command or not, aroused in the first place a certain curiosity, but such feats do not represent anything which is likely to be of use in this country.

BRITISH POLICE DOGS

The dogs required for English and Scotch police are for detection and defence.

For our need very alert, sagacious and self-controlled animals are required, and while they must be capable and assist their own constable masters in cases of ambush and attack, they must not have the slightest trace of actual ferocity in their nature. Our police are already supplied with many such native breeds. They find them useful in patrolling country lanes and suburban neighbourhoods, where persons intent on burglary and petty pilfering of all sorts may seek shelter behind shrubs and hedges until the constable has passed by. Such a dog will be trotting a little ahead, and will be quite aware that it is there to detect and give warning of anyone in hiding. This it will quickly do—running back to the policeman, who can investigate the cause of alarm, and use his own discretion as to the next proceeding. Pure Airedales, and all sorts of Airedale crosses, are excellent for this work Pure Retrievers and Retriever crosses can also be highly commended, and the same can be said of many Collie crosses. Such dogs suit their environment better than these foreign dogs would do, and our police have no difficulty in understanding and teaching them their duties.

No elaborate training is required, as the country is full of good representatives of the breeds I have mentioned, and which have a natural aptitude for the work to start with. It only needs the *nightly patrolling with the constables on duty* to bring out the intelligence and faithful conduct lying ready for cultivation. This steady, nightly work with the police, is, however, necessary, and *is the real training.* For this reason properly educated police dogs can never be trained in any quantities for practical purposes by civilians. For how would the ordinarily good citizen care to patrol the streets and roads into the "wee sma hours," as is necessary As a matter of fact, while good dogs are actually paid for by the Watch Committees, and supplied to the police in many of the large towns in the Midlands and the North, who train them themselves, most of the country police supply themselves with dogs of their own finding—very greatly to the increased safety of the community at large.

I started the police dogs in Liverpool and several other large towns about fifteen years ago, and the idea has spread. These were all Airedales, but, as I have already said, there are many other very fine fellows, doing excellent night work, trotting down the dark roads and country lanes with their constables, and which are all alert and full of true widsom and the natural dignity and self-control which they reflect and absorb from one of the finest bodies of men in the world—our British Police.

To interfere with this relationship, which is two-fold, namely the attitude of the policeman to his dog, and that of the latter to the suspected criminal and to the public in general, by introducing German ideas, as represented by their dogs and their training system, would be extremely unwise and dangerous to the public.

As a matter of fact, before the war, the German Police were extremely attracted to our Airedales and Collies. They greatly admired the sagacity and amenableness of our breeds, and they imported large quantities into Germany, taking the trouble to send over agents to collect as many as they could. It was the same with their regiments. I have large numbers of photographs showing our Airedales, etc., parading with the German police, and I have many pictures which show various rifle regiments supplied with quantities of Airedales and no other breed.

Many of their own trainers much preferred them for the work to anything Germany could produce.

In my constant visits to the training schools reviewed abroad before the war, the authorities have said to me, "Ah, if we only had your Airedales and Retrievers and Bloodhounds!" The greater self-control, initiative and scenting powers of our native breeds was greatly appreciated, and as regards discipline—a very much vaunted quality in the German system of training—is there any dog which can equal one of our well trained retrievers or border collies?

With regard to the other tricks which are shown at the German Police dog trials they can be passed by with a few words of comment. The jumping over obstacles is not of any great moment. Any country bred dog can jump 6 ft. with hardly any training. The guarding is what any dog of the right disposition will do almost naturally, and as to the tracking, it is always absurd to anyone who understands true tracking conditions.

Altogether one will see far cleverer tricks done in any travelling circus. People are not accustomed to see men bitten by dogs in this country, whether in padded suits or without, and this little excitement is all there is to these so-called Police Dog Trials.

I have been considerably attacked as the result of my comments in our Press on the imposition of this alien breed, and I am accused of wishing to exclude all foreign dogs from the country. This is far from being the case, however. The world is wide, and there are many very charming foreign breeds coming to us with excellent characters—*viz.*, the Saluchi hounds, Pekinese, Elk hounds, etc., but they are coming in under their true names, neither do they come in with much vaunting that they are better than our own breeds. They come in as gentlemen, and are welcomed as such.

It is well that all men should be able to trade together, and if our people wish to buy German dogs they must be allowed to do so, but they should know what they are actually buying, and the name should be clearly stated.

The petty subterfuges and misrepresentations which have been adopted in connection with this German dog, in order to obtain a sale, are greatly to be deprecated. There is this much to be said for the Germans since the war, in that they are loyal to their own breeds—one does not find Airedales or fox terriers imported into Germany under the name of " Lorraine Terriers ! "

The fact is that dogs are now a very valuable stock, and there is an immense amount of money behind it. The temptation to seize on any form of camouflage which may increase the value of a breed is the cause of much mis-statement.

A common form of such advertisement is a statement, frequently met with in connection with these German " Alsatians," that they were the dogs which helped our soldiers in the war. Of course this is not the case. Many hundreds of dogs helped the soldiers of the British army, but they were all of our native breeds.

The suggestion that our dogs need German or any other foreign breed to teach them how to use their intelligence is ridiculous to all. It is especially so to anyone who has been for many years before the war constantly in touch with foreign countries, and who therefore knows the extreme desire evinced by foreigners to acquire large quantities of our breeds, which they considered in many ways superior to their own, and certainly so in general sagacity and amenableness.

Herr Bungartz, a well-known German trainer, believed in Scotch collies, and used hardly anything else.

During the Russo-Japanese War the Germans sent some of their own sheep dogs to aid the Red Cross in the Russian army. I also sent some Scotch collies which had been trained for this work. The report on the dogs which appeared in one of the Russian daily papers is as follows:—

"Captain Persidsky, of the late Count Keller's staff, writes:

"In finding the missing and wounded, with which the millet-fields are strewn, nothing has succeeded like our pack of seven dogs. The English ones are especially intelligent. In our last engagement twenty-three men were found in unsuspected places."

The "English dogs" here mentioned were some Scotch collies I trained and sent out to Russia at the request of the Dowager Empress of Russia. Afterwards I received the "grateful thanks" and the medal of the Russian Red Cross Society for the work these dogs did; I also received a splendid gold and diamond watch and chain from the Tzar.

It would seem strange that this chapter has to be added at all. As a race, we have always been hospitable and courteous to foreigners. On the whole they have not in the past abused our confidence, and as long as straightforward statement and negotiation is maintained the foreigner has nothing to fear, whether he be human or canine, but the moment facts are distorted and false claims put forward, especially in connection with the capabilities of their hosts, the position is quite reversed, and such unsportsmanlike conduct is greatly resented at once by all Britishers

CONCLUSION

> " Mine is no narrow creed ;
> And He who gave thee being did not frame
> The mystery of life to be the sport
> Of merciless man ! There is another world
> For all that live and move—a better one !
> Where the proud bipeds,who would fain confine
> Infinite goodness to the little bounds
> Of their own charity, may envy thee."
>
> —SOUTHEY. *Lines to his dead dog.*

I TRUST that all I have said in the foregoing chapters will stimulate interest in the animal, which, out of all creation, is nearest to man in sympathy and intelligence.

To those who know the capacity for affection, and devoted service obtainable from the dog, it is a subject of commiseration, when such people are encountered, who have no understanding of this wonderful source of pleasure and useful co-operation.

One small point which probably passes unnoticed by the majority, is the case of our countrymen in all parts of our dominions, in the lonely places of the world, whose only happiness and touch with things intimately good and homely, is brought by the companionship of a dog. One man told me that his little group of devotedly attached terriers had practically saved his sanity during years of irrigation work in a lonely part of India. His experience is exceedingly common, and there are sporting little creatures, breathing ardent British characteristics all over the world, which are not only keeping their own " tails up," but are, metaphorically, helping their masters to do so also, in the face of depressing conditions, of climate, loneliness, and every sort of trying experience.

This service cannot be lightly held, in view of the

immensely important work many of these masters are doing. To keep up the prestige of the British Empire all over the world, is one of the great props on which the whole fabric of civilisation is based. Amalgamation with alien ideals, which are immensely lower than ours, will never accomplish this, and, not understanding this fact, is one of the dangers with which this country is faced at present.

The conservation of British characteristics in our race, for which generations upon generations of our fathers lived and died, and which have ruled the world, not by right of physical force, but by sheer weight of right, spiritual standards, should be the most important object of every true son of Britain to-day.

The dogs of our race which have descended to us from these same fathers, have retained all the mental characteristics received from their masters, and one witnesses the knowledge of this in the behaviour of our typically British breeds when they are with their masters in alien lands. The emphatic impression of conscious superiority over their surroundings, the gracious acceptance of alien service, but with a distinct " thus far and no further " attitude, and the staunch upholding of all that touches what the master is trying to live for, fills one with tender amusement for these humble companions.

Their example might well be imitated by many of our inhabitants.

Many of our dogs, such as the curly coated retrievers, and Sir Walter Scott's lion-hearted little terrier, the dandie dinmont, are almost extinct, and other first class breeds, such as Irish, Yorkshire and Welsh terriers, and even fox terriers, are beginning to languish. Bloodhounds, of noble appearance and ancient British tradition, can almost be counted on the fingers of the hands, and even our bulldog, which has always stood for British character, is out of fashion. I have mentioned this state of affairs to many people, and the reply I often receive is, " Oh, but surely all dogs are the same, no matter what part of the world they come from. They are not the same as people."

Indeed they are! Anyone who has closely studied the aspect of the psychology of the animal creation, in all countries in relation to man, will find that this is true, and we cannot afford to allow anything which stands for British prestige and character to deteriorate, or be pushed to the wall.

In the guise of "fashion," many people rush out unthinkingly to purchase anything under this head without troubling to enquire of what lies behind, and much harm is done in consequence.

In every branch of trade we hear of foreign competition, and I can assure my readers that in no section is this more serious than in the dog world. If it were from France, our allies, it would be serious enough, but when the injury comes from Germany, and with every evidence of the usual underhand forms of exploitation, it is intolerable to all who stand for things British.

For intelligence, reliability of character, courage, humour, and fidelity, there are no dogs in the world which can touch the British native breeds.

To close with a few remarks on training as a whole. I find there is a very vague idea in many peoples' minds, as to the attitude to adopt towards the young growing dog Fathers and mothers who have successfully reared families of children, are sometimes quite at a loss when it comes to bringing up a litter of puppies. My endeavour is to show that there need be no such misapprehension. The methods are, or should be, exactly the same.

With animals, the idea of training by force is one of the mistaken concepts, whereby many good young animals are ruined, and one may find an owner, who has exacted loving obedience and co-operation from his offspring, by the capture in the first place of their devoted affection, adopting an attitude of severity towards the young dog ; or else he may neglect to check an act against discipline, or of disobedience, which in his own child he would have corrected by gentle restraint and an appeal to the better nature, with the result that the only other alternative seems, later on, to be a severe whipping, to cure a fault which need never have been allowed to develop.

Furthermore, as the human child is quick to respond to those who regard it with trusting, wise affection, equally so will the young dog return this attitude. When the adult does not have the faculty of attracting the affection of the young of either specie, one can be quite certain the fault is with him, and a certain coldness and lack of sympathy will be found ingrained in such a nature. Young things are quick to sense this unloving mentality. It acts on them like a cold douche, and as a sensitive plant shrinks at a rough touch, so does this attitude towards them alienate any desire to please.

In thinking over the title of this book, it seems to me that a very curious fact is apparent. The centuries have been sweeping onward with all their progress, inventions, theories, etc., but from the days of thousands of years ago, when the Egyptian kings thought fit to illustrate their tombs with representations of their trusted canine guardians, watch-dogs have remained the same. The necessity for them is as great to-day as it was then. No mechanical invention can replace them, nor has man learned to love his brother sufficiently to be able to dispense with the devoted safeguard offered by his dogs.

By day, the tie of loving companionship is still maintained, and at night, while the master sleeps, the dog keeps guard.

If anything I have said can assist in emphasising and assisting this co-operation between man and his best friend, I shall feel this book has not been written in vain.

I will close with the words of Mr. Vest, an American Senator to a dog.

" The best friend a man has in this world may turn against him, and become his enemy. His son and daughter that he has reared with loving care may become ungrateful. Those who are nearest and dearest to us, those whom we trust with our happiness and good name, may become traitors to their faith. The money that a man has he may loose. It flies away from him when he may need it most. Man's reputation may be sacrificed in a moment of ill-considered action. The people who are prone to fall on their knees and do us honour when success is with us, may be the first to throw the stone of malice when failure settles its cloud upon our heads.

" The one absolutely unselfish friend a man may have in this selfish world, the one that never proves ungrateful or treacherous, is the dog. A man's dog stands by him in prosperity and poverty, in health and in sickness. He will kiss the hand that has no food to offer, he will lick the sores that come in encounter with the roughness of the world. He will sleep on the cold ground when the wintry winds blow and the snow drives fiercely, if only he may be near his master's side. He guards the sleep of his pauper master as if he were a prince.

"When all other friends desert he remains. When riches take wings and reputation falls to pieces, he is as constant in his love as the sun in its journey through the heavens. If fortune drives the master forth an outcast in the world, friendless and homeless, the faithful dog asks no higher privilege than that of accompanying him, to guard him against danger, to fight against his enemies, and when the last scene of all comes, and death takes his master in its embrace and his body is laid away in the cold ground, no matter if all other friends pursue their way, there, by his graveside, will the noble dog be found, his head between his paws, and his eyes sad, but open in alert watchfulness, faithful and true, even unto death."

THE END

PRINTED BY THE ANCHOR PRESS, LTD., TIPTREE, ESSEX, ENGLAND.

Lightning Source UK Ltd.
Milton Keynes UK
UKHW012000190820
368517UK00006B/142

9 781846 640414